Energy and Order
in the Poetry of Swift

Also by A. B. ENGLAND

Byron's *Don Juan* and Eighteenth-Century Literature

Energy and Order in the Poetry of Swift

A. B. England

Lewisburg
Bucknell University Press
London and Toronto: Associated University Presses

©1980 by Associated University Presses, Inc.

Associated University Presses, Inc.
Cranbury, New Jersey 08512

Associated University Presses
Magdalen House
136-148 Tooley Street
London SE1 2TT, England

Associated University Presses
Toronto M5E 1A7, Canada

Library of Congress Cataloging in Publication Data

England, A   B   1939—
    Energy and order in the poetry of Swift.

    Bibliography: p.
    Includes index.
    1. Swift, Jonathan, 1667-1745—Poetic works.
I. Title.
PR3728.P58E5   821'.5   78-75200
ISBN 0-8387-2367-5

Printed in the United States of America

For my mother
and in memory of my father

Contents

Acknowledgments

I owe a considerable debt to a large number of scholars and critics who have influenced my perception of Swift's poetry. In particular, I have been grateful to Harold Williams, for his edition of the poems, and to C.J. Rawson for the criticism he has published during recent years, culminating in *Gulliver and the Gentle Reader: Studies in Swift and our Time.*

Parts of the following study have appeared, sometimes in different form, in *Essays in Criticism, Studies in English Literature,* and *Papers on Language and Literature,* and I wish to thank the editors of those journals for their permission to reprint.

I am also grateful to The Canada Council for generous financial assistance during the period when most of this study was written.

And finally, I thank Elizabeth, Jacyntha, and Matthew England, who provided the most important help of all without, for much of the time at any rate, being aware of it.

Introduction

The following study is not intended to provide an inclusive overview of Swift's poetry. It focuses on a limited group of stylistic or rhetorical tendencies and on a limited number of poems. But I hope that I have provided enough evidence and discussed a sufficient number of Swift's more important poems to demonstrate that these tendencies may reasonably be called characteristics of his poetry. The poems that I have selected for discussion are not the only ones to which the terms of this study are applicable. Some poems I have not described because to have done so would have created unnecessary repetition. Others are omitted because I think that to analyze them in the terms of this study would not much advance already published discussions of them; *Of Dreams*, for example, has already been analyzed by Denis Donoghue in a manner that is quite closely related to the main emphasis of my fourth chapter,[1] and John M. Aden's account of *A Beautiful Young Nymph Going to Bed* suggests that the poem can be considered in terms that bear some connection with those that dominate my fifth chapter.[2]

The stylistic tendencies that I have sought to describe are, roughly speaking, of two contrasting types, and the title of this study is intended to indicate something of their natures. Those tendencies to which I mean to refer (in some cases very approximately) by the word "energy" are discussed mainly in the first three chapters; and what I am concerned with here are various ways in which Swift departs from certain orderly forms of discourse that have traditionally been associated with "Augustan" literature. Chapter 1 focuses on Swift's interest in two related kinds of verbal configuration, one involving the apparent violation of orderly sequence by the force of spontaneous impulse, and the other characterised by an anarchic inventiveness that expresses itself particularly through metaphor. The second chapter also concerns itself with Swift's metaphors, specifically with the way in which they are often arranged so as to subvert or violate certain "logical" structures that are also embedded in the poems; this subversion is sometimes achieved by the violence of a single central image and sometimes by an unruly proliferation of several images. In the third chapter, I have discussed Swift's interest in certain processes of accretion which give rise to sequences of details that do not appear to have been subjected to ordering thematic arrangements; the word "energy" may not seem particularly relevant to much of this chapter, but in some of the works discussed the accumulation of particulars is characterised by a vigor that appears to evade orthodox thematic structures.

Despite the widespread presence of the above tendencies, there are in Swift's poetry many signs of a radically contrasting impulse which causes the subjection of details to alignments that are noticeably ordered and much more consistent with some traditional assumptions about the forms that Augustan literature tends to take. The presence of this impulse is discussed in the fourth chapter, and in several of the poems described there Swift arranges details into rather clear-cut thematic or didactic structures that are often nearly symmetrical in outline, and he does not show an impulse to subvert or violate those structures by other tendencies within the poem. However, the final chapter, while continuing to focus on poems in which such orderly alignments are rather distinctly visible, focuses primarily on their subjection to disconcerting stresses which prevent them from creating the impression that they represent an assured or authoritative mastery of the recalcitrant materials with which they deal.

Now I am aware that what I have referred to by a species of shorthand as "some traditional assumptions about the forms that Augustan literature tends to take" have been rather frequently challenged or questioned in recent years, and it may seem that I am using an outdated concept in order to refer to that syndrome which I shall suggest Swift both adheres to and departs from in his poetry. There have been, for example, Donald Greene's essay on the absence of "Logical Structure" in eighteenth-century poetry,[3] Peter Thorpe's on the "Nonstructure of Augustan Verse,"[4] and David Vieth's on the "Anti-Aristotelian Poetic" of some works belonging to the same period.[5] But while these critics have challenged in a most valuable way several assumptions that have been too easily made, it seems to me that the ideas underlying these assumptions remain relevant to several of the period's major works, perhaps most obviously those by Pope and Fielding; as Martin C. Battestin has amply demonstrated, "balance and proportion and design . . . whether conceived geometrically or as a movement through time towards some predetermined ending" *are* "salient formal features" of a literature that placed special emphasis on an ideal of "Order."[6] On the other hand, as Greene, Thorpe, Vieth, C.J. Rawson and others (including Battestin) have shown, the relationship between the period's major writers and this ideal is often ambivalent. And the present study is an attempt to offer a further contribution to the continuing account of this ambivalence.

At least one aspect of my procedure in the following pages seems to me to require explanation in advance. I have said that in some of the poems I shall discuss Swift aggregates details into miscellaneous clusters without showing an evident impulse to subject those details to ordering thematic arrangements. And this begs an obvious question about the possibility of there being in these poems a thematic arrangement of a kind that I have not been able to perceive. So in order to justify my own analyses I have been forced to argue that some previous interpretations which have claimed that there are certain fairly orthodox thematic patterns in these poems are in fact inadequate. This has meant that a great deal of the third chapter involves a process of disputation that might seem more appropriate to the footnotes than the main text. But such a process has necessarily been central to my attempt to advance my own interpretations of these poems.

If my choice of poems for discussion seems in any way arbitrary or tendentious, I would say that there are certain specific types of rhetorical tendency that I want to demonstrate and that I have naturally chosen to describe the poems that seem to me most clearly to manifest those tendencies; that is why there is some fairly extensive analysis of Swift's Pindaric Odes, even though I do not dissent from the prevailing opinion about the poetic value of these works. However, I would also suggest that the great majority of what have traditionally been regarded as Swift's most valuable and important poems are discussed in the following study. And it is my belief that the tendencies I have sought to describe are important enough to determine the choice of which poems to include and which to omit. As I hope I have already indicated, those tendencies have to do with some large and central questions about the nature of Augustan literature and about the relationships between Swift's work and some of his age's major ideals.

Finally, I should point out that my concerns in this study are for the most part different from those which directed the extended discussion of Swift's poetry that appeared in my earlier book, *Byron's Don Juan and Eighteenth-Century Literature* (Lewisburg, Pa.: Bucknell University Press, 1975). In that book, for example, one of my major interests was in the differences between Swift's poetry and that of Pope, but there is very little of that kind of comparison in the present study. What overlapping there is is mainly confined to the third chapter, where one of the points made in the earlier book is developed in much greater detail, and I hope that this will not appear to constitute undue repetition.

1

"Wild Excursions"

I

WHEN Swift decided to write Pindaric odes at the beginning of his literary career, he committed himself to a highly individualized poetic form with which some very definite rhetorical expectations were associated. Geoffrey Walton has described the Pindaric's function at the end of the seventeenth century as that of providing opportunities for release from certain stylistic and structural rigors: "When normal couplet-writing was becoming too rigorously controlled by 'coolness and discretion' . . . writers attempted, by means of the 'gaudy and inane phraseology' of the ode, to give direct and easy outlet to moods of ecstasy and enthusiasm."[1] However mechanical and fabricated many of the actual exercises in the mode were, the established theoretical concept of the Pindaric was such that for Swift to adopt the form meant that he was showing an interest in configurations quite other than those suggested by the following comment on the workings of his mind: "Swift cultivates some sort of elemental delimitation, a determination . . . to keep his thinking well cut back, to rein in this Pegasus which is the intellect if it ever should want to have its head and venture on a high flight."[2] The Pindaric ode accommodated tendencies which were more or less opposite to this kind of "delimitation," and these tendencies appear throughout Swift's early poems, including those which were not written in the Pindaric form. They also appear in *A Tale of a Tub,* as well as in some of his later poems. So I would suggest that however much he may have been acting under Temple's influence, and however routine the use of the Pindaric form may have been at the end of the seventeenth century, what occurred at the beginning of Swift's career as a poet was a genuinely significant act of choice.

Swift makes it clear in one of his letters that in writing Pindaric odes he felt himself to be imitating Cowley.[3] This feeling was common to most practitioners of the form at the end of the seventeenth century, for it was generally accepted that Cowley had established the fashion. And in order to understand how Swift would probably have perceived the Pindaric ode, one may consider some of Cowley's comments on the form, comments which appeared in the contemporary editions of his works and with which Swift would have been very familiar. What we confront in the various notes and prefaces is Cowley's own version of Pindar's poetry. This version is not entirely accurate, nor does it adequately describe Cowley's own odes,[4] but it does reflect the contemporary attitude to Pindar, and it largely determined the age's concept of what a Pindaric ode was supposed to be like. When Cowley first introduces the subject of the odes, he feels a need to be apologetic about them; " . . . as for the *Pindarick Odes* (which is the third part) I am in great doubt whether they will be understood by most *Readers;* nay, even by the very many who are well enough acquainted with the common Roads, and ordinary Tracks of *Poesie*. . . . The digressions are many, and sudden, and sometimes long. . . . the *Figures* are unusual and *bold*, even to *Temerity,* and such as I durst not have to do withal in any other kind of *Poetry*. . . . The *Numbers* are various and irregular, and sometimes (especially some of the long ones) seem harsh and uncouth. . . ."[5] Cowley's phrases dramatize his sense that he is being very adventurous, even reckless, in imitating Pindar. But they also make some specific points about the kind of rhetoric he is attempting; in particular he focuses on its irregular and seemingly uncoordinated movement and on the boldness of its imagery. Later on, he uses the image of rapidly flowing water to describe the movement of Pindar's poetry: " . . . I term his Song *Unnavigable;* for it is able to drown any *Head* that is not strong built and well *ballasted.* Horace in another place calls it a *Fountain;* from the unexhausted abundance of his Invention."[6] Here, he is commenting on some lines in a poem that he wrote in praise of Pindar, and elsewhere in the same poem he again turns to the image of a powerful outpouring of water which cannot be contained:

> So *Pindar* does new *Words* and *Figures* roul
> Down his impetuous *Dithyrambique Tyde,*
>   Which in no *Channel* deigns t'abide,
>   Which neither *Banks* nor *Dikes* controul.[7]

In all of these comments it is clear that Cowley's emphasis falls on the notion of an unruly creative energy that manifests itself both in metaphor and in the overall development of the poem's meaning. And Dryden focuses on a similar notion when he describes Pindar as a "wild and ungovernable" poet, who is "generally known to be a dark writer, to want Connexion (I mean as to our understanding), to soar out of sight, and to leave his Reader at a Gaze."[8]

When Swift set out to write Pindaric odes, one of his major concerns was to embody within them certain manifestations of such an unruly and exuberant energy. In the *Ode to the King* (1691), for example, the sudden shifts from panegyric to satire seem to derive from an attempt to create that enthusiastic wildness of movement described by Cowley and Dryden. An early instance occurs in the fourth stanza, when, after the initial praise of William for achieving a combination of *"Valour"* and *"Virtue,"* Swift imagines himself looking on at the king's heroism in the battle of the Boyne:

> And now I in the Spirit see
> (The Spirit of Exalted Poetry)
>   I see the *Fatal Fight* begin;
> And, lo! where a Destroying Angel stands,
>   (By all but Heaven and Me unseen,)
> With Lightning in his Eyes, and Thunder in his Hands.[9]

There is clearly something factitious about this, a blatantly contrived working up of "enthusiasm." But the fact that one would not make high claims for it as poetry should not prevent us from attending to what Swift is trying to do. He describes himself as being in a state of extreme excitement as he contemplates the image of the "Destroying Angel." And it is in this state of excitement that he imagines the angel launching into a violent attack on Ireland:

> *In vain,* said He, *does* Utmost Thule *boast*
>   *No poys'nous Beast will in Her breed,*
>   *Or no Infectious Weed,*
> *When she sends forth such a malignant Birth,*
> *When Man himself's the* Vermin *of Her Earth;*
> *When* Treason *there in* Person *seems to stand,*
> *And* Rebel *is the* growth *and* manufacture *of the Land.*

The sudden shift from praise to satire is apparently meant to dramatize the intensely emotional mood that the poet has attributed to himself. We are intended to receive the impression that the poet is so excited by what he has seen in his imagination that the movement of his thought is no longer subject to the logical or conventional procedures of the panegyric. And the suddenness of the shift is therefore an aspect of the Pindaric frenzy or wildness which at this point has taken over the movement of the poem. Moreover, the language of the attack, its rhythms giving the impression of an uncontrollable vitriol, furthers the general sense that this is an outburst not easily subordinated to the demands of logical structure. In the next stanza Swift again moves suddenly from praise to satire, this time upon the Scots. And again it is crucial to the effect he is seeking that he should appear to be carried away, forced by a powerful impulse into an attack which erupts spontaneously and prevents orderly development. We should not reduce these passages to evidence of an inability on Swift's part to "sustain a vision of goodness" (p. 58),[10] for they are functioning elements in the particular kind of rhetorical pattern that he is attempting to construct; as Martin Price has said, speaking of the "Pindaric manner," "its enthusiasm turns largely to satiric fervor in Swift."[11] It is true, of course, that these passages of satire are not utterly disruptive of logical structure because they do implicitly further the eulogistic process by stressing the enormity of what the king must cope with.[12] But this does not alter the fact that, when they occur, they take on the characteristics of violent, unpredictable outbursts that disturb the orderly progress of the panegyric.

Cowley also suggested that the Pindaric manner was characterized by the extreme boldness and ingenuity of its images. And in the *Ode to the King* Swift's imagery tends to grow more and more ostentatiously elaborate as the poem progresses. In both the third and the fifth stanzas the sequence of metaphors by which Swift describes William is rather noticeably ingenious. And in the sixth, when he turns to the subject of the war in France, the image-making process reaches a sort of climax:

> How vainly (Sir) did Your fond *Enemy* try
> Upon *a rubbish Heap of broken Laws*
>   To climb at Victory
>   Without the Footing of a *Cause;*
> His Lawrel now must only be a Cypress Wreath,
>   And His best Victory a Noble Death;
> His scrap of Life is but a Heap of Miseries,
>   The Remnant of a falling Snuff,
>   Which hardly wants another puff,
> And needs must *stink* when e're it dies;
> Whilst at Your Victorious Light
>   All Lesser ones expire,

> Consume, and perish from our sight,
> Just as the Sun puts out a Fire;
> And every foolish *Flye* that dares to aim
> To buzz about the Mighty Flame;
> The wretched Insects singe their Wings, and fall,
> And humbly at the bottom crawl.

In this stanza, Swift seeks to create the illusion that he moves rapidly from image to image because he is impelled by an inventiveness that will not be held in check, and the apparent discontinuity is therefore an aspect of a deliberate rhetorical effect. After the initial image of the defeated French king attempting to climb towards victory upon *"a rubbish Heap of broken Laws,"* Swift begins to describe the last phase of his life by means of a sequence of metaphors. This sequence becomes genuinely outlandish in the line, "His scrap of Life is but a Heap of Miseries," where Swift risks bathos in the attempt at energetic paradox. After this he shifts rapidly from the image of a burned-down candle wick which will "stink" when its flame goes out, to that of a fire being put out by the sun, and finally to that of a singed fly crawling in the bottom of a lamp. Although these metaphors all involve some reference to light and heat, they are not very precisely coordinated, the transitions from one to another are abrupt, and the passage enforces a continual readjustment of the reader's focus. What all of the images in the stanza do have in common, however, is that they express the poet's contempt for the French king and his admiration of William's greater strength. And Swift's purpose is to make it seem that the pressure of these emotions has stimulated a metaphorical inventiveness which is not especially coherent but which is capable of astonishing by its frenzied imaginative vigour.

At the beginning of the *Ode to the Athenian Society* (1692) we again see Swift going to extremes in his manipulation of imagery. After the initial description of Mount Ararat appearing above the waters of the flood, he imagines the possibility that this was the same mountain that the Greeks called Parnassus. With a fairly high degree of speculative audacity, he thus establishes a dramatic image of religious and aesthetic eminence. And Swift then uses this to describe the reemergence of *"Philosophy"* after the wars that have dominated the seventeenth century. A major idea behind the metaphor is that one manifestation of philosophy's resurgence is the work of the Athenian Society, and that the nature of this work is therefore to some extent defined by the grandiose opening image. Swift's muse is now preparing to visit this combination of Ararat and Parnassus in order to bring a "Laurel wreath" (this poem) as a testament to the new age of peace. As he describes the muse's journey, Swift suddenly turns to a new, though related image; from a distance, she sees a "Peaceful and a Flourishing Shore," and she soon discovers that it is "Scatter'd with *flowry Vales,* with fruitful Gardens crown'd":

> It seems some floating piece of *Paradise,*
>   Preserv'd by wonder from the Flood,
> Long *wandring thro the Deep,* as we are told
>   Fam'd *Delos* did of old,
> And the transported Muse imagin'd it
> To be a fitter *Birth-place for the God of Wit;*
>   Or the much-talkt Oracular Grove
>   When with amazing Joy she hears,
> An *unknown Musick* all around,
>   Charming her greedy Ears
>   With many a heavenly Song
> Of Nature and of Art, of deep *Philosophy and Love,*
> *Whilst Angels tune the Voice, and God inspires the Tongue.*
>
>   (St. 2)

This extraordinary picture is in fact a metaphor intended to describe the intellectual world of the Athenian Society. One does not need to go into the matter of what the Athenian Society actually was (I shall come to that later) in order to see that Swift is pushing the imagery to an extreme point here. Pindaric enthusiasm, we are again meant to feel, is carrying the poet beyond the ordinary limits of proportion and rationality, towards metaphors that are genuinely "*bold*" (to use Cowley's word) and that testify to a frenziedly inventive state of mind. Also, one can hardly escape the note of self-display in the passage, the sense that a major concern of the poet is to demonstrate the daring élan with which he can invent and develop an image. Swift draws attention to these features by apologizing for them in the next stanza, where he refers to them as "wild excursions of a youthful pen," and suggests that his enthusiasm has led him to go beyond "the narrow *Path of Sense*." This apology, of course, is in effect a means of defining some of the characteristics that he wants his poem to have. And it bears an obvious relationship to that moment in *A Tale of a Tub* when the author announces that he has "thought fit to make *Invention* the *Master*, and to give *Method* and *Reason* the Office of its Lacquays."[13]

After this point the poem moves, by some rapid and rather abrupt transitions, towards a confrontation with those figures whose philosophic bent will tend to make them detractors of the Athenian Society. In the fourth and fifth stanzas Swift suggests that the most prominent among these will no doubt be the materialists, who will argue that the society's work is merely the consequence of a "*Crowd of Atoms justling in a heap*" rather than of the "wondrous Wit" of certain gifted human beings. And this leads him to the following response:

> But as for poor contented Me,
> Who must my Weakness and my Ignorance confess,
> That I believe in much, I ne're can hope to see;
> *Methinks I'm satisfied to guess*
> That this New, Noble, and Delightful Scene
> Is wonderfully mov'd by some exalted Men.
>
> (St. 6)

He expresses his opposition to the materialists here by two statements of belief. In the first, he asserts that he believes in a great deal that lies beyond sense-perception. In the second, that he believes the *Athenian Gazette* to be the product not of miscellaneous atoms jostling accidentally, but of a creative effort by a group of distinguished men. This second belief is particularly important in this context, I think, because of its relationship to the nature of the poem Swift is writing. His implicit assertion of the primacy of the human will is in some ways similar to Dryden's assertion of the "Providence of Wit";[14] both poets wish to emphasize the power of the human mind to create its own areas of order, and to oppose a philosophy which tends to deny this power. There is, of course, nothing at all surprising in this similarity of viewpoint. But what gives Swift's statement special piquancy is that in this particular poem he shows an interest in configurations that do not convey a very distinct impression of having emerged from an ordering effort of the will. At certain points he goes out of his way to make it seem that the poem's movement is directed by an unpredictable sequence of spontaneous impulses. And it is in this ode, particularly, that Swift seems to have taken very much to heart Cowley's account of the frequency and suddenness of the Pindaric digressions. Again there is a relationship between the poem's development and that of *A Tale of a Tub* in which the author sometimes rather ostentatiously associates ideas without seeming to be guided by a rigorous sense of direction. On certain occasions in the *Ode to the Athenian Society* Swift appears to be trying for an impression of accidental, fortuitous growth, as if to suggest that the poem's movement is not predetermined by a shaping artistic will. A vivid example is the seventh stanza, in which he makes an attempt to define the nature of *"Fame"*. After saying that he "would not draw th' *Idea* from an empty Name," he proceeds to reject another possible means of definition:

> Less should I dawb it o're with transitory Praise,
> And *water-colours* of these Days,

> *These Days!* where ev'n th'Extravagance of Poetry
> Is at a loss for Figures to express
> Men's Folly, Whimsyes, and Inconstancy,
> And by a faint Description make them less.

Here, the movement of the rhetoric is such as to suggest that the mention of "these Days" triggers an immediate and intense response in the poet, and that the next few lines of the poem issue spontaneously from that response. In consequence, a dramatic assertion of the poet's disgust for his contemporaries disturbs and distracts from the progress of the definition. He returns to that definition in the next line, but it is not long before another outburst disrupts the course of the argument:

> *Then tell us what is Fame?* where shall we search for it?
> Look where exalted Vertue and Religion sit
>   Enthron'd with Heav'nly Wit,
>   Look where you see
>   The greatest scorn of *Learned Vanity,*
>   (And then how much a nothing is Mankind!
>   Whose Reason is weigh'd down by Popular air,
> Who by that, vainly talks of bafling Death,
> And hopes to lengthen Life by a *Transfusion of Breath,*
>   Which yet whoe're examines right will find
> To be an Art as vain, as *Bottling up of Wind:)*
> And when you find out these, believe true Fame is there.

What is said in the parenthesis is certainly to some extent related to Swift's initial argument, in that it is a way of emphasizing that there is not much for man to be vain about. But it is protracted to such an inordinate length, and eventually takes on such a potent life of its own, that when the parenthesis is closed and Swift completes his sentence the reader is forced into a considerable effort of recollection. The parenthesis in this way drastically interrupts and impedes the progress of the argument. What appears to happen is that the initial ejaculation ("How much a nothing is Mankind!") leads the poet to dwell on certain specific absurdities by

which he is obsessed. In this way, the growth of the parenthesis is made to seem like a process of compulsive accretion,
instigated above all by intense spontaneous emotion. Such, at
any rate, appears to be the kind of effect that Swift is aiming
for. It is an effect which involves the deliberate disruption of
orderly, consecutive development. And it is as if Swift is
trying to contain within the structure of the poem something
rather like that quality of unpredictable, unarranged flux
which he earlier rejected as a description of the Athenian
Society.

The *Ode to the Athenian Society* is a rather peculiar poem,
and it is sometimes hard to be sure of how sincere Swift is
being. At one point, for instance, he appears to parody his
own Pindaric digressiveness for comic effect. The digression
here is stimulated by Swift's praise in the ninth stanza for the
way in which the Athenian Society has restored to "Queen"
Philosophy her ancient simplicity of dress. This leads him to
a fairly intense expression of his excitement in contemplat-
ing her new appearance: "How fond we are to court Her to
our Arms!" Then, at the start of the next stanza, he suddenly
begins to attack the *"Rebel Muse"* for once again seducing
him into praise of that "Tyrant Sex of Hers." And he follows
this by turning angrily upon the *"fatal and Immortal Wit"* of
the Athenian Society for having conspired with the muse to
"fann th'unhappy Fire" (the *Athenian Gazette*'s praise of
women amounted to a minor liberationist campaign). When
Swift next addresses the Athenian Society as *"Cruel Unknown,"* using the heavy Gothic print that often appeared in
the *Gazette* as a means of emphasis, it becomes difficult to
take him seriously.[15] He continues to attack the society in the
most vehement terms, only extricating himself at the end of a
long diatribe against women by saying that in spite of
everything he is proud to be of the same *"exalted Sex"* as the
society's members. If we are meant to feel that the sequence is
a further instance of spontaneous digression under the pressure of intense emotion, then it is a ludicrously unconvincing

failure. But it seems more likely that Swift is playing with the rhetorical device here, engaging in a sort of stylistic self-display that is meant to surprise by its verve and energy but not to be taken quite seriously. Indeed, the poem as a whole may be intended to create some such impression as this. At the time Swift wrote the poem, he did not know that the anonymous Athenian Society consisted simply of John Dunton (whom he later ridiculed in *A Tale of a Tub*)[16] and a few hack assistants. But he did know that its sole production was the *Athenian Gazette*, in which the society answered readers' questions on a wide variety of topics.[17] The most cursory glance at the *Gazette* makes it clear that an educated contemporary could hardly have regarded it as anything more than an effective dispenser of received facts and intelligent opinion. This would be enough, of course, to give it considerable value, and we know that Temple approved highly of it.[18] But the nature of the poem's subject does mean that the element of hyperbole is more drastic and obtrusive here than in the previous poem, and it would seem to support the possibility that Swift's primary impulse was towards a kind of rhetorical bravura. For the subject matter is such as to make the poem's extreme metaphors and frenzied wildness of movement seem like considerable feats of rhetorical invention.

In both the *Ode to Sir William Temple* (1692) and the *Ode to Dr. William Sancroft* (1692), Swift continues the attempt to make it seem that the movement of his poetry is directed by an exuberant Pindaric energy. But there are now increasing signs of factitiousness in this attempt. In the ode to Temple there is a good deal of evidence to suggest that Pindaric enthusiasm is being exploited as a means of evading and blurring a thematic problem which Swift found insuperable. The problem is created by the fact that he begins with an account of Temple's "Virtue" as essentially active in nature, manifested largely by his performance in the political arena, and then seeks to continue the panegyric by praising his retirement from such activity. The most frenzied rhetoric occurs at two points, first when Swift tries to effect this awkward transition by means of an emotional attack on the corruption of the court (st. 7), and second, when he engages in a "Flight" of enthusiasm for the natural country life (st. 9). But as the poem continues, several details have the effect of implying both that the court is a place where growth and development are possible and that there is considerable value in persisting in a difficult course rather than withdrawing from it (sts. 10 and 11). So the poem becomes deeply ambivalent, and the several bursts of Pindaric energy look very much as if they were contrived as a means of distracting the reader from certain fundamental contradictions. A similar impression of contrivance is given by the *Ode to Dr. William Sancroft*, but here for a rather different reason. There is so much evidence in this poem of careful thematic and metaphoric organization that it is more difficult than usual for Swift to sound convincing when he claims that Pindaric enthusiasm is forcing him to violate a central line of argument. In the first four stanzas, for example, he establishes an image-pattern which defines Sancroft as a sunlike, light-bringing presence, whose steadiness is not accurately perceived by the confused and distorting vision of the multitude. Then, in the fifth stanza, he suddenly attacks this multitude in what he seeks to define as a digression stimulated by "ill-govern'd zeal." But when he begins the attack by asking for an ability to create a "dawn" of sense in the "dark mass," he immediately connects it with a central thematic and metaphorical pattern, and his claim that a spontaneous disruption of the poem's order has taken place is patently unconvincing. Similarly, in the last of the twelve stanzas which were apparently all that Swift could manage to write,[19] the attempt to define his attack on "reformers" as another impulsive outburst on the part of an unchecked muse creates the unfortunate impression of a poet going mechanically through a routine.

II

The *Ode to Sancroft* was Swift's last Pindaric ode, but in his next poem, *To Mr. Congreve* (1693), he again makes the typically Pindaric claim that a strong impulse forces him to violate the ordinary requirements of logical structure. Towards the end of the poem, after a long attack on contemporary criticism, Swift suddenly castigates himself for the direction he has allowed the poem to take: "Perish the Muse's hour, thus vainly spent/In satire, to my CONGREVE's praises meant" (ll. 175-76). He asserts that the poem has not developed in the way he originally intended, and thus implies that its composition has been a spontaneous process in which certain impulses running contrary to an initial plan have taken over. Now the development of this poem is much more commensurate with such a claim than is the development of the *Ode to Sancroft*. And I would suggest that in *To Mr. Congreve* Swift recovers a good deal of that disruptive energy which he has clearly been very interested in from the start.

At an early stage of the poem it is established that Swift's intention is to praise Congreve. The beginning of this praise is considerably delayed by the complaint of Swift's muse (ll. 7-22), who protests that he must have been false in his expressions of love for "retreat" and "innocence" if he is now seeking to bring her into contact with the "vices of the town" (Congreve lived in London). But Swift reproaches her for this outburst, and insists that he is going to make an "off'ring long design'd to CONGREVE's fame" (l. 24). Indeed, he now transforms the muse's protests into a means of praising Congreve; because of the enormous distance between the muse's milieu and that of Congreve, this poem will be "The greatest compliment she ever made" (l. 28). Immediately after this, however, the poem begins to take one of its many surprising turns, as Swift insists upon the distance between Congreve's world and his own in terms that do not clearly tend towards the elevation of Congreve:

And wisely judge, no pow'r beneath divine
Could leap the bounds which part your world and mine;
For, youth, believe, to you unseen, is fix'd
A mighty gulph unpassable betwixt.

(ll. 29-32)

Swift is now aligning himself with his muse, who has just reviled the city environment in which Congreve has chosen to live. And the lofty tone of the lines tends to attribute a degree of moral superiority to the author. After this, Swift insists that his intention is not to elevate himself by praising Congreve, or to try and "surmount what bears me up" like the "wren perch'd on the eagle's wing" (ll. 37-38). But he cannot restrain himself from telling us that "This could I do, and proudly o'er him tow'r,/Were my desires but heighten'd to my pow'r" (ll. 39-40). Here, the self-aggrandizing tendency of the earlier lines becomes more open, and the speaker of this poem now appears to be taking on a character that is hardly commensurate with his ostensible purpose. He feels a need to stress his own essential superiority to the subject of his praise, and his tone verges on the arrogant. Moreover, Swift continues to talk more about himself than about his stated subject as he suggests that "CONGREVE's bays" must be "Godlike" in their force if they can soften a "pride" which

> . . . *well suspends poor mortals fate,*
> *Gets between them and my resentment's weight,*
> *Stands in the gap 'twixt me and wretched men,*
> *T'avert th'impending judgements of my pen.*
> (ll. 45-48)

It could still be argued that this works in such a way as to elevate Congreve, because the impulse to praise him has been a sufficient stimulus for the poet to overcome this pride, to emerge from his "retreat," and to confront a subject involving "poor mortals." But as the poem develops, it becomes clear that what Swift is really absorbed by is the developing confrontation between himself and the "wretched men" who are the objects of his satire. He does for a few lines praise the richness of the "poetic mine" to which Congreve has access (ll. 51-54), but he shifts rapidly to the "indignation" that he experiences when he sees Congreve's wit "Forc'd on me, crack'd, and clipp'd, and counterfeit,/By vile pretenders" (ll. 55-57). And every time that he uses the image of the sun to describe Congreve's mind, his language becomes most vigorous when he is exploiting it as a means of satire; when, for instance, he is focusing on the "fiery froth which breeds/O'er the sun's face" (ll. 69-70) or on the "swarms of gnats, that wanton in a ray/Which gave them birth" (ll. 81-2). Before long, as Swift's dominant impulse takes over, the poem becomes exclusively satiric in emphasis. And what this eventually leads to is an extreme violence of language and imagery that is testament to the poet's intensely excited state of mind. Here, he is describing the "gibberish" that he has heard from a "finish'd spark" pretending to some knowledge of the drama:

> A jargon form'd from the lost language, wit,
> Confounded in that Babel of the pit;
> Form'd by diseas'd conceptions, weak, and wild,
> Sick lust of souls, and an abortive child;
> Born between whores and fops, by lewd compacts,
> Before the play, or else between the acts.
>
> (ll. 121-26)

The kind of violent excess that appears in the phrasing of this attack is to be seen as an aspect of the poem's energy, an energy that runs counter not only to the initially established intention, but also to the ordinary restraints of logical proportion. Just as in the earlier Pindaric odes, it is important that Swift should appear to be carried away by his anger, perhaps even to the point where the violence of the attack is in excess of what its object (the country "lad" who has become a city "spark") would seem to require. And it is now that Swift returns to the note of self-aggrandizement, carrying it to a greater extreme than before:

What bungling, rusty tools, are us'd by fate!
'Twas in an evil hour to urge my hate,
My hate, whose lash just heaven has long decreed
Shall on a day make sin and folly bleed;
When man's ill genius to my presence sent
This wretch, to rouse my wrath, for ruin meant.

                                        (ll. 131-36)

The poet's meeting with this "wretch" is thus being transformed into a major confrontation between himself and
"man's ill genius." In fact, it now appears that this confrontation has become the poem's essential theme. And when
Swift explicitly claims that in the process of composing the
poem he has diverged from his original intention, the claim
is much more convincing than it was in the *Ode to Sancroft*
because it has been preceded by a poetic structure that is
genuinely commensurate with it. At this point, perhaps, one
should acknowledge that it is not unusual in the Augustan
period for a satirist to present himself as being driven by a
strong impulse to transgress certain "rational" limits. Pope
does it, for instance, rather often. But those passages of satire
which Pope describes as spontaneous outbursts never seriously disrupt the logical development of the poem or
violate the reader's expectations in the way that Swift's
passages of satire do in this poem. It is interesting, I think,
that Swift intended this poem to become a prologue to one of
Congreve's plays, and after he had written it he still apparently thought that it could perform this function.[20] But if
Swift seriously believed this, he must have had in mind a very
individual concept of the form. For in a number of ways, he
has radically overturned the reader's ordinary expectations of
what a prologue is like. He has not only turned away from the
conventional purpose of praising the author towards a preoccupation with satire. But he has also become much more
absorbed in himself than in his ostensible subject, and this
self-absorption has been expressed in ways that have tended
to aggrandize himself rather than Congreve. All of this has

clearly been a matter of deliberate rhetorical strategy on Swift's part. And one purpose of the strategy, I would suggest, is to create the impression that there is present within the poem a kind of spontaneous, idiosyncratic energy that tends to disrupt and overspill the limits of a traditional literary form.

It would seem logical that once Swift has castigated himself for diverging from the subject of "CONGREVE's praises," he will return to that subject in the succeeding parts of the poem. But nothing of the kind happens. Instead, the poem now becomes more distinctly autobiographical than it was before, as Swift turns to the subject of his life at Moor Park in Temple's employment. He says that it should not matter to his muse "if mankind be a fool," because she is in the happy situation of being able to please *all that's good among the great* (ll. 177-80). The allusion is indirect and private, and it seems a peculiar turn for the poem to take at this point. Moreover, when Swift suggests that if Congreve knew this "Apollo" he would want to offer his "laurel" only to him (ll. 185-86), he implies that Congreve would be better off at Moor Park than in London—an implication that has been present in other parts of the poem and that tends to undermine its ostensible laudatory purpose. After this Swift once more moves enthusiastically away from the subject of Congreve into an ecstatic description of his rural retreat at Moor Park. He describes a "reverend cave" in which he imagines a "druid" composing poetry in the remote past, and he thinks of the possibility of pursuing the druid's foot-steps "Far in this primitive cell" (ll. 187-96). What appears to be taking place now is a withdrawal into nature and the past, away from a theme associated with the city and the present. Both Swift and the muse are preparing to make this withdrawal together, reconciled and transformed into "two fond lovers" (l. 200) after the disruption that was initially caused by Swift's choice of subject. And it is now clear that this is the climax of a dramatic sequence of events which has become the real centre of the poem's concerns, and for which the subject of Congreve has been only an occasion. The sequence started with Swift's emergence from the "retreat" valued so highly by the muse, it continued in the dramatic confrontation which occupied the greater part of the poem, and it is now concluded by the return of poet and muse to the environment in which they began. This is not to suggest that the poem really has an orderly pattern of development if only one knows where to look for it. For the sequence of events that I have described runs drastically counter to the theme that Swift initially states to be his major concern, and it overturns certain reasonable expectations that he arouses in the reader. As Swift contemplates his withdrawal with the muse, he once again chooses to make us feel that a divergence from his original intention has taken place:

> Since thus I wander from my first intent,
> Nor am that grave adviser which I meant;
> Take this short lesson from the god of bayes,
> And let my friend apply it as he please.
> (ll. 201-4)

It seems here that he has now given up on all attempts to provide the poem with consecutive structure, and is accepting with a shrug what he explicitly defines as its wandering course. He does suggest that he is going to make a last gesture towards his stated program by providing a "short lesson." But that program has now apparently shifted from the offering of praise to the offering of advice, and Swift is very enigmatic about Congreve's application of the lesson. So he is still making it rather difficult for the reader to establish his bearings. And when the lesson comes, it seems very much in keeping with the unpredictable course the poem has run:

> *Beat not the dirty paths where vulgar feet have trod,*
> *But give the vigorous fancy room*
> For when like stupid alchymists you try

> To fix this nimble god,
> This volatile mercury,
> The subtil spirit all flies up in fume;
> Nor shall the bubbl'd virtuoso find
> More than a fade insipid mixture left behind.
>
> (ll. 205-12)

The externals of this are in themselves somewhat disconcerting. For Swift abruptly introduces a passage which is written in a different form from the rest of the poem, and which, he tells us in a footnote, is in fact taken from an earlier ode called *The Poet*.[21] Again he seems to be exerting a fairly drastic liberty in his manipulation of the poem's form. And the meaning of the lines goes a long way towards defining the nature of this liberty. For however the passage may be intended to apply to Congreve's literary career, what it most clearly expresses is an opposition to conventional restraints which may be put upon the imagination. And it confirms the general impression made by the poem that one of Swift's major intentions has been to suggest the presence of a creative energy that is not easily contained within ordinary structural limits.

In the last of this group of early poems, *Occasioned by Sir W—— T——'s Late Illness and Recovery* (1693), Swift yet again suggests that a powerful emotion disrupts the formal pattern that seems to be establishing itself in the poem's early stages. In these early stages, everything that Swift does creates the expectation that the poem is going to focus on Temple's recovery, celebrating it while also remembering the illness. Swift's elaborate description of how the muse appeared to him when he composed the poem seems carefully calculated to suggest this probability:

> Such seem'd her eyes, as when an evening ray
> Gives glad farewell to a tempestuous day;
> Weak is the beam to dry up nature's tears;
> Still ev'ry tree the pendent sorrow wears;

Such are the smiles where drops of chrystal show,
Approaching joy at strife with parting woe.
                                        (ll. 17-22)

The images describe a process in which signs of "woe" are beginning to give way to signs of "joy." And as Swift continues to describe the muse's appearance, he further develops the notion of such a process; he compares her face to the sky after a storm, when the "blest sun" gives "kind dawn of grace" and when the rainbow appears as a sign that "God's dart is shot" (ll. 23-30). An elaborate image-pattern thus establishes an opening mood from which a celebration of Temple's recovery would logically follow. Although in the next few lines it is stressed that Swift is still deeply troubled ("With how undecent clouds are overcast/Thy looks. . . ."), this suggests only that his movement from grief to joy will be impeded, not prevented, by the fact that he is finding it hard to get over the misery he felt during Temple's illness. At this point, the muse sets out to draw him away from his grief and to teach him how "to sing" (l. 36). Her long speech provides the basic materials for a poem of the kind that Swift has apparently been tending towards from the start. In a series of elaborate metaphors, she describes the grief experienced by Temple's household during his illness, and is clearly offering the subject of this grief as a prelude to the theme of "returning joy" (l. 68). One of the major figures in the drama is Lady Temple:

> Mild Dorothea, peaceful, wise and great,
> Trembling beheld the doubtful hand of fate;
> Mild Dorothea, whom we both have long
> Not dar'd to injure with our lowly song;
> Sprung from a better world, and chosen then
> The best companion for the best of men;
> As some fair pile, yet spar'd by zeal and rage,
> Lives pious witness of a better age;
> So men may see what once was womankind,
> In the fair shrine of Dorothea's mind.
>   (ll. 41-50)

It may be seen from this passage that the muse's rhetoric is characterized by some distinctive features. As she describes Lady Temple, she tends to transform her into an idealized, rather impersonal figure, and her language possesses an almost ceremonial order and formality.

It is at the end of the muse's speech that the pattern which has begun to establish itself is abruptly and violently disturbed. For Swift now asserts that he cannot write the kind of poem that he has apparently been moving towards. He says that he is subject to a "grief" which continues in spite of the muse's advice, and which is now going to force him into an act of "irreligion" (ll. 75-78). This act is an attack on his own muse, an attack which emerges from "passion" (l. 80) and is violent in its language:

> Malignant goddess! bane to my repose,
> Thou universal cause of all my woes;
> Say, whence it comes that thou art grown of late
> A poor amusement for my scorn and hate;
> The malice thou inspir'st I never fail
> On thee to wreak the tribute when I rail;
> Fools common-place thou art, their weak
>   ensconcing fort,
> Th'appeal of dullness in the last resort.
>
> (ll. 81-88)

The style of this is completely different from that of the muse's speech. It is more direct and colloquial, and it has the kind of intensity appropriate to what Swift wants us to feel is a spontaneous outburst of passion. The ordered formality of the muse's concept is thus being shattered by an emotion which cannot adjust itself to that concept. Swift's attack upon her increases in energy and violence until it reaches a point at which he questions her very existence and describes her as "a glitt'ring voice, a painted name,/A walking vapour ..." (ll. 101-2). Central to the poem once again, therefore, is a dramatic confrontation involving a high degree of conflict, this time between Swift's own emotion and a rhetorical pattern that has begun to establish itself. Up to this point, Swift has not said very much about the precise nature of the "grief" which makes it impossible for him to comply with the muse's requests. But he begins to suggest something about it when he describes himself as

> . . . an abandon'd wretch by hopes forsook;
> Forsook by hopes, ill fortune's last relief,
> Assigned for life to unremitting grief.
>
> (ll. 108-10)

This makes it clear that it is not, after all, a continuation of the misery caused by Temple's illness that is troubling him. For the grief that he refers to now has been caused by broken "hopes" which have nothing to do with either the illness or the recovery. Swift does not define the nature of these hopes, and even when he does indicate something about their object at the end of the poem, he is still tantalizingly vague; he says that his "few ill-presented graces" have brought only "contempt" when he had hoped for "esteem" (ll. 145-46). In order to understand what he is referring to, we have to turn to the external, biographical facts of his disappointed hopes for advancement in Temple's service. In this last part, then, the poem becomes acutely private, focusing on a personal disappointment to which the poem's ostensible subject is irrelevant—there is no reason to think that Temple's illness and recovery will affect the essentials of Swift's relationship with him. As in the previous poem, Swift has shifted away from the initial subject towards an intense preoccupation with himself and his own emotions. And this preoccupation continues to the end of the poem, where he abandons the muse and poetry because poetry has been one of the means by which he sought "esteem."

This poem, then, becomes a further instance of Swift's early concern with verbal patterns in which certain forms of order, such as consecutive progression and moderating restraint, appear to be evaded or disrupted by contrasting tendencies within the rhetoric. It is not difficult to see that these patterns have some characteristics in common with those which appear in *A Tale of a Tub,* the work Swift began to write soon after his temporary rejection of poetry. At several points in that work, for instance, Swift accumulates metaphors into protracted sequences that seem to be emblematic of an unchecked inventiveness, and he digresses from a central line of argument in ways that have the air of being caused by anarchic processes of association. Also, the self-aggrandizing tendency which appears in *To Mr. Congreve,* and is a primary expression of that poem's radically subversive energy, bears some relationship to the pride in his own powers that so often leads the author of the *Tale* to assert himself with an unruly lack of restraint.[22] A major tendency in critical responses to the *Tale,* of course, has been to attribute its "wild excursions" to a satirized persona rather than to Swift, and this has led to the suggestion that Swift is both imitating and rejecting the characteristics of his early poetry in the work.[23] Such an account, however, depends upon the assumption that Swift is in fact ridiculing these characteristics of the *Tale*'s putative author rather than expressing himself through them. And some recent criticism has, I think rightly, questioned this assumption. C.J. Rawson, for example, has argued that "the tale has at the same time a vitality of sheer performance which suggests that a strong self-conscious pressure of primary self-display on Swift's part is also at work."[24] And John Traugott, in describing the "sheer invention and flamboyant virtuosity" of the *Tale,* suggests that its author "is always Swift, but Swift relieved of responsibility and its decorums and hence liberated and energised."[25] If the *Tale* can with any justification be described in this way, then it can also be seen as in some ways a further development, rather than a rejection, of tendencies that appear in the earlier poems. Indeed, I wish to suggest that these tendencies have a considerable bearing on Swift's later work, and that the early poems are important to his development as a poet for other reasons than the fact that they contain some satire.

III

One work which was written at a very late stage in Swift's career and which has something in common with those structures we have been examining is *On Poetry: A Rapsody* (1733). In Johnson's dictionary a rhapsody is defined as "any number of parts joined together, without necessary dependence or natural connection,"[26] and Swift's poem often has the appearance of being consistent with this definition. In its movement there are several shifts of direction which, when they occur, run dramatically counter to expectations that have been aroused in the reader. And since Swift sometimes creates the impression that these shifts occur under the pressure of impulses and energies that are disruptive of logical structure, the poem's movement takes on a certain resemblance to that which appears in some of the early poems, notably *To Mr. Congreve.*

Swift begins by defining the *"Pride"* (l. 3) and the "Perverseness" (l. 12) manifested by the large number of human beings who aspire to become poets. And in order to stress the folly of such an aspiration, he uses a sequence of analogies drawn from the animal kingdom:

> *Brutes* find out where their Talents lie;
> A *Bear* will not attempt to fly:
> A founder'd *Horse* will oft debate,
> Before he tries a five-barr'd Gate:
> A *Dog* by Instinct turns aside,
> Who sees the Ditch too deep and wide.
> (ll. 13-18)

Here, the successive emphases on height, depth, and width systematically enforce the notion that genuine poetic achievement is extremely difficult. In believing themselves capable of such achievement, Swift insists, human beings show themselves to be less rational than other animals: " . . . *Man* we find the only Creature,/Who, led by *Folly*, fights with *Nature*" (ll. 19-20). This argument, of course, implies an extremely high valuation of poetry, and in the following paragraph Swift establishes some of the reasons for such a valuation:

> Not *Empire* to the Rising-Sun,
> By Valour, Conduct, Fortune won;
> Nor highest *Wisdom* in Debates
> For framing Laws to govern States;
> Nor Skill in Sciences profound,
> So large to grasp the Circle round;
> Such heavenly Influence require,
> As how to strike the *Muses Lyre*.
>   (ll. 25-32)

He argues that, in order for genuine poetic creation to take place, extraordinary capacities are required, capacities that both include and go beyond the extremes of "Valour," "Wisdom," and "Skill" that are referred to here. And in the next three verse-paragraphs he makes it vividly clear that, although the genuine poet will possess these capacities, society will grant him almost no recognition or esteem for them. In this opening sequence, therefore, Swift confronts the would-be poet whom he is addressing with a daunting barrier. But once having made it plain that poetry is a most demanding activity, he does finally begin the task of explaining how best to attempt it:

> How shall a new Attempter learn
> Of diff'rent Spirits to discern,
> And how distinguish, which is which,
> The Poet's Vein, or scribling Itch?
> Then hear an old experienc'd Sinner
> Instructing thus a young Beginner.
>   (ll. 71-76)

It now appears that Swift's purpose in the first seventy lines of the poem has been rather like that of a teacher who is determined to ensure that his pupil recognizes the difficulty of what lies ahead before he will begin the process of instruction. In the above passage he defines himself as a teacher, and he implicitly casts the imagined reader in the role of a pupil who is about to be instructed in the art of poetry (although Swift says that the reader is about to overhear him instructing a third person, namely the "young Beginner," it is the reader who inevitably becomes the recipient of the advice). He suggests that he is going to enable the reader to make an important distinction, between the "Poet's Vein" and the "scribling Itch." And the manner in which he describes his procedure at this point is very similar to the one that Pope adopts in another poem about poetry, when he says that he intends to "instruct the times,/To know the Poet from the Man of Rymes."[27] As Swift begins the process of instruction, his first words are fully in keeping with what the reader has been led to expect:

> Consult yourself, and if you find
> A powerful Impulse urge your Mind,
> Impartial judge within your Breast,
> What subject you can manage best;
> Whether your Genius most inclines
> To Satire, Praise, or hum'rous Lines;
> To Elegies in mournful Tone,
> Or Prologue sent from Hand unknown.
> (ll. 77-84)

It sounds here as if Swift is embarking on a distinctly Augustan *Ars Poetica*, one that begins logically by urging the reader to consider which of the available poetic kinds are most appropriate to his talent. But when he starts to describe the procedures that the aspiring poet must adopt once he has made his choice of genre, the poem suddenly takes a surprising direction:

Then rising with *Aurora's* Light,
The Muse invok'd, sit down to write;
Blot out, correct, insert, refine,
Enlarge, diminish, interline;
Be mindful, when Invention fails,
To scratch your Head, and Bite your Nails.
                                        (ll. 85-90)

What Swift recommends is essentially a series of mechanical gestures. The invocation of the Muse is reduced to the status of a routine, and after giving it a cursory mention Swift goes on to emphasize the importance of some well-known physical procedures for counteracting lapses of the imagination. Almost as soon as the process of instruction has begun, therefore, he appears to be insulting the figure whom he has cast in the role of pupil. He defeats the expectations that have been induced by the establishment of the teacher-pupil relationship, and engages in an aggressive attempt to unsettle the reader. It is as if Swift, in his role as teacher, has decided from the start that his pupil is not, and never will be, a genuine poet. So he bypasses what one would ordinarily assume to be the significant aspects of poetic composition, and focuses strictly on externals, as if he feels that these are the only matters which the reader is likely to understand. He talks in great detail about typology, and how it is used in "printed Trash" to serve the needs of the "dullest Reader" (ll. 91-104). And after this, he focuses on the commercial production of literature, recommending that his pupil should rely on the business acumen of Lintot (ll. 105-10). Swift is already attacking the hypothetical poem that he imagines his pupil to have written—he describes it as having been fitted with a suitably "modish Dress" (l. 105)—and his attitude towards the reader has thus become one of open aggression. Earlier in the poem Swift said that genuine poetic creativity involved the exercise of great human capacities and that, by instructing his auditor in the art of poetry, he would try to enable him to make the crucial distinction between the genuine and the spurious.

But in carrying out the process of instruction, he has departed radically from the kind of pattern that appeared to be establishing itself and from the traditional pattern of the *Ars Poetica*. And the impression is given that these patterns are being disrupted by the author's intense feelings of hostility towards modern literature. Swift's procedure at this point in the poem, then, bears some relationship to the way in which, in *To Mr. Congreve*, he makes it seem that certain radical energies and emotions force him to subvert the traditional structure of the prologue form.

After this, Swift maintains the note of aggressive contempt as he describes the manner in which the reader/pupil must respond to the "Judgement of the Town" (l. 125) upon his hypothetical poem; if that judgement is negative, Swift says, "you" must not admit yourself to be the author—otherwise, "you must bear the whole Disgrace,/'Till some fresh Blockhead takes your Place" (ll. 141-42). But when he comes to describe the aspiring poet's second and third attempts, he does finally offer the kind of advice that the early stages of the poem appeared to be leading towards:

> But first with Care imploy your Thoughts,
> Where Criticks mark'd your former Faults.
> The trivial Turns, and borrow'd Wit,
> The *Similes* that nothing fit;
> The *Cant* which ev'ry Fool repeats,
> Town-Jests, and Coffee-house Conceits;
> Descriptions tedious, flat and dry,
> And introduc'd the Lord knows why.
>
> (ll. 149-56)

Here, Swift addresses himself to some genuinely significant aspects of literary composition, and his manner of approach is clearly aligned with the conventions of the Augustan *Ars Poetica*. He focuses on the importance of originality, but also on the need for a rational and coherent relationship between parts, for similes that "fit" the matter being described and for descriptions that are relevant to the poem's argument. Almost as soon as the poem has settled into this fairly orthodox instructive manner, however, a further shift of direction occurs. Swift hypothesizes that one of the aspiring poet's initial errors was an excessive use of initials and blanks rather than the full names of the individuals under attack, and that his readers were consequently uncertain about whom he was referring to:

> A publick, or a private *Robber;*
> A *Statesman,* or a South-sea *Jobber.*
> A *Prelate* who no God believes;
> A ———, or Den of Thieves.
> A Pick-purse at the Bar, or Bench;
> A Duchess, or a Suburb-Wench.
>
> (ll. 161-66)

In this passage, instruction in the art of poetry gives way to social and political satire. The sequence of satiric juxtapositions obviously goes far beyond what is necessary for the making of the instructive point, and it appears that a new interest is momentarily directing the poem's movement. This interest is soon, in fact, going to become a dominant force. But first, as Swift again takes up his enumeration of literary errors, yet another tendency disrupts the orderly process of instruction that had begun to establish itself:

> Or oft when Epithets you link,
> In gaping Lines to fill a Chink;
> Like stepping Stones to save a Stride,
> In Streets where Kennels are too wide:
> Or like a Heel-piece to support
> A Cripple with one Foot too short;
> Or like a Bridge that joins a Marish
> To Moorlands of a diff'rent Parish.
> So have I seen ill-coupled Hounds,
> Drag diff'rent Ways in miry Grounds.
> So Geographers in *Afric*-Maps
> With Savage-Pictures fill their Gaps;

And o'er unhabitable Downs
Place Elephants for want of Towns.
                    (ll. 167-80)

Swift begins by defining a serious literary fault, but as he develops the sequence of comparisons he shifts away from a concern with instructive definition towards a process of sheer accretion that is disproportionate to the poem's argument. There is, of course, an element of parody in the sequence that is capable of playing a part in an instructive process.[28] But the accumulation of images is protracted so far, and takes on such an energetic life of its own, that it eventually seems to emanate from an author who is absorbed by a multiplicity of analogous particulars for their own sake, rather than for the sake of the initial subject. Also, the passage clearly involves an elaborate display of the author's ingenuity, and it is made to appear that an irrepressible inventive energy suddenly becomes a major influence in the development of the poem.

From this point on, the poem quite clearly becomes what it has been threatening to become from the moment at which Swift started to instruct the would-be poet—namely, a satire on contemporary literature, rather than an education in the art of poetry. And this literary satire leads more and more persistently towards satire on contemporary politics. At times the movement from the one to the other has the appearance of being compulsive, as if instigated by an irrepressible hostility. An example of this occurs soon after Swift has suggested that his pupil-reader should engage in the "profitable Game" (l. 184) of writing poems in praise of the king. He first emphasizes the fact that although a king is to be defined as an embodiment of "ev'ry Virtue" (l. 192) while he is alive, once dead he automatically becomes a *"Devil* in Hell" (l. 206). In this manner, Swift attacks the hypocrisy of poets who write the sort of panegyric that he is ironically recommending, and the passage thus plays a part in the developing satire on contemporary literature. But as soon as he imagines the king in Hell, he also imagines him to be surrounded by his

"Ministers of State," and this leads him to develop at some length the image of those ministers transformed into "Imps," and plying in Hell the dishonest "Arts" by which they were characterized on earth (ll. 207-18). The major function of such an image is obviously not to further the satiric definition of literary hypocrisy, but to enable Swift to attack some contemporary political activities about which he feels strongly. And this sudden movement from the literary to the political appears to derive from a process of compulsive association that was stimulated by the initial image of the dead king in Hell.

As the poem develops, however, one is increasingly made to feel that these shifts of emphasis are determined by a thematic pattern that steadily becomes more evident. For one thing, Swift's contemptuous instructions to the would-be poet begin at an early stage to focus on the politics rather than the art of poetry. And once he has conducted his pupil to the point at which he becomes an adept in these politics, and sets himself up as a *"Conoisseur"* (l. 276), Swift begins to establish what is perhaps the central thematic concept of the poem, namely a parallel between the literary and the political communities (ll. 263-78). This parallel is rather steadily maintained until the end of the poem, and it enables Swift to move from literary to political satire without creating a sense that the poem's development is uncoordinated. Indeed, in the middle and later stages of the poem there is a good deal of evidence to suggest that an orthodox process of thematic structuring has taken place; for example, when Swift compares the "State of War" that dominates the literary community with that which dominates the animal kingdom, and attributes a greater logic to the behavior of animals than to that of mankind (ll. 319-34), he returns to a concept that we have seen him establishing in the first paragraph of the poem. This is not to say, however, that the poem at any point settles into a predictable pattern, for there is an energetic variety in the satiric techniques by which Swift describes the nature of the literary community. And the poem does not, finally, arrive at a point of rest. Just before his conclusion Swift writes two passages of extended parody, in which he imitates the procedures adopted by sycophantic poets who compose eulogies of the royal families and of Walpole (ll. 411-64). The parodies are characterized by a high degree of rhetorical order, but that order is clearly spurious because it derives from a persistent falsification of reality.[29] Although Swift continues after this to heap ironic praise upon the king, his manner becomes hectoring and colloquial, as if he is growing impatient with the procedures he is ridiculing (ll. 471-80). And in the concluding paragraph there is a total breakdown of the ritualized order that appeared in the parodies:

> Translate me now some Lines, if you can,
> From *Virgil, Martial, Ovid, Lucan;*
> They could all Pow'r in Heaven divide,
> And do no Wrong to either Side:
> They'll teach you how to split a Hair,
> Give -------- and *Jove* an equal share.
> Yet, why should we be lac'd so straight;
> I'll give my ***** Butter-weight.
> And Reason good; for many a Year
> ----- never intermeddl'd here:
> Nor, tho' his Priests be duly paid,
> Did ever we *desire* his Aid:
> We now can better do without him,
> Since *Woolston* gave us Arms to rout him.
> (ll. 481-95)[30]

Swift is still ironically praising the king; he refers to the manner in which the Roman poets attributed equal power to Jove and to Caesar, only to insist that George's power is in fact greater than that of God. But his imitation of the attitudes that he perceives in the contemporary panegyrics has now brought him to utter what he must have regarded as blasphemy. And as Swift continues to adopt the manner of a poet who engages in such blasphemy with jaunty eagerness, it appears that he is carried by a wave of anger towards one final compulsive shift of direction; when he says that God has not "intermeddl'd" here for a long time, that we have never really wanted his help anyway, and that Woolston's theology has provided us with a means to do without him, Swift creates the impression that the primary impulse at work is no longer the desire to satirize bad poetry but a compulsive urge to attack a contemporary theologian whom he despised. In a sense, however, the passage could be regarded as a climactic demonstration of the type of mentality dominating the literary world that Swift has attacked, and as thus bringing the poem's satiric argument to a dramatic and finalizing conclusion. Similarly, when Swift writes *"Caetera desiderantur"* after the last line of the poem, his claim that the manuscript is incomplete becomes susceptible of two interpretations— first, that the poem ends abruptly, at a point where it appears to be moving suddenly in a new direction, because the rest of it has been lost,[31] and second, that after the delineation of such extreme and total chaos, there is really no more to be said. This concluding paragraph, therefore, is in certain ways turbulent and unruly in its rhetorical pattern (the barrage of dashes and asterisks furthers such an impression), but it does also bring the poem's argument to a kind of climax. It thus resembles the poem as whole. For although the movement of the *Rapsody* involves several disconcerting shifts of direction, a fairly high degree of thematic coordination does eventually emerge. The sudden shifts tend to occur most frequently in the early stages, and in certain respects it appears that the poem progressively settles into a coherent thematic pattern. But some central terms of that pattern are implicit in the poem's beginnings. And because of this, I think it can be said that Swift manages both to create the impression that certain unruly energies are involved in the poem's growth, and ultimately to include those energies in an ordered rhetorical unit. The poem thus differs from *To*

Mr. Congreve in the degree of orthodox thematic patterning that it ultimately achieves; its movement is not quite so disruptively "wild" as is the movement of the earlier poem. But in spite of this, there are enough resemblances between the two works to suggest that, at a late stage in his career, Swift was still interested in the creation of effects similar to those which he had been preoccupied by in the early poetry.

2

The Subversive Image

A S we have seen, it is very often through metaphor that the disruptive energy of Swift's early poems expresses itself. At various times in these poems, Swift will invent metaphors that involve drastic gaps between tenor and vehicle, he will protract the elaboration of metaphors to extreme lengths of ingenuity, and he will allow metaphors to proliferate into unruly sequences. These various forms of rhetorical extravagance tend to be subversive of certain neo-classical orthodoxies such as restraint, proportion, and coherence. And when Swift took up poetry again after his temporary rejection of it, he did not eliminate such tendencies, even though the poetry he now began to write was obviously very different from what he had written earlier. In his use of metaphor, he continued to show an interest in configurations that subverted certain orthodox patterns of coherent development.

One particularly vivid manifestation of such an interest is the parodying of formal logic which often accompanies Swift's development of an image. And in order to approach this matter, it is useful to recall some of the ways in which he parodies the logician's procedures in the major prose works. In *A Tale of a Tub, An Argument against Abolishing Christianity,* and *A Modest Proposal,* he uses some traditional structures of syllogistic argument in ways which are ironic and which imply that these structures are not in themselves adequate to the situations with which they ostensibly cope. This has been put in another way, of course; namely that Swift invents speakers who employ the forms of logical argument but who do not seem to be of particularly admirable intelligence or sensitivity. In the *Argument,* for instance, although the speaker is basically right that it would be better not to abolish Christianity, his carefully arranged syllogisms are for the most part absurd, and in the *Proposal,* the more cogent the speaker's demonstration of his thesis becomes, the more grotesque is its insensitivity; in both works the reader has to move beyond the surface "logic" in order to understand Swift's definition of his subject. However one describes the technique, it is clear that the important meanings which Swift wishes to express in these works are not expressed directly by means of the "logical" structures which appear on the surface, but indirectly by means of Swift's subversive manipulation of those structures (or of his logicians); it has been suggested, for instance, that on several of those occasions when the speaker of the *Tale* tries to be painstakingly logical, he succeeds in "proving" the truth of some obviously absurd fallacies, and thus appears to be deluded by his own rigid thought-processes.[1] The techniques of formal logic which appear in these works are reduced to devices by which Swift may conduct the reader along a clearly marked path into ironic complexities which are outside the logician's scope. And one consequence of this is that Swift's attitude towards the traditional procedures of logical argument seems to be somewhat less than respectful. This attitude does not, of course, manifest itself consistently in Swift's work. But it certainly appears in several of his poems, especially when he is engaged in the development of metaphor. Indeed, in the poems that I shall discuss in this chapter, Swift not only shows a certain disrespect for rigid argumentative procedures, but at times comes very close to ridiculing formal, consecutive logic of any kind.

One of the earliest poems that Swift wrote after his resumption of poetry was *The Problem* (1699), in which he analyzes the rumour that Charles, the second Earl of Berkeley, *"stinks"* when he is in love. Swift recognizes the difficulty of believing that so "sweet a Passion" (1. 3) could express itself in this way, and he proposes to solve the problem by a process of logical argument:

> But now, to solve the Nat'ral Cause
> By sober, Philosophick Laws,
> Whether all Passions, when in Ferment,
> Work out, as Anger does in Vermin?
> (ll. 13-16)

In these lines he adopts the stance of a natural scientist who is going to be very rigorous in his determination of the issue; he is going to follow "sober, Philosophick Laws" as he develops the arguments that will lead to a logical solution. But such a stance has already been made to look absurd by the initial definition of the problem to be solved. And it is subjected to a further assault as Swift starts to bring examples and analogies to bear upon the issue: "We read of Kings," he says, "who in a Fright,/Tho' on a Throne, wou'd fall to sh—" (ll. 19-20). Immediately after this, Swift begins to analyze a traditional metaphor that he claims is relevant to the problem:

> Beside all this, deep Scholars know,
> That the main String of Cupid's Bow,
> Once on a Time, was an A— Gut,
> Now to a nobler Office put,
> By Favour, or Desert preferr'd
> From giving Passage to a T—.
> But still, tho' fixt among the Stars,
> Does sympathize with Human A—.
> Thus when you feel an hard-bound B—
> Conclude Love's Bow-String at full Stretch;
> Till the kind L—seness comes, and then
> Conclude the Bow relax'd again.
> (ll. 21-32)

Certain phrases in this passage appear to suggest that the analysis of the image is a further stage in the development of a logical argument. The appeal to the authority of "deep Scholars," the use of words like "Thus" and "Conclude," and the precise attention to physiological detail, are some of the ways in which Swift imitates the manner of a systematic logician. But such a manner is of course ludicrously inappropriate to what is really going on. It is clear that Swift is seeking to heighten the comedy of the poem by creating an absurd contrast between the procedures of logical debate and the scurrilous image that he is developing. And the force of that image reduces the logician's stance to a transparent sham.

A few years later, Swift used a similar technique in *The Description of a Salamander* (1705). The argument of this poem is provided with an obtrusively neat structure. After a general preamble about the reasons why great men get their nicknames, Swift turns specifically to Lord Cutts, who had been given the name of "Salamander" for his bravery under fire. In order to establish more clearly the reasons for this nickname, Swift twice juxtaposes a sequence of details from Pliny's description of the salamander with a sequence of analogous details about Cutts's personality and career. The comparison is divided into two linked pairs of verse-paragraphs; the first two paragraphs are exactly equal in length, the fourth fractionally longer than the third, as Swift brings his case to a climax. Besides giving his argument this almost symmetrical pattern, he adopts the tone of a meticulously logical investigator; in order to avoid making any subjective judgments, he will follow a long-established authority:

> *Pliny* shall prove what we affirm:
> *Pliny* shall prove, and we'll apply,
> And I'll be judg'd by standers-by.
> (ll. 26-28)

Not only is the argument to be studiously objective, but it is also to be developed consecutively; each successive paragraph begins with a word stressing the care which has been taken—"FIRST," "SO," "FARTHER," "SO." Thus, Swift goes through the motions of logical, reasonable discussion, adopting the manner of one who is conscientiously and rather deliberately bent on demonstrating the truth of a proposition. But the actual purpose of the comparison, and the direction which it is going to take, become clear with the first group of details which Swift recites from the *Natural History:*

> FIRST then, our Author has defin'd
> This Reptil, of the Serpent kind,
> With gawdy Coat, and shining Train,
> But loathsom Spots his Body stain.
> (ll. 29-32)

Pretending to be clinically exact in his exploration of a given analogy, Swift associates Cutts with a series of repulsive physical images. The military hero had been given his nickname because of the salamander's supposed ability to resist heat:

> FARTHER, we are by *Pliny* told
> This *Serpent* is extreamly cold,
> So cold, that put it in the Fire,
> 'Twill make the very Flames expire.
> (ll. 47-50)

So by analogy Cutts becomes a cold, chilling influence, able to resist heat because of his aged insensitivity:

> SO have I seen a batter'd Beau
> By Age and Claps grown cold as Snow,
> Whose Breath or Touch, where e'er he came,
> Blew out Love's Torch or chill'd the Flame.
> (ll. 57-60)

The carefully systematic conduct of Swift's argument thus leads towards a cluster of images which expresses an intensely

emotional response; just as the salamander "Spues a filthy
Froth" of "Matter purulent and white" which causes "Lep-
rosy," so the "Filth" which Cutts "ejects" brings "Pox" to
the bodies of the women with whom he comes into contact.
And it begins to look as if Swift is using the extended analogy
in order to give some degree of shape to the expression of his
disgust. But if we simply say that he employs the procedures
of logical argument in order to give cogency to his attack,
then I think we fail to do justice to the poem's (admittedly
rather limited) complexity. For the analogy is developed in
such an obtrusively neat fashion, and the imagery to which it
leads is so violent in its debasing force, that the poem's
language finally has the effect of running dramatically counter to the nature of its structural surface. Clearly, the systematic structure of the poem is not intended to deceive anyone.
Swift may imitate the procedures of logically consecutive
argument, but he is manifestly engaged in another sort of
activity than that. Moreover, as the logician's methodology
comes to seem less and less appropriate to what Swift is
actually doing, another and different kind of logic steadily
asserts itself. For by continuously making the reader associate
Cutts's personality and career with the ugly details about the
salamander, Swift enforces a connection which is not rationally demonstrated but which is extremely difficult to
resist. The reader is not persuaded to believe the analogy
valid, in the way that he might be persuaded to accept a
carefully argued proposition, but he is made to hold the two
sets of details so closely together in his mind as he reads the
poem that he finally has to make a strenuous effort of the will
if he is going to separate them. The salamander in this way
becomes a metaphor for Cutts, and there is in the poem an
almost irresistible logic of imagery which pushes aside the
kind of logic which the poem parodies. The poem thus
expresses a kind of contempt for the structures of formal
argument, first by abusing them, and then by replacing and
overwhelming them with another kind of "logic" altogether.

In *The Fable of Midas* (1712) Swift again works out a debasing analogy with a parade of argumentative rigor and precision. The poem is divided into almost exactly equal halves, in the first of which Swift tells the story of Midas, and in the second relates the details of that story to the political career of the Duke of Marlborough. The poem thus resembles *The Description of a Salamander* in that it possesses a near-symmetrical outline which is calculated to give an appearance of rigorously logical progression. But again the impression of logicality is transparently spurious. In his initial account of how Midas gained and lost the power of transforming all he touched into gold, Swift establishes a set of details so concretely that there is no escaping them for the rest of the poem:

> He *chip't* his *Bread,* the Pieces round
> Glitter'd like Spangles on the Ground:
> A Codling e'er it went his Lip in,
> Would strait become a *Golden* Pippin:
> He call'd for Drink, you saw him Sup
> *Potable Gold* in *Golden Cup.*
>
> (ll. 3-8)

He begins the second part by making the connection between Midas and Marlborough in a quietly reasonable tone, as if attempting to explain an analogy as clearly and precisely as he can:

> This Tale inclines the gentle Reader,
> To think upon a certain *Leader,*
> To whom from *Midas* down, descends
> That Virtue in the Fingers ends:
> What else by *Perquisites* are meant,
> By *Pensions, Bribes,* and *three per Cent?*
>
> (ll. 41-46)

As Swift continues to describe Marlborough's career, he constantly refers back to the story of Midas, making the comparison with a painstaking attention to detail like that which we would expect of a logician. But while he pretends in this way to be engaged in a form of discursive argument, attempting to establish a definition of Marlborough by a process of analogy, what he actually does is to set up a debasing metaphor and then keep insisting on it until the reader cannot get it out of his mind.[2] The kind of image to which this technique constantly leads is not, of course, a kind which tends to characterize conscientious discursive argument:

> But *Gold* defiles with frequent Touch,
> There's nothing *fouls* the Hands so much:
> And Scholars give it for the Cause,
> Of *British Midas* dirty Paws.
>
> (ll. 67-70)

Even here, while enforcing such an image (and "gold" was slang for excrement), Swift cannot resist pretending to be studiously logical; it is on the authority of "Scholars" that he explains Marlborough's dirty hands. The poem thus resembles *The Description of a Salamander* in that it invokes the formalities of rational, consecutive argument only to reduce them to devices by which a damning metaphor can be fastened upon the object of Swift's satire. In the stolidly deliberate transition from the first part of the poem to the second Swift clearly parodies the methods of the conscientious logician. But again, such methods are clearly not intended to deceive anyone—the logic of the poem is too openly the logic of satiric metaphor rather than the logic of rational argument—and because of this they cannot be regarded as providing a kind of built-in cogency to Swift's attack. On the contrary, the poem once again seems to make fun of the structures of logical discourse by blatantly abusing them.

When Swift uses structures of this kind in order to develop a metaphor, he does not always include within them such clear echoes of the logician's phraseology as he does in the above poems. In *A Simile, on Our Want of Silver, and the only Way to remedy it* (1725), for example, the parody of formal logic is not so evident, but the poem's symmetry of structure has an effect rather like that which we have seen in *The Fable of Midas*. In the first part of the poem Swift establishes an image of the *"Silver"* moon being thrown into eclipse by devious and unnatural means:

> As when of old, some Sorc'ress threw
> O'er the Moon's Face a sable Hue,
> To drive unseen her magick Chair,
> At Midnight, through the dark'ned Air;
> Wise People, who believ'd with Reason
> That this Eclipse was out of Season,
> Affirm'd the Moon was sick, and fell
> To cure her by a Counter-spell.
>
> (ll. 1-8)

This "Counter-spell" involves a high degree of dramatic action, as "Ten Thousand Cymbals now begin/To rend the Skies with brazen Din." And the action is successful; the "Cloud" is dispelled, the "Hag" is driven into Hell, and the moon is able to show her *"Silver* Face" again. Swift's short narrative creates a vivid picture of devious and selfish evil first creating unnatural conditions and then being routed by "Wise People." And he now proceeds to relate this picture to the economic situation which was created in Ireland when William Wood was granted a patent to mint new copper coinage for the country:

> So, (if my Simile you minded,
> Which, I confess, is too long winded)
> When late a Feminine Magician,
> Join'd with a *brazen* politician,
> Expos'd, to blind the Nation's Eyes,
> A Parchment of prodigious Size;
> Conceal'd behind that ample Screen,
> There was no Silver to be seen.
>
> (ll. 17-24)

The images established in the first part of the poem are now being used to express an intense hostility towards the Duchess of Kendal and Sir Robert Walpole. And when Swift goes on to describe the hoped-for defeat of the new economic measures, the strength of his feeling is again apparent. He suggests that the *"Draper"* will use his "Counter-Charm" (Swift's own *Drapier's Letters*) so vigorously and so loudly that all Ireland will hear, the paper on which Wood's patent is written will "shrivel," the two conjurers will be driven "to the Devil," and the consequence of their defeat will be that "Our Silver will appear again." This exuberantly narrated triumph of good over evil is the climax of a poem in which Swift has used an extended simile (which at times becomes a metaphor) to express violent indignation. The simile has not only been developed with a meticulous, step-by-step attention to the details of parallelism, but it has also been set within a symmetrically structured framework. For the poem is divided into two paragraphs of sixteen lines, the first devoted to the establishment of the major image, and the second to its application. Embodied by the poem's outline, therefore, is an obtrusive and very strict logicality of design which would appear to imply that the poem progresses according to the dictates of rational and systematic argument. But the emotional animus of the poem's images runs drastically counter to the claims implicitly made by this framework. And the symmetrical structure of the poem is in fact made to look like a patent fabrication, its meticulous tidiness comically inappropriate to what Swift is really engaged in.

In the above examples, it is the violence of a central image that subverts the impression of logical order given by the poem's structure. Elsewhere, Swift creates similarly subversive effects by means of an energetic and unruly proliferation of images. A tendency towards this kind of proliferation shows itself in *Vanbrug's House* (1703), which was written quite soon after his resumption of poetry. When Swift later came to revise this poem, apparently under the influence of

Addison,[3] one of the main alterations he made was to remove
a metaphor which he had clearly been persuaded to regard as
insufficiently coordinated with the poem's central line of
argument. And in order to understand the position which
this metaphor occupied, one has to consider the original
version of the poem in some detail. Swift conceived the idea
for the poem when John Vanbrugh started to build a house
for himself on the site of the ruined Whitehall. Working on
the notion that the house was financed by the profits accruing
from Vanbrugh's plays, Swift wrote a poem which focuses on
the contrast between ancient and modern literature. He begins by considering the traditional image of the poet as
builder, an image deriving from the "Pythagorean notion . . .
that the same numbers which govern harmony in music and
poetry govern architecture as well."[4] In one sense, he burlesques this image by developing it in literal detail and making
it sound absurd:

> Sonnets and Elegyes to Chloris
> Would raise a House about two Storyes;
> A Lyrick Ode would Slate; a Catch
> Would Tile; an Epigram would Thatch.
> (ll. 9-12)

But he also uses it to introduce an attack on Vanbrugh and on
the modern literature he is taken to represent. For when he
suggests that modern poets no longer have access to this
"Art" (l. 13) or "Power" (l. 7), he exploits the notion as a
metaphoric expression of the power of the ancient poets and
as a means of diminishing the reader's sense of what the
modern poet is capable of achieving. Further on in the poem,
this ancient concept is specifically applied to Vanbrugh's
house, which becomes a metaphor for the decline of literature
from the way it once was. And the poem concludes with a
series of metaphors and analogies emphasizing that decline.
This noticeably coordinated sequence of ideas and images is
at one point interrupted, however, by an image that does not

clearly connect with the dominant architectural motif. Immediately after developing the idea that modern poets do not have access to the building power of the ancients, Swift begins to develop an analogy between a modern playwright and a silkworm:

> There is a Worm by Phoebus bred,
> By Leaves of Mulberry is fed;
> Which unprovided where to dwell,
> Consumes it self to weave a Cell.
> Then curious Hands this Texture take,
> And for themselves fine Garments make.
> Mean time a Pair of awkward Things
> Grew to his Back instead of Wings;
> He flutters when he Thinks he flyes,
> Then sheds about his Spaun, and dyes.
>
> (ll. 29-38)

After initially establishing the image in this way, Swift spends a further sixteen lines in relating it to the modern playwright, thus engaging in the fairly elaborate protraction of a metaphor. It was this metaphor that he later decided to eliminate from the poem, and it is not difficult to see why he did so. For although there is a momentary link with the building motif in the fact that the silkworm "Consumes itself to weave a Cell," and although the image does reinforce the pervading contempt for the moderns, it diverges in a radical way from the steady concentration on architectural imagery that is maintained in the rest of the poem. Because of this, one can see why Addison might have felt it should be removed. In the revised version of the poem, the silkworm image is replaced by a much more extensive development of the image of Vanbrugh as poet-builder and by a careful and repetitive underlining of the point that Vanbrugh's house is small because the creative and intellectual content of his plays is small. In this way, the linear development of the poem becomes more strictly coherent than it was in the first version. But although the elaborately developed silkworm image may in this way be regarded as an excrescence, its removal does deprive the poem of a certain kind of vitality. For the metaphor embodies certain energies of hostility that, disruptive though they may be, make the revised version of the poem look rather stiffly formalized. In Swift's application of the image to the modern playwright, a fairly high degree of verbal intensity keeps on manifesting itself; after emitting his "tawdry Stuff," this "Insect of the Age" moves rapidly towards an ugly death:

> And now he spreads his little Fans,
> (For all the Muses Geese are Swans)
> And borne on fancy's Pinions, thinks,
> He soars sublimest when he Sinks:
> But scatt'ring round his Fly-blows, dyes;
> Whence Broods of insect Poets rise.
>   (ll. 48-54)

The metaphor thus suggests the presence of energies not easily contained by the type of "logical" framework that Swift eventually imposed. And this first version of the poem shows Swift tending towards a metaphoric abundance which is unruly in the sense that it comes into conflict with what he later conceived to be the requirements of orderly discourse.

In *The Virtues of Sid Hamet the Magician's Rod* (1710), the proliferation of images departs much more radically from these principles of logical structure. The poem involves a thoroughgoing escape from rational, consecutive discourse, and as such it might seem a fairly typical example of an Augustan poet taking a sort of holiday from his more serious duties. But the presence in Swift's work of those tendencies which I have described above suggests the possibility that *Sid Hamet's Rod* is symptomatic of a distinctive and deeply rooted attitude of mind. The poem is an attack on Sidney Godolphin, written soon after he had been deprived of his post of Lord Treasurer. There are elements in it of what might have been a rationally conducted argument, if the rational conduct of an argument had been Swift's concern; Godolphin is accused, for instance, of both greed and dishonesty. But while we are vaguely aware that he is being accused of vices which are quite susceptible of cogent moral definition, such as that which Pope might have given them, the poem does not engage us in the rational contemplation of moral issues. Instead, it provides us with a highly entertaining sequence of analogies, in which Godolphin's vices are simply taken for granted, and which is so vivid and ingenious that we feel no inclination to question its accuracy.

Godolphin had been requested by the queen to break his staff of office, and the image of the staff is used by Swift as the starting-point for a display of destructive analogical wit. He begins by comparing it to the rod of Moses, which was "harmless" while he held it in his hand, but became a "devouring Serpent" when he put it down. Godolphin's staff, however, changed in the opposite way:

> His *Rod* was honest *English* Wood,
> That, senseless, in a Corner stood,
> Till Metamorphos'd by his Grasp,
> It grew an all-devouring Asp;
> Would hiss, and sting, and roll, and twist,
> By the meer Virtue of his Fist.
>
> (ll. 7-12)

When this momentarily useful comparison is worked out, Swift finds a wholly unrelated image in the divining rod; Godolphin's staff of office pointed towards sources of profit as unerringly as the divining rod was supposed to point towards gold:

> In *Scottish* Hills found precious Ore,
> Where none e'er look'd for it before;
> And, by a *gentle Bow*, divin'd
> How well a *Cully*'s Purse was lin'd:
> To a forlorn and broken *Rake*,
> Stood without Motion, like a Stake.
>
> (ll. 29-34)

Next, just as the rod of Hermes could put mortals to sleep and send "departed Souls" to the underworld, so Godolphin's powerful staff could cloud the minds of Parliament and "drive . . . *Souls to Hell*" (ll. 34-42). From classical mythology Swift then turns to a more commonplace reality, forcing into relevance the image of a fishing rod:

> *SID's* Rod was slender, white, and tall,
> Which oft he us'd to *fish* withal:
> A *PLACE* was fastned to the Hook,
> And many Score of *Gudgeons* took;
> Yet, still so happy was his Fate,
> He caught his *Fish*, and sav'd his *Bait*.
> (ll. 43-48)

After this emphasis on a fairly ordinary acquisitiveness, he next finds an analogy in the world of magic, and through this he insists again on the obscure and corrupt power that Godolphin wielded in office; Swift suggests that whereas a magician describes a circle with his wand in order to keep evil spirits away, "Sid" described his own huge circle in order to create a space within which they could throng around him (ll. 49-58). After this, the last in the series of classical analogies is made:

> *ACHILLES's* Scepter was of Wood,
> Like *Sid's*, but nothing near so good.
> (ll. 59-60)

And here Swift's tone grows lighter and more facetious; he openly revels in the absurdity of the poem's progression, seeming to become intoxicated by his own inventive wit and by the game which it is playing. In spite of the heroic ancestry of Achilles' scepter, he suggests, it can't match Sid's. For nothing grew on it; it was just a "sapless Twig." Whereas

> *Sid's* Scepter, full of Juice, did shoot
> In Golden Boughs, and Golden Fruit,

And He, the *Dragon* never sleeping,
Guarded each fair *Hesperian* Pippin.
(ll. 71-4)

The moral point about Godolphin's greed is still being made, of course, but by now it has been reduced to little more than the occasion for a comic performance. Godolphin's attitude towards the staff is next compared to that of a child towards a hobbyhorse. And he is finally reprimanded for being so foolish as to turn the staff into a *"Rod"* for his "own Breech" when he might have continued to use it like a jockey's whip. Such foolishness is likely to mean that the only sort of rod he will have in the future will be "a *Rod* in *Piss*."

Each of the several analogies enforces Swift's criticism of Godolphin in a manner obtrusively different from that in which analogies enforce meanings in logical discourse. Every time he introduces a new comparison, Swift accuses Godolphin of some vice, usually greed, which the comparison has the air of confirming. But the various images and allusions which he brings to bear on Godolphin are simply devices by which Swift makes a repetitive attack seem like an entertaining diversion. The analogies are ingenious, and the reader is constantly entertained by the neatness with which they are worked out. Swift invites us to be amused by his ingenuity, and not to examine very closely the charges that are being made; what engages our attention in each instance is the neatness of the parallelism rather than the nature of the charge which that parallelism is a witty way of making. The entertainment we are offered takes it for granted that Godolphin in office was a greedy, corrupt, and insensitive man, and it does not attempt either a complex rendering or a moral definition of these vices. Instead, the reader is invited to take Godolphin's vices for granted also; and in the process of relishing the wit of the imagery by which those vices are constantly reasserted, he tends to do so. Thus, the poem's technique is constantly subversive of logical thought. Swift seduces his reader away from rational contemplation of the vices he asserts, asking for a different kind of attention from that which we give to logical argument—and by this I mean either the kind of logical argument one might find in discursive prose or the kind which is ordinarily conducted, however much in terms of concrete images rather than abstractions, in responsible satiric poetry. Nor does Swift pretend to be responsible to the ordinary canons of logic. He makes it quite plain that the various analogies are just diverting ways of phrasing an accusation, rather than ways of enriching a moral argument. He is blatantly open in his avoidance of logical thought-processes.

The only kind of logic that the poem does possess is strictly visual in nature. For however varied and miscellaneous the several analogies are, each of them at least involves the presence of an object that bears some sort of resemblance to Godolphin's staff. The poem thus develops its own kind of internal logic, essentially pictorial in nature, which Swift jauntily substitutes for the logic of rational communication. But the logic of *Sid Hamet* is, of course, openly specious—it is based on the assumption that if a large enough number of witty analogies can be forced into an apparent relevance, then the truth of an assertion will seem to have been demonstrated. In this poem ingenuity itself is offered as a form of comic "proof." And while it would perhaps be going too far to suggest that Swift implicitly mocks the logician's procedures here, the poem very clearly arises out of an effort to avoid consecutive logical discourse and to substitute for it another and radically different kind of communication.

In *Sid Hamet* certain things are said about Godolphin which might have formed elements in a morally critical argument; beneath all the ingenuity there is a serious and intellectually appraisable meaning. It is the manner in which that meaning is communicated which makes the poem look like a deliberate evasion of logical discourse. But in *A Serious Poem upon William Wood* (1724) there is not even this vestige of a meaningful content. The poem again works almost entirely through the vehicle of analogy. And this time Swift brings into play any phrase, tradition, or anecdote in which the word "wood" occurs and which can be used to make fun of his opponent. But the analogies are not in this instance devices by which he reasserts a moral deficiency (the nearest Swift gets to this is when he calls upon the old tradition about the *"Devil"* speaking from the *"Trunk* of an *Oak")*. Rather, they are images by which he exuberantly communicates anger. Many of the analogies simply describe situations in which a longing to do violence to Wood is gloriously fulfilled; Swift's exploitation of the phrase *"Hewers* of WOOD" (ll. 1-4) is a vivid instance of this, and so is an anecdote about a carpenter boring a hole in a wooden image of a saint (ll. 71-80). For the purposes of this poem, Swift adopts the *persona* of an irrepressible jester, proud of his vigorously eclectic talent: "I ne'er could endure my Talent to smother,/I told you one Tale, I will tell you another" (ll. 69-70). Such a stance is very appropriate to the nature of what Swift is actually doing. He attributes to himself a high degree of inventive energy in the accumulation of anecdotes, analogies, similes and metaphors that can be used to denigrate Wood, and he suggests that he is not going to subject this energy to any kind of restraint. In the poem as a whole, the sequence of images is wildly, exuberantly miscellaneous, lacking any coordinating factors other than the word "wood" and an adaptability to the expression of Swift's anger; the first of these factors provides only a fortuitous verbal connection rather than any thematic relationship, and the second is not a cohesive force because the poem is in large part a demonstration of Swift's ingenious capacity to adapt almost anything to the attack on Wood (such as the title of Wycherley's play, *Love in a Wood*). Thus, instead of selecting and ordering details so as to construct a form which acts as a defense against multiplicity, Swift appears to embrace that multiplicity, seeking to immerse himself in an infinite variety of particulars that are only marginally or accidentally related to one another. In a sense, the poem's structure is a comic parody of the workings of the unifying imagination; for Swift brings a wide variety of images to bear upon his theme, and thus shows a good deal of inventive power, but the relationships between the images are blatantly tenuous and the pattern they form is chaotic rather than homogeneous. At any rate, the movement of the poem is well calculated to suggest the presence of an inventive energy which, under the stimulus of an intense emotion, becomes exuberantly disruptive of logic, proportion, and coherent form.

At certain points in the poem, however, Swift pretends that he is using the procedures of an orthodox logician. After professing to be puzzled by the ability of such an *"Obscure"* rogue as Wood to attract so much attention, he offers an explanation based on venerable scientific authority:

> I own it hath often provok'd me to Mutter,
> That, a Rogue so *Obscure* should make such a Clutter,
> But antient *Philosophers* wisely Remark,
> That old rotten WOOD will *Shine* in the *Dark*.
>
> (ll. 5-8)

And a little further on, he pretends to arrive at a conclusion about Wood by a process of careful, systematic investigation. First he defines the problem: "I hear among Scholars there is a great Doubt/From what Kind of Tree this WOOD was Hewn out" (ll. 25-26). Then he brings before the reader four different solutions which others have offered, only to reject them one by one, and finally to arrive at what he considers to be the truth: "But I'll tell you the Secret, and pray do not Blab,/He is an old *Stump* cut out of a *Crab*" (ll. 35-36). The processes of rational argument are thus mimicked for the sake of comedy. And the element of parody only underlines the extent to which "logic" has been subverted in this poem.

The exuberant multiplicity of images that appears in both the above poem and *Sid Hamet's Rod* is also a major characteristic of *The Bubble* (1720). The poem is a satire on those associated with the South Sea project, and Swift takes as his starting-point the notion that the managers of the project deluded investors into believing the South Sea to be a rich source of financial gain. This notion leads him at once into the image of the sea as a distorting medium.

> Ye wise Philosophers explain
> What Magick makes our Money rise
> When dropt into the Southern Main,
> Or do these Juglers cheat our Eyes?
> (ll.1-4)

From the outset, then, the act of investment is being described in metaphoric terms. And a little further on, we find Swift bringing an analogy to bear upon the initial image:

> Thus in a Basin drop a Shilling,
> Then fill the Vessel to the Brim,
> You shall observe as you are filling,
> The pond'rous Metal seems to swim;
>
> It rises both in Bulk and Height,
> Behold it swelling like a Sop!
> The liquid Medium cheats your Sight,
> Behold it mounted to the Top!
> (ll. 9-16)

At this point the development of the poem has a distinctly methodical air about it. Swift establishes the analogy in a meticulous, step-by-step manner, showing an ostentatious care for clarity of explanation, as if he were demonstrating a scientific experiment to a public audience. And what he describes is a clear illustration of the theme he has stated in the opening stanza. His procedure therefore bears some resemblance to that in *The Description of a Salamander*, for a forceful debasing metaphor is again accompanied by a show of careful logicality. Swift then develops the initial metaphor somewhat further, as he describes the water of the South Sea

as a medium in which one can become dangerously immersed; the "deluded Bankrupt . . . plunges in the *Southern
Waves*" and becomes "Dipt over head and Ears—in Debt" (ll.
21-24). And the analogy which follows seems clearly designed
as a further illustration of this danger:

> So, by a Calenture misled,
> The Mariner with Rapture sees
> On the smooth Ocean's azure Bed
> Enamell'd Fields, and verdant Trees;
>
> With eager Hast he longs to rove
> In that fantastick Scene, and thinks
> It must be some enchanted Grove,
> And in he leaps, and down he sinks.
> (ll. 25-32)

Here, the sailor afflicted with tropical fever is first deluded as
he looks at the water, and then drowned in it, so that the
analogy is coordinated with the two aspects of the water-
image that Swift has stressed so far. Consequently, although
by this point the reader is likely to feel that Swift is being
elaborately and perhaps even profusely metaphorical, the
poem still gives the impression that the invention of analogies is being subordinated to the coherent development of a
theme. This impression begins to weaken, however, in the
next sequence of stanzas, when Swift introduces yet another
analogy:

> Rais'd up on Hope's aspiring Plumes,
> The young Advent'rer o'er the Deep
> An Eagle's Flight and State assumes,
> And scorns the middle Way to keep:
>
> On *Paper* Wings he takes his Flight,
> With *Wax* the *Father* bound them fast,
> The *Wax* is melted by the Height,
> And down the towring Boy is cast:
>
> A Moralist might here explain,
> The Rashness of the *Cretan* Youth,

Describe his Fall into the Main,
And from a Fable form a Truth.
(ll. 33-44)

The Icarus image does advance the poem's satiric argument
to some extent, of course, particularly in its emphasis on the
notion that the young investor's "Fall into the Main" is
caused by a refusal to keep "the middle Way." But it is
difficult at this point not to feel that the element of sheer
metaphoric inventiveness has become a primary concern, just
as it did in *Sid Hamet's Rod*. Indeed, the poem soon develops
into an exuberant and indefatigable display of ingenuity, as
Swift continues to address his theme exclusively by means of
analogy and metaphor. When he raises the question of how it
is that *"Fools"* tend to float and the *"Wise"* to drown in that
"dang'rous Gulf," he is led to an image of *"Geese"* being able
to swim in the river Severn when the "Bird of Jove would
sink" (ll. 49-56). He then changes his mind about this diag-
nosis, suggests that the shrewd *"Directors"* of the project are
the ones who really triumph by manipulating the "Fools,"
and proceeds to a further analogy:

> So when upon a Moon-shine Night
> An Ass was drinking at a Stream,
> A Cloud arose and stopt the Light,
> By intercepting ev'ry Beam;
>
> The Day of Judgement will be soon,
> Cryes out a Sage among the Croud,
> An Ass hath swallow'd up the Moon,
> The Moon lay safe behind the Cloud.
> (ll. 73-80)

Here, the ass is an image of the fools who are manipulated,
and the cloud is an image of the directors. Just before and
after this passage, the directors are also described as whales
that "eat up all" and as flying fish that keep dipping into the
ocean for a moisture that paradoxically makes them better
able to fly. It is clear at this point that images are proliferating

with a good deal of energy, that they are becoming more and more multifarious, and that Swift is trying to engage the reader's agreement by an impressive display of his inventive powers. But in each of the above examples, Swift's imagery is relevant to a satiric argument which it in some sense advances, and it can therefore be said that although the metaphoric inventiveness is not exactly subordinated to the development of a theme, at least it has not lost a sense of connection with it. In the next sequence of analogies, however, a somewhat different impression is given:

> Undone at Play, the Femal Troops
> Come here their Losses to retrieve,
> Ride o'er the Waves in spacious Hoops,
> Like *Lapland* Witches in a Sieve:
>
> Thus *Venus* to the Sea descends
> As Poets feign; but where's the Moral?
> It shews the Queen of Love intends
> To search the Deep for Pearl and Coral.
> (ll. 89-96)

Here, the initial image of the "Femal Troops" attempting to "Ride o'er the Waves" is an ingenious variation on the poem's basic metaphor, and even the reference to *"Lapland* Witches," however ostentatiously farfetched, does not quite suggest that inventiveness is running riot. But in the second stanza, the myth of Venus's descent into the ocean seems blatantly forced into the poem in order to demonstrate that Swift can adapt almost anything to his satiric purpose, especially if it involves some reference to water. When he asks where the "Moral" of the story lies, it is as if he is challenging the reader to predict how he will apply that story to his subject. And when he does apply it, the very gratuitousness of the reference becomes a comic testament to his ingenuity. Such an impression is strengthened by the stanza that follows, in which the poem's development becomes rather like that of *A Serious Poem upon William Wood:*

The Sea is richer than the Land,
I heard it from my Grannam's Mouth,
Which now I clearly understand,
For by the Sea she meant the *South*.
(ll. 97-100)

This is the first in a series of traditional sayings or phrases that are now forced into the poem's increasingly motley texture. A little further on, for example, Swift adapts a passage from Ecclesiastes with a jaunty display of his capacity to improvise:

Upon the Water cast thy Bread,
And after many Days thou'lt find it,
But Gold upon this Ocean spred
Shall sink, and leave no mark behind it.
(ll. 133-36)

And eventually, it ceases to matter whether or not the adapted saying contains any reference to water; Swift brings in the old phrase about how some people "build Castles in the Air" by suggesting that directors "build 'em in the Seas" so as to delude their subscribers (ll. 165-68). Thematically, of course, Swift is repeating himself now, and has become preoccupied with the working of ingenious variations on the poem's original metaphor. When he advises his reader to imitate the "Dogs of *Nile*" which have learned to avoid the crocodiles "lurking" in the river (ll. 177-80), it is clear that the analogy has been introduced to extend and color the proliferation of images rather than to clarify a theme. Immediately after this, Swift develops the most obtrusively farfetched analogy in the poem:

Antaeus could by Magick Charms
Recover Strength whene'er he fell,
Alcides held him in his Arms,
And sent him *up in Air* to Hell.

Directors thrown into the Sea
Recover Strength and Vigor there,
But may be tam'd another way,
Suspended for a while in Air.
                                        (ll. 181-88)

According to the myth, Antaeus was given new strength whenever he touched the ground, but was eventually killed when Hercules crushed him while holding him in the air. The relevance of this myth to the poem's subject is not immediately apparent, and when Swift proceeds in the next stanza to make the connection he gives a particularly dramatic display of his ingenious capacity to improvise. What happens here is very much like what happens in the poem on Wood, for the analogy is not just absurdly contrived, it is also introduced in order to express anger rather than to participate in a coherently developed moral criticism.

In this poem, then, Swift again shows himself willing to embrace a diverse multiplicity of images without subordinating that multiplicity to a "logical" thematic framework. An unruly process of association, combined with an agile wit, manages to bring into the poem's compass an astonishing variety of materials, and this variety is not a testament to the unifying power of his imagination but to his disregard for orthodox concepts of coherence. Morris Golden has drawn attention to what he calls the "grotesque lunacy" of the poem's scheme, and has suggested that "As soon as [Swift] approaches the bubble, the whole world of man's delusion through time, multifariously detailed and deliberately incoherent, assails him; and in his less guarded medium of verse, he welcomes the chaos."[5] While I do not think that all of the materials in *The Bubble* can be brought under the rubric of the "world of man's delusion through time," it does seem to me that Golden describes the poem's structure very well. Once gain, a radically subversive energy expresses itself through a profusion of images that is deliberately "incoherent" and miscellaneous.

3

Enumerations, Miscellanies, and the Irreducible Particular

IN the three poems I have just examined, Swift deliberately creates verbal patterns which involve allusion to a varied multiplicity of items, and which do not give the impression that this multiplicity is being subjected to a particularly strong coordinating pressure. In fact, Swift seems to imply that an exuberantly inventive energy, under the stimulus of strong emotion, goes beyond the limitations ordinarily imposed by concepts of relevance and coherence so as to embrace an unruly miscellany of details. There is thus a strong centrifugal tendency in these poems, a tendency away from containing systems of thematic organization towards an involvement with that multiplicity of disparate items which according to neoclassical theory should remain strictly external to the poem's structure. In the previous chapter, we have seen such a tendency appearing in poems where Swift's major concern is with the proliferation of analogies and metaphors. But it appears in other types of context also, and is in fact a major presence in his poetry.

In the early version of *Baucis and Philemon* (1706), for example, there is a proliferation of concrete detail that Swift later came to feel was not adequately subordinated to the poem's thematic structure. It is a well-known fact that Addison persuaded him to alter the first version drastically, and

that the longest of the excised passages was the description of
how the villagers react to the saints' request for shelter.[1] One
needs to quote only part of this passage in order to illustrate
the vigor with which Swift accumulates details:

> One swore he'd send 'em to the Stocks,
> A third could not forbear his Mocks,
> But bawl'd as loud as he could roar,
> You're on the wrong side of the Door.
> One surly Clown lookt out, and said,
> I'll fling the P—pot on your head;
> You sha'n't come here nor get a Sous
> You look like Rogues would rob a House
> Can't you go work, or serve the King?
> You blind and lame! tis no such Thing.
>
> (ll. 33-42)

However vivid twenty-two lines of this may be, it is not
difficult to see why Addison would have recommended their
removal. For the passage is like Swift's extended development
of the silkworm image in *Vanbrug's House,* in that it involves a high degree of local concreteness but is not completely assimilated into the pattern of the poem's argument;
while it needs to be established at the beginning of the poem
that the saints did not receive any hospitality until they
reached the house of Baucis and Philemon, it is unnecessary,
and in fact disproportionate, to do so with such a prolonged
interest in colorful individualization. Moreover, if it is true,
as Eric Rothstein has argued,[2] that a major purpose of the
poem is to counteract Ovid by attributing to Baucis and
Philemon an unthinking materialism of outlook, then such a
strong emphasis on the villagers' lack of hospitality is not
very well coordinated with the poem's theme because it tends
by a process of contrast to elevate Baucis and Philemon into
admirably unselfish figures. There are several reasons, therefore, why Swift and Addison might have felt that the passage
constituted a form of "concrete excess,"[3] and that its elimina-
tion would provide the poem with a more strictly coherent

linear structure. But I would suggest that the presence of the passage in the early version is at least as significant as its absence from the later, and that it is symptomatic of an important tendency.

In certain poems one can see Swift moving away from the development of an apparently significant theme towards a concentration on specifics which neither advance that theme nor in fact take on any generalized meaning at all. Such a movement appears, for example, in *To Charles Ford Esq. on his Birth-day* (1723), in which Swift takes issue with his friend for wanting to leave Dublin in order to live in London. Most of the poem focuses on a comparison of the two cities, and it sometimes appears that this comparison is leading to large moral distinctions. Swift asks, for instance, why Ford should want to live in London, where he would only "look on Vice triumphant round,/And Virtue trampled on the Ground" (ll. 41-42). And he suggests that, whereas the inhabitants of London are likely to meet "A hundred Whores in ev'ry Street," hardly "half a Score" may be found in the whole of Dublin (ll. 105-8). But although such distinctions do appear, Swift persistently evades them and the type of morally evaluative argument in which they would be capable of participating. He underplays the contrast between the two cities by suggesting that it really does not amount to anything very significant:

> The Diff'rence but amounts to this,
> You bury, on our Side the Channell
> In Linnen, and on Yours, in Flannell.
> You, for the News are ne'r to seek,
> While we perhaps must wait a week.
>   (ll. 100-104)

In order to convince Ford that there is no large distinction to be drawn, Swift enumerates several miscellaneous items belonging to the two locales. He suggests that there is not much difference between "St. James's Park," "Pell-mell," and the

Thatched House, on the one hand, and "Stephen's Green,"
"Dawson Street," and the Deanery House on the other (ll.
59-66). He then puts together a catalog of the several people
between whom Ford will be choosing:

> The Dean and Sheridan, I hope,
> Will half supply a Gay and Pope,
> Corbet, though yet I know his Worth not,
> No doubt, will prove a good Arbuthnot:
> I throw into the Bargain, Jim:
> In London can you equall Him?
>   What think you of my fav'rite Clan,
> Robin, and Jack, and Jack, and Dan?
> (ll. 73-80)

The list continues beyond this point, but the above passage is
sufficient to make it clear that the major focus of the poem is
upon a cluster of specific items that take on no generalized
thematic import, and are of strictly personal interest. The few
moments at which larger implications are raised are thus
overwhelmed by a multiplicity of localized details which
Swift enumerates in the form of a miscellaneous catalog.

If, in *To Charles Ford Esq.*, Swift's interest in the accumulation of localized detail leads him away from the
development of a general theme, in *The Journal* (1721) a
similar interest stimulates the creation of a poem which does
not appear to possess a thematic structure at all. The title of
the poem suggests a good deal about Swift's intentions, and
in the early stages he apparently seeks to capture something
like that unstructured multiplicity which one associates with
the concept of a journal:

> Begin, my Muse, first from our Bowers,
> We issue forth at different Hours;
> At Seven, the *Dean* in Night-gown drest,
> Goes round the House to wake the rest:
> At Nine, grave *Nim* and *George* Facetious,
> Go to the *Dean* to read *Lucretius*.

> At Ten, my Lady comes and Hectors,
> And kisses *George,* and ends or Lectures:
> And when she has him by the Neck fast,
> Hawls him, and scolds us down to Breakfast.
> (ll. 7-16)

There is an element of structure here, of course, but it is merely the structure of temporal succession, and it does not imply the presence of an organizing thematic principle. In fact, Swift seems very careful to avoid establishing the kinds of relationships between items which would suggest that they are being selected and juxtaposed in order to express a theme. There is, perhaps, a potentially thematic contrast between the gathering of the men to read Lucretius and the violent interruption brought about by "my Lady," but although a somewhat similar event occurs a little later, this contrast does not become a major issue; it is simply a characteristic of two among a succession of moments. What Swift appears to be engaged in is an enumeration of events, rather than an organization of them into patterns which would attribute to the life at Gaulstown a set of defining characteristics. And the rhetorical pattern continues to create this impression as Swift's narrative moves beyond breakfast-time:

> We squander there an Hour and more,
> And then all hands, Boys, to the Oar
> All, Heteroclit *Dan* except,
> Who neither time nor order kept.
> But by peculiar Whimseys drawn,
> Peeps in the Ponds to look for Spawn:
> O'er sees the Work, or *Dragon* rowes,
> Or spoils a Text, or mends his Hose.
> Or—but proceed we in our *Journal,* ....
> (ll. 17-25)

Swift says here that when he describes "Heteroclit *Dan"* he is digressing from the journal-like pattern that the poem has followed so far. And this does help to define the major structural characteristic that the first part of the poem has—an hour-by-hour enumeration of a typical day's events. But although Swift is indeed digressing in that he describes a figure whose activities do not conform to the dominant temporal routine, the nature of the digression is in a crucial way like the nature of the poem as a whole. For in the sequence of activities that are attributed to Daniel Jackson, there is a lack of that kind of relationship between individual details which would lead towards coherent, "rounded" characterization. Swift tells us that Dan is eccentric ("Heteroclit") in his disregard for "time" and "order," and that he is subject to "peculiar Whimseys," but the details which follow do not give the impression that they have been carefully selected and organized so as to form a portrait of an eccentric character. They are, for one thing, rather miscellaneous in nature; the investigation of the ponds could perhaps be regarded as a form of "Whimsey," but the rowing of *"Dragon"* is basically the same kind of exercise as the others are involved in at this time (it is just a different boat), and the reading and mending are quite ordinary activities that do not bear any definitive relationship to the others that are mentioned. The expectations aroused by the introductory lines on Dan are thus in a sense defeated, and the miscellaneous quality of the sequence creates the impression that Swift is not organizing details in order to define a character so much as recording them in the form of a list. Moreover, Swift goes out of his way to suggest that the details of the passage do not come together as the result of a preconceived formulation of a character, but through a process of spontaneous accretion which has to be interrupted.

When Swift takes up his journal again after this digression, he writes a passage which has from the time of its first appearance been recognized as an allusion to the Last Judgment:

> At Two or after we return all,
> From the four Elements assembling,
> Warn'd by the Bell, all Flocks come trembling,
> From Airy Garrets some descend,
> Some from the Lakes remotest end.
> My Lord and *Dean,* the Fire forsake;
> Dan leaves the Earthly Spade and Rake,
> The Loyt'res quake, no Corner hides them,
> And Lady *Betty* soundly chides them.
>
> (ll. 26-34)

No doubt the major reason for this allusion has to do with what it expresses about the relationship between Lady Betty and the rest of the household, and this is the second of the two occasions on which her presence is described as being rather forceful. But there is another aspect of the passage's ironic comedy which is very relevant to the way the poem is developing. For one of the major characteristics of the Last Judgment is that it is an occasion on which the human race will be divided into two groups and thus decisively classified. In this passage, however, although each individual is neatly allocated to one of the four elements, no ordering generic classification is felt to be even potentially present. The various activities of the several individuals remain strictly miscellaneous, and Swift does not provide the sort of detail that might make Lady Betty's chiding of them seem anything other than arbitrary. Indeed, he never does subject the varied materials of the journal to the type of classifying arrangement which would imply that a judgment is being made on them. And by a process of ironic contrast, therefore, Swift's allusion reinforces the impression of miscellaneousness that the poem's details constantly tend to make.

As Swift brings his account of the day's activities to a close, the poem's major rhetorical technique becomes more and more prominent:

> Now stinted in the short'ning Day,
> We go to Pray'rs, and then to play,
> Till Supper comes, and after that,

We sit an hour to drink and chat.
'Tis late, the old and younger Pairs,
By *Adam* lighted walk up stairs:
The weary *Dean* goes to his Chamber,
And *Nim* and *Dan* to Garret clamber:
So when this Circle we have run,
The Curtain falls, and we have done.
                              (ll. 51-60)

In the first few lines of this passage, Swift takes great care to
avoid making the reader feel that he is doing anything other
than enumerating a succession of events. He provides only a
flat, uncharacterizing statement of each activity, and his
emphasis on the phrase "after that" makes it seem that the
only reason why one item follows another in the progress of
the rhetoric is that it was the next thing that happened in the
chronological course of the day. The sequence of events that
Swift enumerates does, of course, have a high degree of
temporal regularity, and this provides it with an ordered
framework. But there is a contrast between this framework,
which is simply derived from the chronological routine of a
typical day, and the miscellaneous nature of the several
activities, upon which Swift refuses to impose a unifying
thematic structure.

At the end of the above passage, Swift implicitly compares
the succession of the day's events to the progress of a play.
Since a play is a literary form which tends to involve a
constructed sequence rather than a mere succession of events,
it seems reasonable to assume that Swift's comparison is
ironic; the progression of the "journal" has in fact been
precisely the opposite of that which one ordinarily associates
with a play. And when Swift develops the analogy further in
the next few lines, he appears to confirm the prevailing
impression of irony:

I might have mention'd several facts,
Like *Episodes* between the Acts;
And tell who loses, and who wins,

Who gets a Cold, who break their shins.
How *Dan* caught nothing in his Net,
And how his Boat was over set,
For brevity I have retrench'd,
How in the Lake the *Dean* was drench'd:
It would be an Exploit to brag on,
How Valiant *George* rode o'er the *Dragon;*
How steady in the Sterne he sat,
And sav'd his Oar, but lost his Hat.

(ll. 61-72)

These incidents that he says he might have mentioned sound
much more like the kind of material out of which a play
might be made than do the items that he has already enumer-
ated. For they involve such things as dramatic action, climax-
es, and sharply defined emotional experience. Instead of
simply telling us, for instance, that the characters played
cards and rowed boats (which is what he did in the first part),
he says that he might have told us who lost, who won, who
fell overboard, and who navigated with poise and skill. At
this point, then, it appears that a significant shift of direction
may be taking place, away from the enumeration of un-
characterized details that are not thematically related towards
the narration of incidents which are at least coordinated in
that they all involve dramatic action. But the poem's prevailing tendency towards the miscellaneous soon begins to show
itself again as Swift follows the above sequence of mini-
dramas by turning to several briefly noted characterizing
features of the various individuals at Gaulstown; he mentions, for example, "How skilfully *Dan* mends his Nets" (l.
75) and "how the *Dean* delights to vex/The Ladys, or Lam-
poon the Sex" (ll. 77-78). It is true that the second part of the
poem does differ from the first in that it involves a much
greater degree of individualizing characterization. But it is, if
anything, more miscellaneous, more like an uncoordinated
catalogue of items than the first part because it no longer
involves reference to a regularized time-sequence. Swift now
seeks to create the impression that he is listing the items that

he "might have mention'd" more or less in the order that they
come into his head, and that their accumulation is subject to
no predetermined framework; as he approaches the subject of
Dean Percival's wife he says that "now there need no more be
said on't," but then launches into a lengthy characterization
of her as if impelled by spontaneous impulse, and when he
beings to talk about Baron Rochfort's political views he says
that he is going to do so only "since I have gone so far on."
Eventually the catalog of things he "might have mention'd"
becomes as long as the initial catalog of the daily activities,
growing as if by a process of spontaneous accretion.

In the concluding section of the poem Swift begins to write
as if he were dealing with a large, traditional theme:

> But you, who are a Scholar, know
> How transient all things are below:
> How prone to change is human life,
> Last Night arriv'd *Clem* and his wife.
> (ll. 115-18)

But the portentous tone of the first three lines is already being
undermined by the dry, matter-of-fact manner of the fourth.
And as Swift continues to describe the effects of the new
arrivals, the large abstractions give way to a miscellaneous
cluster of specifics:

> This Grand Event half broke our Measures,
> Their Reign began with cruel Seizures;
> The *Dean* must with his Quilt supply,
> The Bed in which these Tyrants lie:
> *Nim* lost his Wig-block, *Dan* his Jordan,
> My Lady says she can't afford one;
> *George* is half scar'd out of his Wits,
> For *Clem* gets all the dainty bits.
> (ll. 119-26)

The arrival of Clem and his wife is described as a "Grand
Event," and Swift has suggested that it is an example of life's

transience. But when he goes on to describe the changes that are caused by it, they do not appear to be as significant as we have been led to expect by the portentous introduction. Swift does not, for instance, make it clear that any fundamental change in the character of life at Gaulstown is taking place (this would be difficult, since he has not really attributed a defining character to that life). What happens instead is that there is a shifting around of several physical objects as the established members of the household have to give up various items to the newcomers (this is the only apparent reason why these newcomers are defined as "Tyrants"). Now it is true that for the Dean, Nim, Dan, and George, the loss of these items constitutes massive change. And what Swift may be attempting to suggest is that the life at Gaulstown does not possess any central, unifying characteristics (other than a temporal regularity), but that it does consist of a number of miscellaneous activities and objects, so that when any one of these is removed or shifted the characters feel that a significant change is taking place. If the poem makes any "statement" at all about the life at Gaulstown—and it cannot completely avoid doing so—I would suggest that this is what it is.

In a recent essay, however, Aubrey Williams has argued that the details of *The Journal* are not nearly so miscellaneous as I have suggested, and it is necessary at this point to consider his analysis at some length.[4] He sees the poem as a "comment on the inherent dissatisfactions of mortal life, no matter how tranquil and secure that life may seem to be, at first, amid the patterns of rural retreat" (p. 230). In order to establish this reading, Williams suggests that the several details of the first part of the poem work towards a coherent, unifying definition of one version of the country life: "the first half of *The Journal* proceeds to describe a country day which seems to exemplify . . . a life of mild bucolic labours along with conviviality of conversation and tranquillity of mind" (p. 232). But such an analysis does not appear to take into account the rather violent presence of Lady Betty, and the two occasions on which she is a disruptive force. And when Williams turns to the second part of the poem, it seems to me that he again attributes to the sequence of items a unity that it does not really possess. He suggests that this second part "constitutes a gloss on the first—a gloss that is . . . crosshatched with darker lines of human discontent" (pp. 230-31), and that the poem now "proceeds by a systematic shattering of the atmosphere of bucolic tranquillity and conviviality established in the first half" (p. 235). It is true that this part of the poem includes references to defeat, illness, and discomfort, but it also includes references to victory, skill, and poise. And the manner in which Williams discusses Dan at this point in his essay shows the degree of pressure which he is sometimes forced to exert upon the poem's details in order to contain them within the thematic pattern he is arguing for. For he suggests that "Dan, who has so far appeared the assured and expert fisherman, is now seen to have 'caught nothing in his Net,' and we are further told, indeed, 'how his boat was over set'" (p. 235). In fact, nothing has been said about Dan's qualities as a fisherman until this point, so that there simply is not this clear thematic contrast between the references to him in the first part and those in the second. Moreover, if this second part is to be regarded as unified by a steady emphasis on "discontent," it is difficult to understand why it contains, along with the references to Dan's catching nothing and to his boat being overset, references to Nim's successful hunting of hares and to George's poised navigation. When Williams comes to the character sketches of Dean Percival and his wife, he suggests that they are related to the prevailing theme of the poem's second part in that the two figures are interlopers who disturb the "peace" of the household. It is true that they are both boring and irritating characters who talk too much about their respective obsessions, and that there is thus a connection between them. But if the "theme" which Williams suggests is present in the poem's second part is not, as I have argued, really there, then this connection between the two characterized figures obviously doesn't relate them thematically to the part of the poem in which they occur. Williams also suggests that since Mrs. Percival talks so much about her troubles, her presence intensifies the second part's emphasis on the "petty cares, mischiefs, and mischances so common to the human lot—and so noticeably absent from the first part of the poem" (p. 235). But again, I have tried to show that such an emphasis does not dominate the poem's second part. And in any case, if Mrs. Percival's speech is intended to participate in such a theme, it is somewhat more miscellaneous than one would expect it to be; it involves reference to domestic triumphs as well as disasters, and its crucial line appears to be "Tells ev'rything that you can think of" (1. 91). Now Williams's essay is about as sensitive an attempt to discover an orthodox kind of thematic unity in *The Journal* as one could expect to find, but it constantly raises problems such as those I have mentioned. There *is* a difference between the first part of the poem and the second, but it is not of the clearly thematic kind that he suggests. In the first part Swift lists the events that happen in a regular sequence every day, and in the second he adds several further items which were not included in his account of the daily routine; these additional items tend to be more dramatic, more unusual, or more individualized than those in the first part, but they are no less miscellaneous.

Working from what he considers to be a clear-cut thematic distinction between the two parts of the poem, Williams finds that *The Journal* implicitly enforces an argument or a statement which is essentially moralistic in nature. He makes much of Swift's early reference to Lucretius and of the Epicurean concept of tranquillity which Lucretius celebrated (p. 231). And he suggests that "the second half of Swift's poem directly challenges any notion that man can achieve perfect tranquillity of mind or indolence of body in this life, no matter how idyllic the circumstances of his rural retreat may be" (p. 240). The poem thus becomes a sort of "dispute with Lucretius," a "controversion given to a poetic genre that had come to be associated with a whole set of soft-headed Epicurean notions," and it effects an "overturn of the illusions about human nature fostered in earlier poems of country life" (pp. 240-41). Now while it will be clear from my own analysis that I do not regard the poem as possessing an ideational content of this kind, it does seem to me that Williams's comparison between *The Journal* and "earlier poems of the country life" is extremely useful. In an estate or country house poem (which is what, in a sense, this is), Swift's contemporary reader would have expected to find some form of ideal order attributed to the country life, and a fairly high degree of overt general significance derived from the poet's rendering of this order. What Swift does in *The Journal* is to frustrate such expectations. But he does not "challenge" the concept of ideal order by emphasizing the human limitations which make its achievement impossible. Instead, he replaces it by a miscellany of items which is irreducible to the type of thematic coherence that most readers of literature instinctively seek. Our tendency to classify and categorize the details we confront in our search for "meaning" is thus frustrated by a poem belonging to a genre that usually accommodates that tendency more willingly than most. The details of *The Journal* persistently evade the containing thematic structures that we may seek to impose on them, and indeed, Swift often attempts to create the impression that these details are included simply because they were elements in the life at Gaulstown, rather than because they participate in the development of any theme. It thus appears that the multifariously detailed "external" reality that provides the materials for the poem asserts its presence more strongly than any thematic discipline emanating from the poet's mind. This is not to say that Swift abandons his role as artist, or that the items in the second part of the poem really do accumulate by a process of spontaneous accretion. On the contrary, what I have attempted to describe is a calculated rhetorical effect.

It seems to me that Swift works towards a similar effect in *A Description of the Morning* (1709):

Now hardly here and there an Hackney-Coach
Appearing, show'd the Ruddy Morns Approach.
Now *Betty* from her Masters Bed had flown,
And softly stole to discompose her own.
The Slipshod Prentice from his Masters Door,
Had par'd the Dirt, and Sprinkled round the Floor.
Now *Moll* had whirl'd her Mop with dext'rous Airs,
Prepar'd to Scrub the Entry and the Stairs.
The Youth with Broomy Stumps began to trace
The Kennel-Edge, where Wheels had worn the Place.
The Smallcoal-Man was heard with Cadence deep,
'Till drown'd in Shriller Notes of *Chimney-Sweep*.
Duns at his Lordships Gate began to meet,
And Brickdust *Moll* had Scream'd through half the Street.
The Turnkey now his Flock returning sees,
Duly let out a Nights to Steal for Fees.
The watchful Bailiffs take their silent Stands,
And School-Boys lag with Satchels in their Hands.

In this poem, as in *The Journal*, there is implicit reference to a poetic genre with which certain fairly definite rhetorical expectations were associated, and again Swift's poem does not fulfil these expectations. In this case, it is the typical Augustan dawn-scene that Swift is referring to, and in a valuable essay Roger Savage has provided all of the background information we need about the type of "elevated *descriptio*," based on classical precedent, that his contemporaries tended to use when approaching the subject.[5] In order to illustrate what the "Augustan stock-responses to Swift's title" (p. 176) would have been, Savage quotes a passage from Edward Bysshe's *British Parnassus* which "offers the fullest Augustan embodiment" (p. 175) of the typical dawn-topos, and he makes it clear from this that Swift's poem is "basically mock-*descriptio,* a comic imitation of the classical ideal" (p. 177). The element of burlesque extends beyond the initial reference to Aurora leaving the bed of Tithonus: "Warbling larks and tuneful linnets become coalmen and chimney-sweeps . . . the shepherd-swain about to wake and sound his pipe becomes the turnkey counting his flock of thieves as they come in from the night pasture, . . ." and so on (p. 177).

That there is a relationship between Swift's poem and the type of description Savage refers to, and that Swift's poem in some sense controverts the type, are amply and convincingly demonstrated. But when Savage goes on to investigate the precise nature of the relationship and the controversion, it seems to me that his account becomes seriously open to question. First of all, he prepares the ground for the investigation by means of the following passage: "It is not enough just to say that Swift is using ironic imitation of the classical *belle nature* as an enabling device, as his means of rendering the immediate nature of contemporary London. Burlesque of this sort can hardly be neutral, cannot juxtapose two jarring natures without implying some sort of judgement. If low reality makes a mockery of high art in the *Morning,* with which does the blame lie?" (p. 181). While I would agree that the element of burlesque in the poem cannot be neutral, I would suggest that it might possibly lead to something less censorious than an apportionment of "blame." But I shall return to that problem later. First, I want to consider Savage's account of the kind of "judgement" that he feels the poem implies. At several points, he argues that the blame lies on both sides: "Tradition is weighed in the balance with 'the representation of vile things,' and it is the balance which animates the poem. Both sides have things to be said in their favour, but both are found wanting. . . . Swift both chafes at the classical ideal because it seems so little relevant to the reality he sees in the Strand, and is drily ironic about the reality he sees in the Strand because it will not live up to the standards set by the classical ideal" (p. 185). It will be noticed that at the heart of this account there is a sense that the reality of the Strand is "vile," or, as Savage calls it elsewhere, "ugly" (p. 184). In fact, he implies that a much greater degree of "blame" is placed upon London for not measuring up to classical standards than upon the classical standards for appearing irrelevant; after all, by this analysis, it is the inadequacy of London which makes those standards seem irrelevant. So eventually it is suggested that the *descriptor* expresses a "grievance . . . that Modern Town is not Ancient Country" (p. 192), and at various points the Augustan London of the poem is described as "dirty, trivial and immoral" (p. 192), "sordid" (p. 190), and corrupt (p. 185). Savage thus suggests that the details of the poem are coordinated into a unified satiric vision of contemporary reality, and the nature of this vision is indicated by the following statements: "The crowd he points to is slip-shod, raucous and none too clean, and there are obviously as many moral wrinkles and deformities as physical. Along with the brick-dust and coal, gutters and dirty doorsteps, there is Betty's whoring, his Lordship's profligacy, the prison system abused and the need for a secret police of watchful bailiffs" (p. 183). If Swift really intended to create such a monolithic image of London as these terms suggest, it is difficult to understand why he included certain details in the poem. The hackney-coaches at the beginning, for example, bear some kind of a relationship to the signs in nature (such as the first streaks of light in the sky) that herald daybreak in formal *descriptio*, but that relationship is surely not evaluative in the sense that it stresses the inability of hackney-coaches to live up to a classical ideal. Further on, Swift describes Moll as "dext'rous" in the management of her mop and she seems to be preparing for her work in a vigorous, businesslike manner. The youth who is looking for old nails, ill-equipped though he may be, is engaged in a far from despicable activity which in fact possesses considerable ecological value. It is true that the "Smallcoal-Man" and the "Chimney-Sweep" are probably "none too clean," but it seems unreasonable to suggest that their association with dirt is meant to participate in an overall picture of London life as "ugly" or "sordid"; they provide materials and do work that are necessary to city life, and they are surely not to be blamed if they get dirty in the process. I would suggest that a major reason why these two figures are mentioned is simply that they are among the first people to be present on the street in the early morning. And they are like several other particulars in the poem in that they are not reducible to the type of satiric scheme that Savage describes. If such a scheme were really operating, one would expect the poem's concluding line to provide some sort of clinching finality to the indictment. But in that line the final emphasis is not on the lagging of the schoolboys (itself hardly an instance of London's inadequacy), but on the "Satchels in their Hands," which is an observed detail possessing no thematic significance of the kind that Savage attributes to the poem. The fact that this line involves an echo of earlier literary references to dilatory schoolboys does not alter the nature of its structure or its relationship to the rest of the poem. What I am suggesting, then, is that the details of *Morning* are more miscellaneous than Savage's account makes them out to be. And in order to understand the primary impulse behind the poem, I think we need to return to the introduction which originally preceded it in *The Tatler*.[6] Here it is argued that Swift's poem particularly avoids the structures of "Easy Writing, *which any one may easily write.*" By this, *Tatler* means that Swift avoids the set phrases and patterns that had come to be derived from the type of formal *descriptio* discussed by Savage. And it is suggested that he evades these structures by being realistic: "He never forms Fields, or Nymphs, or Groves, where they are not, but makes the incidents just as they really appear." Now it is true, of course, that Swift is engaged in something more complex than a kind of photographic realism, and that the poem contains subtle reference to the type of verbal pattern that it evades; as Savage says, "The goaler's 'flock' return from burlesque fields; the chimney-sweeps and coal-men sing in makeshift groves; Betty takes on the role of a classical nymph, however degradedly she plays it" (p. 183). But we should not allow this to prevent us from recognizing what *The Tatler's* introduction has to say about the type of structure that Swift substitutes for the patterns of elevated *descriptio.* The introduction goes on to say, "For an example of it, I stole out of his manuscript the following lines: They are a Description of the Morning, but of the Morning in Town; nay, of the Morning at this end of the Town, where my Kinsman at present lodges." What *The Tatler* claims for the poem is thus precisely the opposite of Johnsonian generality; the introduction stresses the value of fidelity to a strictly localised segment of the physical world that the poet inhabits, and it implicitly denies that the poem is intended to make a general "statement" about contemporary life by suggesting that the picture would be different if the poet were living in a different part of London. It is true, of course, that the details of Swift's poem are selected for reasons apart from those which the *Tatler* introduction stresses; otherwise, there would not be all those parallels with the typical dawn-topos of formal *descriptio.* But this does not alter the fact that Swift arranges the details into a sequence that is commensurate with the way in which *Tatler* describes the poem; for the several items are sufficiently miscellaneous to suggest that they could be the product of random aggregation in a specific locale at a specific time. Consequently, the poem evades not only the structures of what *The Tatler* calls "Easy Writing," but also the type of containing thematic structure that Savage describes.

I have spent a good deal of time on Savage's essay because in order to establish my own reading of *Morning* it is necessary to consider in some detail readings of the kind that his essay typifies. And I want now to examine another essay which also, it seems to me, attributes to the details of the poem a thematic coordination which they do not have. David

M. Vieth argues that the poem is "a parody of the divine fiat of Creation, 'Let there be light,' by which God imposed Logos upon Chaos" (pp. 303-4)[7] and that the order of God's original creation is here replaced by the "disorder" of contemporary London. By disorder he does not mean the type of miscellaneous aggregation that I have suggested is an aspect of the poem's structure. On the contrary, Vieth's interpretation is designed to rescue the poem from the notion that its details are miscellaneous: "The reading of 'A Description of the Morning' as a parody of Creation, as depicting a postlapsarian world of disorder and imperfection, is best supported by its consistent ability to explain the seemingly miscellaneous details in Swift's poem" (pp. 304-5). It will be seen from this that Vieth's interpretation is closely related to Savage's in that the disorder he sees in the poem is defined as an aspect of a fallen world, and is subjected to moral disapproval. And when he proceeds to demonstrate the presence of this disorder, it seems to me that his account creates similar problems. For example, he argues that when Swift describes Moll as whirling her mop with "dext'rous Airs" he is emphasizing an element of "show" in her movements which implies the possibility that she is not going to work with "genuine dexterity and diligence" (p. 305). I would suggest that if Swift had really wanted to subject Moll to this kind of implicit critical evaluation, he would not have left quite so much for the reader to do in order to arrive at it; after all, he has just referred to the prentice as "slipshod" in only "sprinkling" the floors with water to lay the dust instead of cleaning them properly. Vieth also emphasizes the fact that, according to the poem's footnote, the "Youth" is looking for "old nails rather than new" (p. 305). But since he is trying to find nails that have dropped from passing vehicles, it is hard to imagine what other sort he might be expected to find. It surely requires a considerable effort of the will to regard the oldness of the nails, or, later, the fact that the kennel-edge is "worn," as symptoms of the "disorder and imperfection" of a fallen world.

Vieth answers this kind of objection by saying that in *Morning* "meaningful order is so little evident that a full aesthetic response requires the reader to search for it" (p. 307). I would agree that the kind of meaningful order he is looking for is not made evident by the poem, and that its details are, as he says, "seemingly miscellaneous." But why cannot we accept the possibility that one of Swift's intentions in writing the poem was that the details should actually *be* miscellaneous, or, at least, sufficiently miscellaneous to make Vieth's kind of analysis inappropriate? Such a possibility is recognized in the following comment by Rachel Trickett, which manifests a very different response to the poem from those I have been examining: " . . . the tone of precise honesty enables Swift to be at once humorous, ironic, and exact about detail, with a concentrated factual realism which conveys by implication a positive pleasure in observing those phenomena which were usually generalised for attack under the common heading of the tumult and noise of the town."[8] I am not sure how much "positive pleasure" Swift shows in observing some of the poem's details, but I find this comment extremely valuable in its emphasis on the fact that the details are neither "generalised for attack" nor subordinated to a morally evaluative rubric. However, if one is convinced that the poem's details are sufficiently miscellaneous to be irreducible to the type of moralistic statement that Vieth and Savage propose, one must eventually face the question of what Swift's purpose was in putting a poem together in this way. The question is partially answered, of course, by the *Tatler* introduction and the fact that Swift is writing a poem which in its structure is genuinely commensurate with the terms of that introduction. But I think that the relationship between Swift's poem and the elevated *descriptio* which it parodies amounts to something more than the *Tatler* introduction suggests. It seems to me important that the kind of description that Swift parodies is characterized by a particularly evident exertion of a shaping, ordering art upon the materials that the poet derives from the external world; the ideal pastoral world and the "harmonious, elevated landscape" (Savage, p. 176) of these descriptions are manifestly the products of such a highly selective and coordinating art. It is true, of course, that all poetry (including *A Description of the Morning)* is created by a process of selection and organization. But the ordering imposition of art upon nature is not always so obtrusive as in formal *descriptio,* which follows such clearly defined idealizing patterns. Because of this, I would suggest that the aggregation of miscellaneous and irreducible particulars that occurs in *A Description of the Morning* takes on special significance. What Swift opposes to the world of elevated *descriptio* is a reality that is sufficiently miscellaneous to defy ordering attempts at classification and systematization. If it is true that the Augustan poet was preoccupied with "the task of imposing unity on the multitudinous world, of finding some approximation to the order and meaning intended by the Divine Mind itself,"[9] then *A Description of the Morning* seems carefully designed to suggest the difficulty of his task. And the poem suggests this, not because its details effect a moralistic evaluation of London life, but because they remain obstinately irreducible to such an evaluation.

The companion piece to the above poem is *A Description of a City Shower* (1710), and it too has been subjected to the kind of analysis which suggests that its details are more coherently organized towards a morally evaluative end than I believe them to be. The poem involves several allusions to the first book of Vergil's *Georgics,* particularly to the description of a storm in harvest which that book contains. And once again, the main problem of interpretation has to do with the relationship between the poem's details and the kind of poetry with which they are implicitly compared. By quoting from the "Essay on Vergil's *Georgics*" which Addison wrote as a preface to Dryden's translation, Roger Savage establishes that the typical Augustan concept of the georgic resembled the concept of elevated *descriptio* in that it emphasized the strong presence of an idealizing art: "Georgic *mimesis* demands a high antique decorum to turn raw nature into *la belle nature,* a nature fit for sublime art. Mean scientific fact must be embellished with beauty and grandeur; image and expression must be heightened with ornament and grace...." (p. 186). When Swift begins his poem by imitating Vergil's enumeration of the signs that portend rain, it soon becomes clear that, whatever art he is exerting upon his materials, it is not of this idealizing kind:

> Careful Observers may fortel the Hour
> (By sure Prognosticks) when to dread a Show'r:
> While Rain depends, the pensive Cat gives o'er
> Her Frolicks, and pursues her Tail no more.
> Returning Home at Night, you'll find the Sink
> Strike your offended Sense with double Stink.
> If you be wise, then go not far to Dine,
> You'll spend in Coach-hire more than save in Wine.
> A coming Show'r your shooting Corns presage,
> Old Aches throb, your hollow Tooth will rage.
>
> (ll. 1-10)

In the first book of the *Georgics* the great majority of the signs which indicate change in the weather are found in the constellations of the stars, so that the details which Swift enumerates here seem by comparison very earthbound. This is one very simple, and not necessarily evaluative, contrast. But Savage argues that further specific contrasts indicate that a critique of contemporary London is embedded in the poem's details, and in order to demonstrate this he quotes the following lines from Dryden's translation of the *Georgics:*

> And that by certain signs we may presage
> Of Heats and Rains, and Wind's impetuous rage,
> The Sov'reign of the Heav'ns has set on high
> The Moon, to mark the Changes of the Skye . . .
> The Crow with clam'rous Cries the Show'r demands,
> And single stalks along the Desert Sands.

The nightly Virgin, while her Wheel she plies,
Foresees the Storm impending in the Skies,
When sparkling Lamps their sputt'ring Light advance,
And in the Sockets Oyly Bubbles dance.
(I, 483-86 and 533-38)[10]

Savage describes the relationship between the above lines and
the opening lines of Swift's poem in the following way: "An
alley-cat for the austere crow, corns and toothache for the
distant moon, a poor citizen with drain trouble for the virgin
at her spinning-wheel; this is the poor best the city can offer,
however orotund the language in which it is presented. And
this is the theme of the *City Shower* throughout—the ludicrous attempt of an imperfect, trivial London to live up to
classical dialects and situations" (p. 187). Now it seems to me
that this effort to demonstrate an evaluative parallelism
between the two passages involves a certain amount of strain.
The reference to Swift's "Cat" as an "alley-cat", for example,
is not really justified by the words of the poem. Similarly, the
description of Vergil's "crow" as "austere," while it helps to
establish a neat contrast, is based on a rather selective approach to the text; the crow may stalk the desert alone, but she
is also "clam'rous." And Swift's references to corns and
toothache hardly seem intended to illustrate "the poor best
the city can offer"; they are, rather, symptoms of the inescapa-
bly physical condition of all human beings. For reasons such
as this, I would suggest that the details of Swift's passage do
not quite cohere in the orderly thematic fashion that Savage
proposes.

The above attempt to reduce this cluster of details to
thematic order is very restrained, however, compared to that
of Brendan O Hehir, who argues that it represents the city's
"corruption."[11] He finds evidence of this corruption not only
in "the stink of sewage," which is perhaps capable of lending
itself to such an idea, but also in the "throbbing of corns and
toothache," which surely is not—and he does not mention
the "pensive Cat" (p. 202). O Hehir's essay is intended to

"make plain an impressive meaning, even a serious moral" (p. 195) that he believes to be present in the poem. And before he attempts to demonstrate this meaning, he makes the following assertions: "If the 'City Shower' is a mock georgic, the inference is reasonable that its mockery has a target, the poem a satirical or moral aim. A non-mock georgic would have a similarly didactic end, for the genre falls, in Addison's words *(Essay on the Georgics),* 'under that Class of Poetry which consists in giving plain and direct Instructions to the Reader; whether they be Moral Duties . . . or Philosophical Speculations . . . or Rules of Practice'" (pp. 196-97).[12] Addison's stress on the didacticism of the georgic is thus enlisted as a means of attributing a similar didacticism to Swift's mock georgic. And as O Hehir proceeds to demonstrate what he considers to be the "moral aim" of the poem, he places great emphasis on the fact that Swift at one point refers to London as a *"Devoted* Town." The adjective is in one sense, of course, an ironic comment on the religious life of London. But it also possessed an earlier meaning of "doomed," which Swift appears to be exploiting here. O Hehir brings to bear upon the poem several instances in classical literature of "divinely-ordained floods" portending the "falls of cities" (p. 206), and concludes that London, believing itself to be the heir of Troy and Rome, is here being defined as a city that is doomed because of its corruption. In order to demonstrate the presence of this corruption, he focuses not only on Swift's account of the omens of rain, but also on the following passage which describes some of the consequences of the downpour:

> Now in contiguous Drops the Flood comes down,
> Threat'ning with Deluge this *Devoted* Town.
> To Shops in Crouds the dagged Females fly,
> Pretend to cheapen Goods, but nothing buy,
> The Templer spruce, while ev'ry Spout's a-broach,
> Stays till 'tis fair, yet seems to call a Coach.
> The tuck'd-up Sempstress walks with hasty Strides,

While Streams run down her oil'd Umbrella's Sides.
Here various Kinds by various Fortunes led,
Commence Acquaintance underneath a Shed.
Triumphant Tories, and desponding Whigs,
Forget their Fewds, and join to save their Wigs.

(ll. 31-42)

Seeking some common, unifying factor in the behavior of the citizens, O Hehir comments: "Hypocrisy, or falseseeming, is the essence of their natures. The 'daggled Females' crowd the shops for shelter, 'pretend' to bargain for goods, 'but nothing buy.' The 'Templer spruce . . . Stays till 'tis fair, yet *seems* to call a coach.' Tories and Whigs, in face of the threatening deluge, discard their ostensibly principled differences and reveal their true common purpose, to 'save their wigs'" (pp. 202-3). I would suggest that this account again imposes on Swift's details a much greater degree of condemnatory meaning than they will bear. It is true that the second line of the passage, and especially the tone of *"Devoted,"* appears to suggest that a moralistic condemnation is going to be made. But the sequence of items that follows persistently evades the type of evaluative categorization that we may be led to expect. The behavior of the women in the shops, while it certainly involves an element of pretence, hardly seems intended as an example of morally corrupt "Hypocrisy"; it is, rather, a natural and harmless attempt on their part to avoid looking awkward in a potentially embarrassing situation. The "Templer spruce" is no doubt rather vainly preoccupied with his public image, but his self-conscious behaviour is here a subject of mild comedy rather than of moralistic condemnation. As for the "tucked-up Sempstress," we are told that she is carefully dressed for the rain, that she is walking rapidly, and that she carries an "oil'd" umbrella; as characterizing details, these hardly seem calculated to participate in a satire on hypocrisy.[13] And finally, it is true that the "common purpose" at this moment for politicians of both sides is to "save their Wigs." But does this indicate a hypocritical

disregard for "ostensibly principled differences," or the actual irrelevance of these differences in an emergency? Would the
Whigs demonstrate a greater moral integrity by staying outside the "Shed" if they see that it is full of Tories? Because of
such problems as these, it is only with a considerable degree
of strain that the items in Swift's passage may be marshalled
under such large, unifying banners as "Hypocrisy" and
"falseseeming." In fact a major point seems to be that, in the
emergency caused by the shower, "various Kinds" are
brought together by "various Fortunes," and the miscellaneousness of the items therefore has a significant function. It is important that the several individuals do not form a
homogeneous group, and that the one factor which connects
them is an entirely fortuitous one, their common subjection
to the shower.

I would suggest, therefore, that *A Description of a City
Shower* contains neither "an oblique denunciation of cathar-
tic doom upon the corruption of the city" (O Hehir, p. 206)
nor a morally evaluative contrast between London and the
epic world (Savage). And I think it may be useful at this point
to return to Addison's emphasis on the didacticism of the
georgic form, in order to consider the possibility that one
characteristic of a mock georgic might logically be the absence of didacticism. If the writer of georgic creates a world
from which "plain and direct Instructions" even with regard
to "Moral Duties" (Addison, *Essay on the Georgics*) tend to
emerge, it is conceivable that a major interest of the writer
who parodies the georgic may be in creating a world which
does not make such instructions readily available. Brendan O
Hehir demonstrates that "in both classical and neoclassical
literature the overflowing of a river was often the portent of
civil disorders or destruction" (p. 202), and he argues that
Swift presents us with an image of a London so corrupt as to
invite another such destruction. But might not a major
characteristic of downpours and floods in contemporary
London, as opposed to those in classical literature, be that

they portend nothing? Vergil makes it plain that he regards the storm in the *Georgics* as a phenomenon of immense significance. It is perceived as an expression of anger deriving from the "Father of the Gods," a warning that causes a significant experience, fraught with moral implications, for all of those who are subject to it: "Deep horrour seizes ev'ry Humane Breast,/Their Pride is humbled, and their Fear confess'd...."[14] But what of the experience of the templar, the sempstress, the Tories and the Whigs in Swift's poem? The effects of Swift's shower are so "various" (l. 39) that they cannot be resolved into any generalizing description at all. And the one unifying element, the physical experience of the rain, is so fortuitous and superficial that it only emphasizes the essential miscellaneousness of the crowd. The reality of life that Swift perceives in London is not, therefore, something that can be very well contained within the ordering didactic frameworks of georgic poetry. In his world, the signs of impending change in the weather form an unruly conglomeration of items that include stationary cats, stinking drains, and old aches. And this world is made to seem too fragmented and diverse to be consistently reducible to an evaluative thesis.[15]

Swift's tendency to construct sequences of details that take on the characteristics of the catalog, or the list, shows itself also in *The Furniture of a Woman's Mind* (1727), where he accumulates a large number of satiric comments into a sequence that is ostentatiously unstructured. It is typified by the following passage:

> Her Learning mounts to read a Song,
> But, Half the Words pronouncing wrong;
> Has ev'ry Repartee in Store,
> She spoke ten Thousand Times before.
> Can ready Compliments supply
> On all Occasions, cut and dry.
> Such Hatred to a Parson's Gown,
> The Sight will put her in a Swown.

> For Conversation well endu'd;
> She calls it witty to be rude; . . .
>
> (ll. 9-18)

There is a fairly strong coordinating factor here, of course, in that all of the comments refer to aspects of the woman's mental vapidity. Also, each comment possesses an extremely neat, self-contained structure of its own. But the several items do not appear to have been arranged into the type of structure that progresses consecutively from a starting point towards a conclusion. On the contrary, a strong impression is created that the order of the items could be altered without any damage being done to the integrity of the sequence. Swift cultivates this impression rather assiduously, and at the end of the poem he draws emphatic attention to it:

> O Yes! If any Man can find
> More virtues in a Woman's Mind,
> Let them be sent to Mrs. *Harding;*
> She'll pay the Charges to a Farthing:
> Take Notice, she has my Commission
> To add them in the next Edition.
>
> (ll. 57-62)

Here, Swift deliberately throws the form of his poem open, implying that the sequence could go on indefinitely provided that additional materials could be thought of. And by suggesting that items could be added to the poem without any damage to its structure, he implicitly defines that structure as an aggregation, or accumulation of details rather than an ordering arrangement of them. A similar impression is given by the structure of another poem, *Directions for a Birth-day Song* (1729), in which Swift satirizes and parodies the poet laureate's tributes to the royal family. First, he goes through a list of the appropriate gods to whom the king may be compared. And as he does so, he constantly suggests that the poem's development is characterized, not by the formation of items into a satiric argument, but by an enumeration of them;

for example, he says at one point, "Dismissing Mars, it next must follow/Your Conqu'rer is become Apollo" (ll. 57-58), and later, "Next call him Neptune with his Trident" (l. 97). He claims that one item is added, not because of a prearranged determining structure, but because it occurs to him in the process of composition: "One Compliment I had forgot,/But songsters must omit it not" (ll. 129-30). And he once again throws the list open to additions by the reader: "Of Gods I only quote the best,/But you may hook in all the rest" (ll. 149-50). After the enumeration of gods that might be referred to as a means of praising the king, he turns to an enumeration of other members of the royal family who may also be profitably eulogized. And again he suggests that the poem is developing by a process of accretion rather than according to a predetermined argument: "But now it comes into my mind,/We left a little Duke behind" (ll. 199-200). There *is* a central theme in the poem, of course, which has to do with the falsity of Eusden's odes. But around that theme the items tend to proliferate into a pattern that is ostentatiously loose and unstructured, and Swift constantly draws attention to this aspect of the poem's development. In this way it is made to appear that, rather than holding rigorously at bay the multiplicity of false images that he associated with Eusden's odes, Swift, in the process of parodying it, becomes sufficiently absorbed by that multiplicity to allow it a considerable degree of sprawling life.

Swift's imitation of Horace's *First Ode of the Second Book* (1714) shares certain structural characteristics with the two poems I have just discussed. The ode to which Swift alludes is a closely organized brief meditation addressed to Pollio, who is writing a history of the civil wars. After emphasizing the difficulties and even the dangers of such a subject, Horace expresses a hope that Pollio will soon resume his career as a tragic dramatist. This topic then leads him into the central section of the ode, where he contemplates the tragic character of the events that Pollio must describe in the history. And finally, he turns away from the sombre mood induced by this contemplation, expressing his desire for a lighter and more joyful vein. Swift obviously felt that this poem could be used as a device for satirizing Richard Steele, who was at the time engaged in writing a much-publicized political pamphlet called *The Crisis*. In the imitation, Swift portrays Steele as having interrupted his career as a comic dramatist in order to write the pamphlet, and, after describing what he imagines will be its melodramatic content, he finally suggests that both he and Steele should concern themselves with less solemn matters. But although these parallels are enough to establish a loose relationship between the imitation and Horace's ode, it was clearly Swift's intention to write a poem that differed utterly from its classical predecessor, not only in its subject matter but in its whole rhetorical structure. A noticeable feature of Swift's poem is that the several items he brings to bear upon Steele do not appear to be very carefully coordinated. There is a predominant emphasis on Steele's rash self-assertiveness, and everything that Swift mentions tends in one way or another to ridicule Steele. But the poem is ostentatiously loose in its structure, and the several items are not formed into a progressively developing satiric argument. For example, when Swift summarizes the plot of a play that he says Steele is planning to write (ll. 43-48), he makes that play sound ridiculous, but does not enforce any more precise relationship between its subject matter and the progression of the poem's meaning. And when, in the next verse-paragraph, he ridicules the claim to astrological skill that Steele once made in the *Tatler*, no sense is given that we are moving from one stage to another of a structured sequence. That both of these items tend to damage Steele's standing in the eyes of the reader provides only the most rudimentary cohesive factor. And it is difficult to escape the impression that the several denigratory comments that Swift accumulates are tending at this point to become miscellaneous. It is clear, at any rate, that they are not coordinated in such a way as to make them participate in a moral-satiric argument of any kind. A conclusion about Steele is certainly reached—namely, that he is unsuited for state affairs—but it is reached by the sheer aggregation of reductive items rather than by the formation of them into a progressive sequence. Also, this conclusion remains a strictly personal comment on Richard Steele, and in this sense it is an appropriate ending to a poem in which the several items brought to bear upon the satirized object have not been formed into the kind of pattern that leads towards significant generalization. These characteristics rather clearly illustrate one of the ways in which Swift "imitated" the classics. It is a way which suggests that the ordered forms of classical literature are not easy to reproduce when one is dealing with the multifarious specifics of contemporary reality.[16]

A Character, Panegyric, and Description of the Legion Club (1736) was, like the above poem, stimulated by a specific occasion; the Irish House of Commons had voted to deprive the clergy of certain tithes that were legally due to them.[17] And in the poem Swift attacks not only the House as a whole, but also several of its individual members. It often appears, in fact, that the poem's structure is determined more by Swift's desire to express his animosity towards these various individuals than by any desire to coordinate his references to them into a coherent thematic argument or pattern. In one sequence, for example, after ridiculing John Wynne for his tendency to sleep during debates until woken up so that he can give his automatic vote for "the Court" (ll. 163-72), Swift launches into the following attack on John and Robert Allen:

> THOSE are *A——s, Jack* and *Bob,*
> First in every wicked Jobb,
> Son and Brother to a Queer,
> Brainsick Brute, they call a Peer.
> We must give them better Quarter,
> For their Ancestor trod Mortar;
> And at *Hoath* to boast his Fame,
> On a Chimney cut his Name.
>
> (ll. 173-80)

The relationship between these items and what has just been said about Wynne is not such as to suggest that Swift is engaged in the progressive development of a theme or argument. Nor are the items in the above passage connected with one another in any way that provides a sense of thematic direction; indeed, the movement from the fact that the Allens are related to a "Brainsick" peer to the fact that one of their ancestors was an architect who worked for Lord Howth is obtrusively discontinuous. It thus appears that Swift is using an essentially miscellaneous aggregation of items that have little in common apart from the fact that they can all, in one way or another, be forced into the service of invective.

A certain degree of thematic coordination is provided, however, by the two central images which define the Irish Parliament house as both a lunatic asylum and a kind of Hell. In a recent essay, Peter J. Schakel has focused on these images in order to show that they establish a unified emblematic setting by means of which Swift fuses the two concepts of "madness" and "damnation."[18] Schakel is particularly concerned with the motif of damnation, and by demonstrating that there are several allusions in the poem to the Bible and to the *Aeneid* (specifically to Aeneas's journey to the underworld in the sixth book), he argues that Swift "fuses the classical Hades with the Christian Hell, thus uniting his disparate Christian and classical sources and universalizing the moral scope of the poem" (p. 433). Schakel concludes that these images and allusions enforce a consistent emphasis on the "impiety" of the various members of Parliament for their "betrayal of patriotic duty" and their "sacrilege" against the Church; the several individuals referred to by Swift thus "illustrate a general theme" (p. 437), and are to be judged against a "universal standard for the condemnation of corrupt legislators" (p. 438).

Such an analysis as Schakel's attributes to the poem a high degree of structural and thematic coordination. But in fact the two central metaphors referred to above are not sustained with as much consistency as he suggests. At certain points Swift attacks individual members of the House without characterizing them in any precise way as either inmates of an asylum or inhabitants of Hell/Hades; the sequence about Wynne and the Allens that I referred to earlier is an example of this, and Schakel has some difficulty in containing the passage within the thematic framework he describes—suddenly the details of Swift's poem become "ironically unlike" the details from the *Aeneid* with which they are compared (p. 434), and Schakel admits that what parallels he can find are "fairly incidental" (p. 435). Moreover, it is by no means clear that what Swift says about Wynne and the Allens defines them as guilty of the particular kind of "impiety" that Schakel regards as the poem's central unifying theme. For reasons such as this, I would suggest that neither the two major images, nor the narrative involving himself and the muse that Swift constructs around them, are maintained with the kind of consistency that would provide the poem with a thoroughgoing structural coherence.

Although there is in the poem some orthodox thematic structuring of the kind that Schakel describes, there is also a good deal of evidence to suggest that its composition was directed by certain interests to which that type of structuring is of minimal importance and perhaps, indeed, irrelevant. Immediately after the paragraph about the Allens, for example, Swift attacks three members called Clements, Dilkes and Harrison, in the following terms:

> THERE sit *C——s, D——,* and *H——,*
> How they swagger from their Garrison.
> Such a Triplet could you tell
> Where to find on this Side Hell?
> *H——,* and *D——,* and *C——,*
> Souse them in their own Ex-crements.
> (ll. 181-86)

It is true that there is a reference here to the Christian concept of Hell, and that this is capable of playing a part in the kind

of thematic structure that Schakel describes. But the incantatory repetition of the three names, which is the dominant
rhetorical feature of the passage, hardly seems to emanate
from an author whose major preoccupation is with logical
thematic argument. And if we want to relate Swift's procedure to traditional literary archetypes, it seems less useful at
this point to think of the Bible or the *Aeneid* than to consider
some of the things that Robert C. Elliott has to say about
primitive Irish satire of the ninth and tenth centuries.[19]
Elliott quotes a passage from one of these early satires in
which the sheer repetition of the satirized object's name is a
major rhetorical device, and he describes the sequence as a
kind of magical "incantation" (p. 38): "The stylization is
more magical than literary, consisting chiefly in the accentu-
ated repetition of the victim's name. Magicians everywhere
employ the technique, for the name is the man, and when it is
entrapped in the mysterious bonds of magical verse, the man
himself is entrapped" (p. 39). It seems to me that this comment is distinctly relevant to the above lines from Swift's
poem. And indeed, I would suggest that certain other of
Elliott's remarks about these early satires have a bearing on
Swift's procedure in *The Legion Club*. At one point, for
example, he says that "the closer the primitive satires are to
magic, the less 'meaning', in the discursive sense, are they
likely to have" (p. 37). And in this connection he quotes from
the anthropologist Bronislaw Malinowski, who describes the
kind of "meaning" which tends to characterize magical
incantations: "It will not be . . . a meaning of logically or
topically concatenated ideas, but of expressions fitting into
one another and into the whole, according to what could be
called a magical order of thinking, or perhaps more correctly,
a magical order of expressing, of launching words towards
their aim" (p. 37).[20] In the last-quoted passage from *The
Legion Club,* the repetition of names and the image of the
satirist's victims being soused in their "own Ex-crements" do
not express any ideas that could play a part in a thematic

argument, but they are strategies of verbal attack in which words are launched "towards their aim" somewhat in the manner that Malinowski describes. Similarly, at those points when Swift's aggregation of items becomes miscellaneous, as in the sequence about Wynne and the Allens, his words are not related to one another in such a way as to form a sequence of "logically concatenated ideas," but they are roughly connected in that they all express a single mood of unremitting aggression. And if there is a genuinely sustained cohesive factor in the poem, it is the sheer vituperative energy which is present in every area. This has been well described by Denis Donoghue, who talks about the manner in which the poem's invective "develops energy and momentum from its own resources, once it has started," and about how the poem's images are "driven by an energy which is engendered as one line is generated from another."[21] The attack on Marcus Antonius Morgan illustrates the manner in which this omnipresent force influences the movement of the poem. Swift's indictment of Morgan for having betrayed both his university and the Church is in some ways very amenable to the kind of analysis that Schakel is preoccupied by. Indeed, he relates the passage in a most precise way to the pattern of classical and Christian allusion that he is seeking to establish, and he also demonstrates that it involves a further emphasis on the impiety that he regards as the poem's central theme (pp. 435-37). Since the passage is the last in a series of attacks on individual members of the House, it would seem from Schakel's analysis that it forms a logical climax to a progressively developing thematic pattern. But the passage follows immediately after the attacks on Wynne, the Allens, Clements, Dilkes, and Harrison. And we have seen that these three attacks are not related in any close thematic way either to one another or to the indictment of Morgan. What this means is that, if there is a factor linking the four attacks into a coherent sequence, it is not the presence of an orthodox or "logical" thematic principle. But Morgan was the chairman of a committee that began the process by which the clergy were to be deprived of their tithes, and because of this he was the individual towards whom Swift felt the most intense anger. The attack upon him is therefore the natural climax of a pattern which derives whatever unity it has from a prevailing emotion rather than from a thematic argument. This emotion gives rise to an unflagging vituperative energy which expresses itself through an often miscellaneous catalog of items and which does not require that these items should be brought into a "logical" order or structure.

Another poem which frequently takes on the appearance of an unsystematic catalog is *Mrs. Harris's Petition* (1701). The petition is addressed to the "Lords Justices of Ireland," and it requests both their "Protection" and "a Share in next *Sunday's* Collection" (ll. 70-71). Mrs. Harris needs their help, she says, because she has lost all of her savings, and in the poem she describes this catastrophic event and her unsuccessful attempts to find the money. She thus has a clearly defined story to tell and a clearly defined purpose for doing so, and somewhere beneath the poem's surface lies the concept of how a petition of this kind might logically be constructed. But Mrs. Harris is not being logical, and from the start her narrative runs wildly into an excess of circumstantial detail; she tells the justices about such things as the exact position in which she carried her purse and the specific words she said to her friend Mary when she discovered the loss. As her narrative gathers energy, she finds it impossible to limit herself to details that are even remotely relevant:

So I was a-dream'd, methought, that we went and search'd
    the Folks round,
And in a Corner of Mrs. *Duke's* Box, ty'd in a Rag, the
    Money was found.
So next Morning we told *Whittle*, and he fell a Swearing;
Then my Dame *Wadgar* came, and she, you know, is
    thick of Hearing;
Dame, said I, as loud as I could bawl, do you know what
    a Loss I have had?

Nay, said she, my Lord *Collway's* Folks are all very sad,
For my Lord *Dromedary* comes a *Tuesday* without fail;
Pugh! said I, but that's not the Business that I ail.
Says *Cary,* says he, I have been a Servant this Five and
    Twenty Years, come Spring,
And in all the Places I liv'd, I never heard of such a
    Thing.
Yes, says the *Steward,* I remember when I was at my Lady
    Shrewsbury's,
Such a thing as this happen'd, just about the time of
    Goosberries.

                                                            (ll. 22-33)

Mrs. Harris clearly feels an urgent need to include in her
petition every detail of the incident that she can remember.
She does not select or organize the several items. Instead, the
pressure of immediate feeling stimulates an uncoordinated
process of recollection and association. Later in her speech,
when she tells the justices about her efforts to persuade the
chaplain (Swift) to solve her problem, Mrs. Harris is further
diverted by feelings that are quite extrinsic to the matter at
hand; it is rumored that the chaplain is her "Sweet-heart" (l.
50), she is clearly very interested in him, and she goes into
great detail about such things as his dislike of being called
"Parson" (l. 54), and his offended reaction to being treated, as
he puts it, as if he were a *"Conjurer"* (l. 58).

   Now the rhetorical structure of this poem obviously derives
from the fact that Swift is dramatizing the manner of a highly
individualized speaker. But in some ways this structure is like
a caricature of tendencies that Swift shows in certain contexts
where he is not in fact engaged in such dramatization. We
have seen, for example, his interest in verbal patterns that
involve digression under the stimulus of intense feeling, that
appear to develop by processes of spontaneous accretion, or
that accumulate miscellaneous and localized details without
subordinating them to a thematic design. One work in which
Swift shows a continuous interest in expressing himself
through such patterns is the *Journal to Stella,* and I would

like at this point to digress from the poetry in order to consider some aspects of what Swift does in that work. It is true, of course, that the journal is very private and was not intended for publication. But I would suggest that what one confronts in it are extreme versions of certain types of rhetorical interest that appear in several of the poems I have discussed.

When Swift first introduces the idea of the journal, he says: "Henceforth I will write something every day to MD, and make it a sort of journal; and when it is full, I will send it whether MD writes or no; and so that will be pretty" (p. 8).[22] Here, Swift implies that the journal is likely to be characterized by a certain formlessness; each letter will end only because the paper is full, rather than because anything in the development of its meaning has led to a conclusion. Elsewhere, this formlessness is attributed to Swift's refusing to select from among the particulars which offer themselves to him: " . . . you must take the days as they happen, some dry, some wet, some barren, some fruitful, some merry, some insipid; some etc.—" (p. 236). He suggests not only that the journal will be miscellaneous in texture, but also that it will grow by a natural process of accretion rather than according to a predetermining design. He describes such a process at one point, when, in the course of speculating about a future appointment, he raises the question of whether some information he has heard is accurate or not: "The talk now grows fresher of the duke of Ormond for Ireland, although Mr. Addison says he hears it will be in commission, and Lord Gallaway one. These letters of mine are a sort of journal, where matters open by degrees; and, as I tell true or false, you will find by the event whether my intelligence be good; but I don't care twopence whether it be or no" (p. 53). It is essential to what Swift wishes to achieve that he should appear unconcerned whether or not a prediction about a future event is accurate. For he is not, in most of the *Journal*, making statements about how various particulars have come to form sequences or patterns. Instead, he is reporting on those particulars as they present themselves to him from moment to moment, on the *process* by which they will eventually become sequences. This apparent concern for reproducing one kind of process should make us skeptical of the notion that Swift had "little or no interest in process" and that for him "nothing was interesting until it revealed itself in form or until it could be forced into that degree of definition."[23] In the *Journal* he is interested in precisely those stages in the succession of events which are antecedent to the appearance of form and definition. Swift is also interested in recording for Stella those movements of thought which precede the making of finished or coherent statements. One of his stylistic intentions in the *Journal* is that he should appear to communicate everything that passes through his mind in the process of writing: " . . . you must have chat, and I must say every sorry thing that comes into my head" (p. 568). So we find Swift attempting to make language imitate the incoherent, discontinuous movement of his experience and his thoughts. He will reproduce on paper all of those interruptions which disturb and impede the progress of composition: "I left the company early tonight at lord treasurer's; but the secretary followed me, to desire I would go with him to W——. Mr. Lewis's man came in before I could finish that word beginning with a W, which ought to be Windsor" (p. 371). Here, rather than mending the broken sequence, Swift draws attention to it. Similarly, if a sound from outside his room distracts him as he is writing, he will not exclude it: "(here is a restless dog crying Cabbages and Savoys plagues me every morning about this time, he is now at it, I wish his largest cabbage was sticking in his throat)" (p. 581). The implication is that nothing which comes into his consciousness is irrelevant. And at moments like these Swift seems exuberantly aware that his style offers him an unlimited freedom to embrace a miscellany of details.

In much of the *Journal to Stella*, then, there is an energetic pursuit and accumulation of multifarious specifics without an accompanying impulse to subject those specifics to ordering arrangements. One would hardly expect, of course, in a journal written to inform Stella about the day-to-day progress of his life in London, that Swift would show a particularly careful attention to thematic patterning. But it is clear that from an early stage in the process of writing the journal he felt an acute interest in the types of verbal configuration which that process made available to him. I have attempted to show that an interest in similar configurations appears in several of his poems. And to consider the *Journal to Stella* in this context is a way of showing that, however surprising the tendencies I have described may seem to be in the author of the sermons and several of the political essays, those tendencies are by no means limited to the poetry.

4

The Ordering Design

SWIFT seems to have been fascinated by the types of verbal structure that are suggested by the concept of a "journal," and in *The Journal of a Modern Lady* (1729) he again seeks to embody some of those structures in a poem. In this instance, however, although the poem has several characteristics in common with those I discussed in the previous chapter, there are also signs that Swift is taking a rather different approach to his materials, and one that is more consistent with some traditional notions of what "Augustan" literature tends to be like. The title of the poem suggests the possibility that its structure will be determined less by a thematic argument than by the actualities of temporal succession, and that Swift is going to engage in a process of enumeration rather than of ordering arrangement. At an early point, indeed, he declares that he does not intend to impose any kind of authorial pressure upon the materials with which he is dealing. "I but transcribe" (l. 28), he insists, and thus defines himself as an essentially passive figure who is going to transmit the succession of incidents that constitutes "a Female Day" (l. 35) without shaping it into a thematic pattern. In order to stress the passivity of the stance that he is taking towards his materials, he claims that he is writing about them only because he has been "Compell'd" to do so by the woman to whom the poem is addressed (l. 30), and that his muse is "Unwilling" (l. 34) to assist him. However, Swift also says that the poem will be a "Satyre" (l. 30), and that he will transcribe not only a succession of events but also "common Slanders" upon the female sex (l. 31). This suggests that his presentation of the incidents will be informed by a prevailing critical attitude. And the passage as a whole indicates that although the *Journal* will record events without overtly transforming them, those events will not simply be miscellaneous, but will be expressive of a dominant concept.

So he begins where we would expect a journal of the day's events to begin, by describing the moment at which the "modern Dame" wakes up. But when he emphasizes the fact that this moment occurs at "Noon" (l. 38), an implicit critical evaluation is also established. And the following description of the waking process is commensurate with the initial stance that Swift has adopted:

> She stretches, gapes, unglues her Eyes,
> And asks if it be time to rise;
> Of Head-ach, and the Spleen complains;
> And then to cool her heated Brains,
> Her Night-gown and her Slippers brought her,
> Takes a large Dram of Citron Water.
>
> (ll. 42-47)

Swift's language in this passage renders the physical experience of waking and the woman's first actions in a manner that has the air of being very direct. The events take place in the poet's imagination, of course, but Swift's account of them is sufficiently bare and unelaborated to create the impression that it does not go beyond what would be strictly necessary for the direct reporting of some observed physical actions.[1] At the same time, however, such a disordered waking at such an hour indicates that something is wrong with the life-pattern being described, and the passage thus participates in a process of satiric evaluation. In the passage that follows, where

Swift mimics the inane conversation between the woman and her maid, Betty, his rhetoric is again consistent with the authorial stance that he has taken up. It at once becomes clear that the preoccupations of the two women are being implicitly defined as trivial, and that the passage contributes to the developing satiric scheme. But once again a noticeable feature of the sequence is the apparent directness with which Swift records the details that the speakers are concerned with. Here, for example, is a brief extract from the conversation:

> Madam, the Goldsmith waits below,
> He says, his Business is to know
> If you'll redeem the Silver Cup
> You pawn'd to him? - "First shew him up.
> Your Dressing-Plate, he'll be content
> To take, for Interest *Cent. per Cent.*
>
> (ll. 56-61)

The rhetorical pattern of these lines is rather dramatically commensurate with Swift's definition of himself as an untransforming recorder of events. And his willingness to admit so much trivial and very nearly miscellaneous clutter into the texture of the verse indicates that he wants to include a full rendering of the chaotic multiplicity of detail which is a characteristic of the life-pattern being dramatized. The poem in large part involves an attempt to render that multiplicity, without seeming to impose an artistic order upon it, yet at the same time to effect a significant evaluation of it. In practice, Swift tends to alternate between extended mimicry of the characters' inane speech-patterns and definitive satiric statements about them. An extract from the woman's dinner-table conversation (ll. 101-8), for instance, is followed by the comment that it is all "paultry Stuff" (l. 109) and an example of the "battered, stale, and trite" language that "modern Ladies call polite" (ll. 112-13).

Frequently in the poem, Swift shows a tendency towards the use of the catalog. And this tendency is not limited to the passages of extended mimicry, where we would expect it to appear. At one point he uses a series of abstract nouns to define the characteristics of the several "Prudes, Coquets, and Harridans" (l. 119) who join the "Modern Lady" for her "Ev'ning Tea." These abstract nouns, such as *"Pride,"* *"Scandal,"* and *"Hypocrisy"* (ll. 124-26), attribute to the events being described a high degree of generalized ethical significance. But although Swift is engaged in a process of thematic definition here, the passage as a whole does not possess the kind of order or proportion that would place it in radical contrast to those passages in which Swift is imitating the inanities of the protagonist's life-pattern:

> Now enters over-weening *Pride,*
> And *Scandal* ever gaping wide,
> *Hypocrisy* with Frown severe,
> *Scurrility* with gibing Air;
> Rude *Laughter* seeming like to burst;
> And *Malice* always judging worst;
> And *Vanity* with Pocket-Glass;
> And *Impudence* with Front of Brass;
> And studied *Affectation* came,
> Each Limb, and Feature out of Frame;
> While *Ignorance,* with Brain of Lead,
> Flew hov'ring o'er each Female Head.
> (ll. 124-35)

Swift makes a fairly studied literary joke, of course, by placing such a passage of Spenserian allegorization in this context. But the relationship between the structure of the passage and the rest of the poem is interesting for reasons other than this. For Swift not only renders the traditional abstractions very barely, as if to suggest that the process he is engaged in does not go far beyond one of enumeration, but he also protracts the sequence in such a way as to make it eventually take on that quality of crowded multiplicity which he renders in so much of the poem. And it is not surprising when, immediately afterwards, Swift suggests that the sheer multitudinousness of the "Modern Lady"'s world is difficult to cope with; he would need more than "An Hundred Thousand" tongues, he says, in order to be capable of fully rendering the "Sum" of that world's inanities (ll. 136-43). In the verse-paragraph that follows, Swift again turns to the structure of the catalog in response to this multiplicity. After making the moral-satiric point that "foolish Females" tend to be "most severe" on those "Vices" in which they themselves have the "greatest Share" (ll. 150-53), he goes on to provide a series of illustrative examples. He gives the women fictional names such as *"Mopsa,"* *"Chloe,"* and *"Hircina,"* just as Pope does in the *Epistle to a Lady,* and it is clear that he is arranging a series of type-figures into a sequence which demonstrates a general satiric principle. But even though Swift engages in a process of thematic definition here, the sequence of examples again becomes imitative of the crowded multiplicity that characterizes the "Modern Lady"'s world. Only one of the portraits is extended beyond the length of a couplet, and in an oddly protracted sequence of eighteen lines (ll. 156-73) Swift mentions twelve different names. It is obvious that he includes a much greater number of items than would logically be required for the enforcement of the satiric point. And what again appears to happen is that, although Swift brings a degree of order to the world he perceives by imposing a thematic principle on it, the sheer multiplicity of that world does manage to assert itself and to find its way into the poem's rhetoric.

Later in the poem, when he comes to the subject of the nightly card-playing between the "Lady" and her friends, Swift again defines himself as a passive recorder of the materials he confronts:

> How can the Muse her Aid impart,
> Unskill'd in all the Terms of Art?
> Or in harmonious Numbers put
> The Deal, the Shuffle, and the Cut?
> (ll. 220-23)

Here he suggests that those materials present him with a serious problem because he is rendering them directly, rather than through such elegantly transforming structures as those which Pope used when confronting a similar subject in *The Rape of the Lock.* And when Swift goes on to render the conversation that takes place during the card-game, the poem's rhetorical structure again becomes consistent with such a stance. For the inane and trivial details of that conversation are presented in a manner which provides very little evidence of transforming activity on the part of the author. The women's talk focuses mainly on the mechanics of cheating, which they all believe themselves to be victims of, and the following few lines are illustrative of the whole:

> "I saw you touch your Wedding-Ring
> "Before my Lady call'd a King.
> "You spoke a Word began with H,
> "And I know whom you mean to teach,
> "Because you held the King of Hearts:
> "Fie, Madam, leave these little Arts.
> (ll. 252-57)

When this kind of talk is protracted for more than thirty lines, it is evident that Swift's interests at this point go beyond the enforcement of a satiric evaluation, and that he becomes absorbed in the multitudinous specifics of the woman's world for their own sake. The same thing could no doubt also be said of Pope in his own satires on women, but neither Pope nor the other major Augustan satirists allow into the texture of their poetry anything like the amounts of seemingly untransformed clutter that Swift admits here. Once the extended mimicry is over, however, Swift again makes a summarizing critical comment on what he has rendered (ll. 270-75). And at the end of the poem there is a further combination of journal-like naturalism and satiric evaluation. The poem comes to a conclusion only when Swift's narrative reaches the point at which the woman retires "to Bed" (l.

293); it has been a journal, and its dominant structural principle has been the temporal progression of the events in the woman's day. But Swift also points out that she retires with "empty Purse, and aching Head" (l. 292), that her husband is already "sleeping" (l. 293), and that the "Watchman" is announcing the beginning, rather than the end, of the day (ll. 282-83); in all of these details, it hardly needs to be said, a considerable amount of satiric evaluation is implicit. In the poem as a whole, therefore, although Swift does register the details of the modern lady's life in a way that seems essentially enumerative and not directed by a preoccupation with ordering thematic arrangements, the presence of a rather orthodox kind of satiric theme *is* felt in the poem, and however protracted and unstructured the catalogs may be, they do tend to reinforce that theme most of the time.

In several of Swift's poems, in fact, there is quite clearly an impulse to bring the details of his experience into orthodox types of thematic alignment, and *An Apology to the Lady C—r—t* (1725) offers a fairly vivid example of how such an impulse asserts itself. Swift describes the incident on which the poem is based in an elaborate subtitle: "On Her Inviting Dean S—F—T To Dinner; He came accordingly, but, Her Ladyship being Abroad, went away: At Her Return, She enquired for him; and not hearing of him, sent the next Day to invite him again: When he came, he went to make an *APOLOGY,* for his going away, but my Lady wou'd accept of none but in Verse." As a subtitle this is unusually protracted and detailed, suggesting the possibility that Swift's major concern in the poem will be with the faithful rendering of an actual incident. And in the early stages of the narrative he shows a considerable interest in circumstantial particulars, as the following description of Lady Carteret's return demonstrates:

> My Lady now returning home
> Calls, *Crach'rode, is the Doctor come?*
> He had not heard of him—*Pray see,*

'Tis now a Quarter after three
The Captain walks about, and searches
Thro' all the Rooms, and Courts, and Arches;
Examines all the Servants round,
In vain --- no Doctor's to be found
My Lady could not chuse but wonder:
Captain, I fear you've made some Blunder;
But pray. To morrow go at Ten,
I'll Try his Manners once again;
If Rudeness be the Effect of Knowledge,
My Son shall never see a College.

(ll. 57-70)

For most of this passage, Swift's rhetoric creates the impression that his primary concern is with the untransforming reproduction of actual incidents. It does not matter whether or not Lady Carteret did in fact speak the words that are attributed to her. What is important is that the nature of the rhetoric is such as to suggest that certain specific incidents are being directly transcribed rather than being shaped into patterns that develop a thematic argument. In the last two lines of the passage, however, there is a degree of potentially thematic characterization, which suggests the possibility that the details of the incident are being to some extent arranged so as to express a significant distinction. And in fact, although Swift does accumulate large amounts of strictly circumstantial particulars, he shows an interest from the start of the poem in an organizing principle of thematic contrast which eventually leads to a high degree of significant generalization. Although the narrative is based on an actual incident, Swift at no point introduces either his own name or that of Lady Carteret. Instead, he refers to himself as "the Doctor" and to Lady Carteret as the "Lady," thus attributing to them both an essentially generic identity. And the central contrast of the poem is between the kind of environment to which the doctor belongs and the environment into which he is brought by the lady's invitation. At the beginning of the poem, Swift describes the doctor as a "grave Divine" (l. 5) who long ago "had bid the Court farewel,/Retreating silent to his Cell" (ll. 13-14). And he is defined as a humble figure who finds it very difficult to believe that he is being invited into Lady Carteret's world; as he approaches Dublin Castle, his bearing is "Sheepish" and he "trembles at the Thoughts of State" (ll. 31-32). Swift's procedure is illustrated very clearly when he describes the moment at which he discovered that Lady Carteret was not at home:

> My lord's Abroad; my lady too;
> What must the unhappy Doctor do?
> *Is Capt.* Crach'rode *here, pray? - No.*
> *Nay then 'tis time for me to go.*
> Am I awake, or do I dream?
> I'm sure he call'd me by my Name;
> Nam'd me as plain as he cou'd speak:
> And yet there must be some Mistake.
> Why what a Jest shou'd I have been,
> Had now my Lady been within.
>   (ll. 41-50)

In the first four lines of this Swift appears to be simply reporting the confused particulars of the actual event. But in the rest of the passage he engages in a process of characterization which tends to form those particulars into a thematic pattern; the doctor decides to leave so quickly because his acute sense of inferiority makes him feel that there must have been a mistake, and this sense of inferiority derives from the fact that he is being brought out of his appropriate environment into an alien one. It is clear at this point that Swift is transforming his own experience of the incident into a sort of illustrative fable. And the thematic stylization of the event continues in the second part of the poem, where Swift describes a visit that the lady now pays to the doctor in order to reassure him that she is not offended by his mistake. The doctor decides that he will entertain her in a manner that is appropriate to his own nature:

> He'd treat with nothing that was Rare,
> But winding Walks and purer Air;
> Wou'd entertain without Expence,
> Or Pride, or vain Magnificence;
> For well he knew, to such a Guest,
> The plainest Mails must be the best;
> To Stomachs clog'd with costly Fare,
> Simplicity alone is rare.
>
> (ll. 99-106)

The rhetorical structure of this passage is carefully organized for the purpose of thematic definition, as Swift develops a point-by-point contrast between two ways of life. Instead of "costly Fare" and "Magnificence," there is to be plain food and "Simplicity." The lady is to be entertained in the doctor's environment, which is a natural one characterized by fresh air and "winding Walks." And Swift develops this contrast further by suggesting that, instead of "Spoils of *Persian* Looms" (l. 109), he will offer her roses that shine with "native Lustre" and possess a "Beauty that needs no Aid of Art" (ll. 114-15). Having established in such a systematic way the distinction between the two environments, Swift now describes the consequences of transposing the lady into the one that is appropriate to the doctor. She does her best to praise what he offers her:

> But yet, tho' seeming pleas'd, can't bear
> The scorching Sun, or chilling Air;
> Frighted alike at both Extremes,
> If he displays, or hides his Beams;
> Tho' seeming pleas'd at all she sees,
> Starts at the Rust'ling of the Trees;
> Can scarsely speak for want of Breath,
> In half a Walk fatigu'd to Death.
>
> (ll. 212-18)

The lady's response to the doctor's world is thus an almost exact counterpart of his response to hers. And the doctor draws from this a conclusion which is calculated to "vindicate" (l. 130) his earlier mistake. In a carefully organized speech he explains that he was made uncomfortable because he was placed in an environment that was alien to him, just as she is now made uncomfortable for the same reason. The thematic argument that has been implicit in the poem from the beginning is thus brought to an elegant conclusion, and the details of an actual incident have been arranged into an ordered pattern possessing a high degree of general significance.

Another poem which was stimulated by a specific occasion but which is in the end quite other than "occasional" in nature is *A Libel on D——D—— And A Certain Great Lord* (1730). Swift wrote the poem in response to Patrick Delany's "Epistle To His Excellency John Lord Carteret Lord Lieutenant of Ireland,"[2] and he not only ridicules Delany's aspirations for additional preferment but also attacks Carteret's conduct of his office. Since the poem focuses both on a particular incident and on some localized, contemporary issues, it bears a considerable potential for becoming like those poems that derive their character from Swift's preoccupation with immediate and sometimes miscellaneous particulars rather than with general themes. But from the start Swift widens the context in which we are to contemplate both the occasion and the issues:

> Deluded Mortals, whom the *Great*
> Chuse for Companions *tete à tete,*
> Who at their Dinners, *en famille*
> Get Leave to sit whene'er you will;
> Then, boasting tell us where you din'd,
> And, how his *Lordship* was so kind;
> How many pleasant Things he spoke,
> And, how you *laugh'd* at every *Joke:*
> Swear, he's a most facetious Man,
> That you and he are *Cup* and *Cann.*
> You Travel with a heavy Load,
> And quite mistake *Preferment's* Road.
>
> (ll. 1-12)

In the opening phrase of this he adopts an authoritatively didactic and rather lofty attitude towards the materials of the poem, and in the last couplet he defines the situation of these "Deluded Mortals" in a manner that stresses the generalized and admonitory significance which it bears. In the main body of the passage, however, Swift also dramatizes that situation by rendering some particular details that he imagines it to comprise. By mimicking the speech-patterns and the colloquialisms of a deluded individual, he makes it seem that the generalizing definitions are based upon an awareness of several specific actualities (actualities, indeed, that are closely connected with Swift's perception of Delany and Carteret, and thus with the immediate occasion of the poem). And in the passage as a whole, a union of naturalistic specificity and didactic generalization is achieved. A similar union is achieved in the two verse paragraphs that follow; Swift first dramatizes the coldly aloof response that "my *Lord*" is likely to make if his dinner-guest gives any hint of his own "Int'rest," and he then defines this response as an illustrative example of how great men regard the "Men of Wit" whom they occasionally patronize (ll. 13-32).

After this, Swift brings to bear upon the poem's argument the experiences of several literary figures who had been led to expect assistance from ministers of state, but who were disappointed. He mentions Congreve, Steele, Gay, and Addison, with all of whom he had personal relationships at one time or another, and in describing each instance he goes into a good deal of specific contemporary detail. But he also at several points modifies the actual facts of their experiences so as to make them more precisely relevant to the poem's thematic argument than they would otherwise be.[3] The four writers are thus transformed into lucid *exempla* illustrating, first, how foolish it is for "Men of Wit" to expect significant assistance from the ministers of state who patronize them, and second, the corruption which is the defining characteristic of those ministers. Through the instances of Congreve and Addison,

Swift also seeks to demonstrate the damaging compromises that must so often be resorted to if the writer's frustrated ambitions are eventually to be fulfilled. And it is this which leads him to introduce the example of his friend Pope, who managed to place himself above "the Reach of Want" (1. 84) without enslaving himself to powerful men. Swift has thus organized a sequence of contemporary allusions into a pattern which both defines the object of his satire and also establishes the positive value of integrity by which that object is evaluated. And he continues to develop the poem's argument in a highly structured way when he compares the services that can be offered by "Men of Wit" to those provided by the *"Journey-Men"* who are of much greater practical value to ambitious politicians:

> At Table you can *Horace* quote;
> They at a Pinch can bribe a Vote:
> You shew your Skill in *Grecian* Story,
> But, they can manage *Whig* and *Tory:*
> You, as a *Critick,* are so curious
> To find a Verse in *Virgil* Spurious;
> But, they can *Smoak* the deep Designs,
> When *Bolingbroke* with *Pult'ney* Dines.
> (ll. 95-102)

Here, the issues are defined with great clarity through a series of neatly balanced oppositions between literature and politics, and between the writer's knowledge of a classical tradition and the journeyman's experience of present political realities. At the same time, the process of thematic definition is considerably vitalized by the rhythms of colloquial speech and by a vivid sense of contemporary specifics.

It is at this point that Swift focuses directly on the occasion which stimulated the poem, and begins to discuss the relationship between Delany and Carteret. The "you" whom he now addresses is not the typical example of the patronized "Man of Wit" that he has been concerned with so far, but

Delany himself. And he attributes to Delany a belief that he is
free from the kinds of problem that the poem has defined:

> But, Rev'rend *Doctor*, you, we know,
> Cou'd never Condescend so low;
> The *Vice-Roy*, whom you now attend,
> Wou'd, if he durst, be more your Friend;
> Nor will in you those Gifts despise,
> By which himself was taught to rise.
>
> (ll. 111-16)

Delany will argue, says Swift, not only that Carteret values
the attributes of learned men and would reward them gener-
ously if he were free to do so, but also that Carteret is an
essentially virtuous figure. Swift responds by granting that
"This may be true" (l. 121), but insisting that Carteret's role as
Lord Lieutenant of Ireland has been strictly defined by the
corrupt Walpole, that he is performing an essentially evil
function in that role, and that he really has nothing but the
"Offals of a *Church* distress't" to offer as "bait" to those
whom he patronizes (ll. 129-31). Swift's reply to Delany is thus
very closely related to the central themes in the poem, in that
it stresses the corruption of Carteret in his role as statesman
and warns Delany against expecting any significant favours
from him. But what is also noticeable around this point is
that the movement of the poem is becoming more flexible
than it has so far been; Swift now confronts Delany on the
subject of a specific and immediate occasion, and the overtly
structured patterns of didactic exposition give way to the
rhythms of interpersonal conversation. This new tendency in
the poem's rhetoric continues to establish itself, as Swift next
suggests what Delany's response to the above arguments will
be:

> But, here again you interpose;
> Your favourite *Lord* is none of those,
> Who owe their Virtues to their Stations,
> And Characters to Dedications.
>
> (ll. 135-38)

What Delany now argues in order to defend his patron is that Carteret possesses both genuine "Virtues" and genuine "*Learning*" (l. 140). Swift's immediate rejoinder is to agree with this estimate of Carteret as an individual, but again to insist that it is his "*Place*" rather than his "*Virtues*" (l. 146) which determines his behavior in Ireland. And this leads him to a definitive conclusion about the subject of the debate: "I do the most that *Friendship* can;/I hate the *Vice-Roy*, love the man" (ll. 151-52). With this renewed emphasis on the inescapable corruption of political office, the conversational give-and-take between Delany and Swift arrives at a major crux of the poem's thematic argument, and the personal confrontation over an immediate issue has thus enabled Swift to achieve a high degree of significant generalization.

In the concluding paragraphs of the poem, Swift juxtaposes two contrasting definitions of the role that Carteret plays in Ireland. First there is Delany's, according to which Carteret is an "*Angel* sent by *Heav'n's* Command," who is too "gentle" to relish his mission, and who feels "*Compassion*" for the "guilty Land" that he has been sent to destroy (ll. 161-70). And then there is Swift's:

> So, to effect his *M——h's* ends,
> From *Hell* a *V——* DEV'L ascends,
> His *Budget* with *Corruptions* cramm'd,
> The Contributions of the *damn'd;*
> Which with unsparing Hand, he strows,
> Through *Courts* and *Senates* as he goes;
> And then at *Beelzebub's Black-Hall,*
> Complains his *Budget* was too small.
>
> (ll. 185-92)

The image expresses an intense animosity towards the satirized object, and since it follows upon a didactic argument that has been conducted with a good deal of logical rigor, it may appear reminiscent of those moments in Swift's poetry at which, I have suggested, some form of linguistic violence comes into conflict with or subverts a rationalistic structure.

Here, however, the effect is not of this kind, for a number of reasons. First, the ethical argument that precedes the image is not so obtrusively and rigidly rationalistic in structure as to create an irreconcilable discrepancy between its order and the image's violence; it has involved, for instance, something of the flexibility and emotional interplay that characterizes urgent conversation. Also, the image itself is not protracted in any way that is disproportionate to the poem's overall structure. And finally, although that image expresses a high degree of antipathy towards certain individuals, it also extends the generalizing satiric argument in which it participates. It is true that Swift explicitly defines the passage as having been stimulated by violent emotion: he describes himself as a man "Who, from [his] Soul, sincerely hate[s]/ Both ――― and *Ministers of State*" (ll. 173-74). But he also claims that it is based upon a more rational and accurate observation of political life than Delany is capable of; he says that he looks at the court "with stricter Eyes,/To see the Seeds of *Vice* arise" (ll. 175-76), and that his own definition of Carteret's behaviour is superior to Delany's because it involves more "Truth" (l. 194). The nature of the passage, and its relationship to the rest of the poem, are not such as to make us question his claim that these rationalistic concerns were aspects of its motivation. Indeed, it emerges as the powerful climax of a satiric argument that has been both precisely articulated and intensely felt. And in the *Libel*, Swift appears to reconcile certain rhetorical tendencies that we have elsewhere seen in states of uneasy coexistence; for the poem involves a high degree of ordering thematic arrangement, much specific and localized detail, and a considerable violence of imagery.

In several of Swift's poems, details are subordinated in a rather rigorous way to a generalizing thematic structure. In *The Progress of Poetry* (1720), for example, he develops the notion that poetic creativity is conditioned by the physical state of the poet, and the details of the central image are

consistently organized so as to define that notion. In the
opening lines of the poem, Swift begins to establish the terms
of what is going to become a systematically worked-out
analogy:

> The Farmer's Goose, who in the Stubble,
> Has fed without Restraint, or Trouble;
> Grown fat with Corn and Sitting still,
> Can scarce get o'er the Barn-Door Sill:
> And hardly waddles forth, to cool
> Her Belly in the neighb'ring Pool:
> Nor loudly cackles at the Door;
> For Cackling shews the Goose is poor.

All of the details that are included here work to define the
particular type of inertia that the poem's argument is concerned with. And in the next eight lines, Swift proceeds with
equal care to develop a thematically significant contrast;
when the goose is forced to graze on the "barren Common"
she becomes "lank and spare," and in this condition she flies
energetically above the ground, uttering what Swift ironically refers to as "Sounds harmonious." Having thus established the basic terms of his satiric argument, Swift now takes
the next step of transforming the goose-image into an extended analogy:

> Such is the Poet, fresh in Pay,
> (The third Night's Profits of his Play;)
> His Morning-Draughts, 'till Noon can swill,
> Among his Brethren of the Quill:
> With good Roast Beef his Belly full,
> Grown lazy, foggy, fat, and dull:
> Deep sunk in Plenty, and Delight,
> What Poet e'er could take his Flight?
> Or stuff'd with Phlegm up to the Throat,
> What Poet e'er could sing a Note?
>
> (ll. 17-26)

The selection of detail here is guided by an obtrusive concern for relevance and thematic relationship. And the careful drawing of parallels is continued in the poem's final paragraph, where the poet, reduced to a starving condition, becomes "exalted" in spirit, rises high on "Wings of Paper," and "sings" energetically as he flies. The poem is thus brought to a definitive conclusion, and provided with an almost exactly symmetrical structure. Since this structure contains a central image of considerable debasing force, *The Progress of Poetry*, like the *Libel on D—— D——*, bears a superficial resemblance to those poems I discussed in the second chapter, in which there is a subversive conflict between a violent metaphor and an ordered framework. But in this instance the nature of the central image is not such as to make the poem's symmetry of structure look like an absurd fabrication. Here, the image is not a means by which Swift engages in the type of personal invective to which a rationalistic framework is comically inappropriate. It is true that Swift has a particular kind of poet, rather than all poets, in mind, and that when he describes the ecstatic response of *"Grub-street"* to the poet's song he assigns him to a particular locale. But Grub-street had a generic significance for Swift as well as for Pope. And when he describes the manner in which the poet's "Spirit" becomes "exalted" as a consequence of his physical condition, Swift transforms his subject into a comic example of the ineluctably physical nature of man. The poem's central image, therefore, does not work in the same way as the salamander-image that he applied to Cutts or the Midas-image that he applied to Marlborough. Nor does it possess the kind of angry, disruptive violence that characterizes Swift's use of those metaphors. Because of this, the image does not develop an unruly life of its own that comes into conflict with the poem's highly ordered framework. Instead, that framework appears to give supportive and confirmatory shape to Swift's development of the metaphor, so that image and structure work harmoniously together both to satirize the Grub-street poet and to define a theme of some general significance.

138 ENERGY AND ORDER IN THE POETRY OF SWIFT

Another poem which possesses a noticeably high degree of rhetorical order is Swift's imitation of *Horace. Book I. Ode XIV* (1724). Here, the ship of state metaphor that dominates Horace's ode is adapted by Swift so as to form a comment on Ireland's political situation. The poem thus refers to some very specific contemporary issues, and especially to certain acts committed by the English government. But Swift constantly transposes these issues into large, traditional terms, and the poem is characterized by an elevated formality of utterance. The following lines clearly illustrate his procedure:

> Unhappy Ship, thou art return'd in Vain:
> New Waves shall drive thee to the Deep again.
> Look to thy Self, and be no more the Sport
> Of giddy Winds, but make some friendly Port.
> Lost are thy Oars that us'd thy Course to guide,
> Like faithful Counsellors on either Side.
> Thy Mast, which like some aged Patriot stood
> The single Pillar for his Country's Good,
> To lead thee, as a Staff directs the Blind,
> Behold, it cracks by yon rough *Eastern* Wind.
>
> (ll. 9-18)

Here, it is probable that the "Oars" and the "Mast" are references to individual figures who were crucial to Ireland's stability. But in this poem Swift wants to achieve something like the purity and elevation of phrasing that appear in Horace's ode. So he does not include proper names because that would be to introduce an element of localized particularity that in this case he wants to hold at a distance. Thus, although he modifies Horace's terms so as to make them more precisely relevant, he does not depart from the tone and spirit of the classical poem. It is true that around the middle of Swift's poem there are some specific references to England, Ireland, and Scotland, but this involves a very limited degree of particularity which is a necessary means of placing the traditional image in a contemporary context.

Elsewhere, his adaptation of the image tends towards a sentificus generality of tone:

> In Ships decay'd no Mariner confides,
> Lur'd by the gilded Stern, and painted Sides.
> So, at a Ball, unthinking Fools delight
> In the gay Trappings of a Birth-Day Night:
> They on the Gold Brocades and Satins rav'd,
> And quite forgot their Country was enslav'd.
>
> (ll. 47-52)

It is clear that Swift's poetic response to Ireland's situation is radically different in this instance from that which we saw in the poem about William Wood. Here, he uses the precedent of Horace as a means of transposing that situation into terms which are sanctioned by a long poetic tradition. It is true that he departs considerably from the classical ode in the details that he includes, and his own poem is more than three times as long as Horace's. But the manner and the tone in which he develops the central image suggest that he has used the ode as a means of ordering and shaping his response to Ireland's predicament. And Swift's technique of imitation is thus more or less opposite to that which we saw him adopting in the satire on Steele.

The above poem is not the only occasion on which Swift used classical imitation as a means of imposing rhetorical order on experiences that elsewhere gave rise to less structured responses. We know, for instance, from the *Journal to Stella* and other sources, that his relationship with Harley in 1713 was a very complicated one indeed. But in *Part of the Seventh Epistle of the First Book of Horace Imitated*, he uses the classical poem as a means of describing that relationship in the terms of a clear-cut, somewhat formulaic narrative. Horace's poem has the sharply defined purpose of demonstrating some of the problems that are involved in both the giving and the receiving of patronage. It focuses on the relationship between the pleader Phillippus, who is distinguished, rich, and a leading member of the community, and the auctioneer, Volteius Mena, who is a fairly ordinary citizen of solid character and modest means. After overhearing Volteius praise the country life, Phillippus, on a whim, provides him with a farm. But Volteius runs into all kinds of difficulties, and is soon riding in the middle of the night to implore Phillippus to withdraw his patronage. Swift uses not only the outline of this story, but also some of its details, to construct a narrative that purports to describe the progress of his own relationship to Harley. From the start of the poem he establishes a firm thematic contrast between Harley and himself, just as Horace established such a contrast between Phillippus and Volteius; Harley is a great statesman, "the Nation's great Support," and Swift is an unassuming *"Parson"* who is "Cheapning old Authors on a Stall" when Harley first notices him (ll. 1-6). The relationship between them is then initiated by a whimsical impulse on Harley's part to "crack a Jest" (l. 15)—the great lord, who is fond of "Mischief" (l. 14), prepares to play a joke on the unsuspecting parson. It is clear at this point that Swift is beginning to construct a narrative in which the characters and their motivations are defined according to a traditional comic pattern. However, when he describes what Harley finds out about the character called Dr. Swift, he introduces several details that are related neither to this pattern nor to Horace's poem, as the following lines illustrate:

> His Works were hawk'd in ev'ry Street,
> But seldom rose above a Sheet;
> Of late indeed the Paper-*Stamp*
> Did very much his Genius cramp;
> And, since he could not spend his Fire,
> He now intended to Retire.
>
> (ll. 41-46)

Especially in his reference to the problems caused by the Newspaper Stamp Duty, Swift moves away from coherently thematic characterization towards the notation of irrelevant and localized particulars. But although his characterization of "Dr. Swift" is longer and more variegated by topical details than Horace's characterization of Volteius, it retains some sort of connection with the classical model, especially in its emphasis on Dr. Swift's solid integrity of character and his modest but solvent financial situation. And when Swift describes the clergyman's response to Harley's invitation to dinner, he again imitates Horace's poem rather closely. The invitation is made at second hand, and Dr. Swift, not believing it to be seriously meant, refuses it. Harley is taken aback, but tries again, and on the second occasion Dr. Swift becomes a humble, confused figure, "sneaking" up to Harley's coach and offering "many a lame Excuse" (ll. 64-65). These details are not only firmly based on Swift's classical model, but they involve a fairly high degree of comic schematization. And this schematization continues as Swift describes the pleasure which the parson begins to take in Harley's company; when he says that "the Gudgeon took the Bait" (l. 80) he both echoes Horace and reemphasizes the comic pattern of the unsuspecting cleric being taken in by the manipulating statesman. At this point in the narrative Dr. Swift accompanies Harley to Windsor, where he admires the rural surroundings and expresses a desire to "be a *Canon* there" (l. 84). But Harley decides that he must become a dean in Ireland instead, and plans a radical transformation of Dr. Swift's state; he says that he only needs to "cross the *Irish* Seas,/To live in Plenty, Power and Ease" (ll. 92-93). We know that the allocation of the deanship was in reality the end product of a long, complicated process involving a high degree of uncertainty and confusion for Swift. But in this poem it is simplified into the form of a whimsical act occurring in the course of a traditionally structured comic narrative. When Dr. Swift is described in his new state, the comic stylization of actual events is pushed to an extreme point:

> Suppose him, now, a *Dean* compleat,
> Devoutly lolling in his Seat;
> The Silver Virge, with decent Pride,
> Stuck underneath his Cushion-side.
>
> (ll. 97-100)

There is a considerable element of caricature in these lines, as the change effected by Harley's manipulation is made to seem both very dramatic and morally illustrative. After Dr. Swift's initial sensation of luxury, his affairs rapidly deteriorate very much in the manner that Volteius's do in Horace's poem. He becomes overwhelmed by the financial complexities of the deanship, "His Tenants wrong him in his Rent" (l. 108), and the local farmers force him to "take his Tythes in kind" (l. 110). Eventually reduced to a desperate state, he takes dramatic action:

> Poor *S——t*, with all his Losses vext,
> Not knowing where to turn him next;
> Above a Thousand Pounds in Debt,
> Takes Horse, and in a mighty Fret
> Rides Day and Night at such a Rate,
> He soon arrives at *HARLEY*'s Gate;
> But was so dirty, pale and thin,
> Old *Read* would hardly let him in.
>
> (ll. 113-20)

The actual return from Ireland that Swift is referring to in this passage occurred because he had been sent for. But he is not attempting a faithful reproduction of actual events, and the narrative he constructs is in fact very remote from those events. It is characterized at this point by the type of emphasis that is appropriate to a morally illustrative fable; the frenzied state of panic in which Dr. Swift rides and his extremely dishevelled appearance testify to the extent of the dislocation that has been effected by Harley's misguided patronage. Finally, the narrative is brought to an elegant and admonitory conclusion, as Dr. Swift implores Harley to return him to his original state:

I have Experience dearly bought,
You know I am not worth a Groat;
But you resolv'd to have your Jest,
And 'twas a Folly to Contest:
Then since you now have done your worst,
Pray leave me where you found me first.

(ll. 133-38)

In these late stages of the poem Swift imitates Horace's narrative very closely. And it appears that he has used the classical model as a means of transposing the complex, difficult reality of his relationship to Harley into a very orderly and clear-cut pattern. In a sense, of course, Swift simply evades that reality, creating instead a highly structured and stylized comedy that is set apart from the confused particularity of his actual experience. But since he does refer to real people and events, it would appear that the poem's effect is meant to derive from some sort of relationship between the stylized narrative and what actually happened. And in that relationship there is no doubt an element of conscious irony, an awareness of the difference between the manner in which events are structured in the poem and the manner in which they are structured in actual experience.

Swift again alludes to some of the above incidents in his imitation of part of *Horace, Lib. 2. Sat. 6* (1714), but this time he transposes them into quite a different set of terms. The central thematic principle of Horace's poem is a contrast between country and city life, and he focuses particularly on the peace that he enjoys in his rural retreat and the vexations that he endures when he visits his patron Maecenas in the city. Although Swift's imitation is much looser in this instance than in the previous poem, he does adopt the thematic framework of the classical model and at one point he imitates its phrasing very closely. Swift begins his poem by stressing the desirability of a comfortable home in a rural scene:

I Often wish'd, that I had clear
For Life, six hundred Pounds a Year,

> A handsome House to lodge a Friend,
> A River at my Garden's End,
> A Terras Walk, and half a Rood
> Of Land set out to plant a Wood.

Although there is an emphasis on financial security here as well, Swift's major preoccupation appears to be with the achievement of peace in a natural environment. And when he goes on to express his contentment with the fact that he does now possess these things, he defines his situation as one in which he is "Remov'd from all th'ambitious Scene,/Nor puff'd by Pride, nor sunk by Spleen." However, he now describes himself as being forced to leave this environment because of a request by Harley, who insists that he is needed in the "Town" (l. 13). This request is transformed into an example of the thoughtlessness which typifies eminent political figures; "The Toil, the Danger of the Seas;/Great Ministers ne'er think of these" (ll. 17-18). As a consequence of it, Swift is forced to suffer a particular kind of vexation which is characteristic of the city, but from which he is free in his rural retreat; when he reaches the court, and attempts to speak to Harley, he is subjected to irritated and jealous comments from other figures who are seeking an audience. And after he has managed to obtain no more than a brief "Whisper" (l. 43) from Harley, he is at once besieged by insistent demands on what people take to be his influence:

> A hundred other Men's Affairs
> Like Bees, are humming in my Ears.
> "To morrow my Appeal comes on,
> "Without your Help the Cause is gone—"
> The Duke expects my Lord and you,
> About some great Affair, at Two—
> "Put my Lord *Bolingbroke* in Mind,
> "To get my Warrant quickly signed;
> "Consider, 'tis my first request.—"
> Be satisfy'd, I'll do my best:—
> Then presently he falls to teize,

"You may for certain, if you please;
"I doubt not, if his Lordship knew—
"And Mr. *Dean,* one Word from you—"
(ll. 49-62)

Both in this passage and in other parts of the poem Swift
carries the mimicry of discordant elements to a considerable
length, but the several bits of conversation are all related to
that contrast between city and country which is the poem's
major thematic principle. Also, it is noticeable that when
Swift satirizes the "Crowd" of petitioners (l. 34), many of
whom are clearly his political enemies, he does not refer to
any of them by name. This procedure is very different from
that which he adopts in another poem, also written in 1714
and focusing on the same subject matter; in *The Author upon
Himself* he attacks by name several figures who are vindic-
tively jealous of his relationship with Harley. In the present
poem, Swift obviously wants to keep that type of particularity to a minimum, as he builds an emblematic fiction
on the basis of a classical precedent. The two major roles in
that fiction are assigned to himself and Harley, and the next
step in the poem's developing structure is a dramatization of
the relationship between them:

'Tis (let me see) three Years and more,
(*October* next, it will be four)
Since HARLEY bid me first attend,
And chose me for an humble Friend;
Would take me in his Coach to chat,
And question me of this and that;
As, "What's a-Clock?" And, "How's the
Wind?
"Whose Chariot's that we left behind?"
Or gravely try to read the Lines
Writ underneath the Country *Signs.*
(ll. 63-72)

This part of the poem contains some precise echoes of
Horace's description of his relationship with Maecenas. And

one hardly needs to compare it with the known facts of Swift's relationship with Harley to recognize that the passage is a highly stylized comic fabrication. It does, however, play a significant part in the thematic structure of the poem, because the passage defines a relationship of such a kind as to make the rumors swirling around it seem ridiculous. In the next section, Swift returns to an account of the court hangers-on who are convinced that his relationship with Harley has admitted him to the highest level of political knowledge. They again subject him to a series of innuendoes and demands for information. And in the concluding lines of the poem, after defining his experience in the city as a futile waste of time, Swift expresses a longing to return to the environment in which he began:

> Thus in a Sea of Folly tost,
> My choicest Hours of Life are lost:
> Yet always wishing to retreat;
> Oh, could I see my Country Seat.
> There leaning near a gentle Brook,
> Sleep, or peruse some antient Book;
> And there in sweet Oblivion drown
> Those Cares that haunt the Court and Town.
>   (ll. 105-12)

Irvin Ehrenpreis has described the elegantly symmetrical structure which these lines complete;[4] the movement of the poem is from the poet's country retreat, to the crowd of hangers-on in the court, to Swift and Harley at the center, back to the deluded crowd, and finally back once more to the country retreat. This highly ordered framework is a means of developing a thematic argument of great clarity. It is noticeable, however, that Swift has achieved such rhetorical order by constructing a fiction (based on classical precedent) that is far removed from the complex reality of the situation it purports to describe. The tension of that reality, rather than being allowed into the narrative, is held at a great distance. So the order embodied by the poem's structure is not threatened or undermined by any subversive forces. As in the previous poem, however, Swift must have been ironically aware of the fictionalizing and stylizing process in which he was engaged. And he must have expected such an awareness to be an aspect of the contemporary reader's response to the poem.

Several of the poems that Swift wrote to Esther Johnson also involve both allusion to a real personal relationship and a very noticeable rhetorical shapeliness. In these instances, however, there is no sense that the order embodied by the rhetoric derives from the kind of stylization which holds the actualities and immediacies of experience at a distance. On the contrary, rhetorical form appears to be both firmly based on and validated by those actualities. The first poem in the sequence, *On Stella's Birth-day* (1719), illustrates this quite clearly:

> Stella this Day is thirty four,
> (We shan't dispute a Year or more)
> However Stella, be not troubled,
> Although thy Size and Years are doubled,
> Since first I saw Thee at Sixteen,
> The brightest Virgin on the Green,
> So little is thy Form declin'd
> Made up so largly in thy Mind.
> Oh, would it please the Gods to split
> Thy Beauty, Size, and Years, and Wit,
> No Age could furnish out a Pair
> Of Nymphs so gracefull, Wise and fair
> With half the Lustre of Your Eyes,
> With half thy Wit, thy Years and Size:
> And then before it grew too late,
> How should I beg of gentle Fate,
> (That either Nymph might have her Swain,)
> To split my Worship too in twain.

Here, Swift manages to achieve a very high degree of structural coordination and at the same time to suggest that he is focusing on the concrete particularities of actual experience. The opening lines are characterized by a carefully realistic tone: first, there is the drily factual statement of Stella's age, qualified in a familiarly conversational manner in the second line, and this is followed by a notation of the fact that not only her age but also her "Size" has been "doubled" in the course of time. This realism of manner then blends into a romantic and pastoral tone when Swift refers to her early appearance as "The brightest Virgin of the Green." Although it would appear that the time for such phraseology is now past, Swift insists that there has been no decline in her essential "Form" because it is composed of the qualities of her "Mind" rather than of her body. In these lines, Swift is turning to a traditional concept by which he introduces a tone of moral idealism into his praise of Stella. The concept is given special piquancy here, of course, by the implications of "largly," which harks back to the awareness of Stella's physical dimensions. But the word in no way subverts the moral idealism of the lines, partly because throughout the poem Swift implies that physical appearance is unimportant compared to spiritual characteristics, and partly because at this point the word's meaning is transferred to a description of Stella's moral and spiritual, rather than physical, dimensions. After this, Swift begins to develop a traditional conceit focusing on the poet's sense that even if the loved one were to be divided into two, the resulting women would have no equals. But again, through his repeated emphasis on Stella's "Size," Swift develops the conceit in a way that involves a steady awareness of physical realities. This emphasis does not undercut Swift's elegantly ordered compliment—rather, it suggests that such a compliment can be made in full awareness of Stella's physical substantiality (the conceit is even turned into a means of stressing that substantiality). And in the final lines of the poem Swift brings the sequence to a conclusion by suggesting that if such a division of Stella were to take place, he would want his "Worship" of her to be similarly divided so that each "Nymph" could receive his love. Here, he returns to the romantic-pastoral note in the references to nymphs and swains, and to the morally idealizing note in "Worship," and he clearly means to suggest that the implications of such words are relevant to his relationship with Stella. But such phraseology has been validated and strengthened by the physical realism that has been a constant presence in the poem. The poem is thus a highly coordinated rhetorical unit which involves both a considerable degree of literary stylization and also a sense that it retains contact with the particularities of actual experience.

In *Stella's Birth-day* (1721), the dominant structural feature is an image that Swift establishes in the opening lines:

> All travellers at first incline
> Where'e'er they see the fairest Sign,
> And if they find the Chambers neat,
> And like the Liquor and the Meat
> Will call again and recommend
> The Angel-Inn to ev'ry Friend:
> And though the Painting grows decay'd
> The House will never loose it's Trade.

The implication of the image is that interior virtues are considerably more important than outward appearances. And Swift soon proceeds to make this implication relevant to his praise of Stella:

> Now, this is Stella's Case in Fact;
> An Angel's Face, a little crack't;
> (Could Poets or could Painters fix
> How Angels look at thirty six)
> This drew us in at first to find
> In such a Form an Angel's Mind
> And ev'ry Virtue now supplyes
> The fainting Rays of Stella's Eyes.
>   (ll. 15-22)

As in the previous poem, Swift exploits a romantic convention—here, it is the comparison of the woman to an "Angel." Again, an emphasis on the beauty she had in her youth blends into an idealization of her present spiritual qualities; Swift perceives in Stella an "Angel's Mind," the virtues of which give light to her fading eyes. And this idealization of her is again substantiated by a perception of the real; her angelic face is now, at the age of "thirty six", somewhat "crack't." As Swift develops the image further, he maintains this realistic note by using the terminology of innkeeping, and at the same time continues to draw attention to Stella's spiritual virtues. She entertains her guests by "plentifully" filling their "Minds" from her "Stock" of "Breeding, Humor, Wit and Sense," while making extremely "reasonable Bills" that put her guests to "small Expense" (ll. 23-30). Swift is clearly taking great pains to ensure that the progression of the poem is metaphorically and thematically coherent. His next step is to ridicule the notion that a "newer Face" outside another inn might tempt Stella's guests away. And in a powerful conclusion he chastises "Cloe" for believing in such a possibility:

> . . . should you live to see the Day
> When Stella's Locks must all be grey
> When Age must print a furrow'd Trace
> On ev'ry Feature of her face;
> Though you and all your senceless Tribe
> Could Art or Time or Nature bribe
> To make you look like Beauty's Queen
> And hold for ever at fifteen.
> No Bloom of Youth can ever blind
> The Cracks and Wrinckles of your Mind,
> All Men of Sense will pass your Dore
> And crowd to Stella's at fourscore.
>   (ll. 47-58)

A tendency towards significant generalization has always been present in the poem, and here Swift's manner is authoritatively didactic. A specific occasion in the life of a woman with whom Swift had a close personal relationship is thus transformed into an illustration of a general truth. And the poetic design which articulates this truth is characterized by a high degree of evident order. The poem does not, however, create the impression that its generalizing force and coordinated structure have been achieved through an evasion of those actualities to which it alludes. Instead, the actuality of Stella, and of Swift's relationship to her, appears to support and strengthen the harmonious structure within which its elements are contained.

In *To Stella, Visiting me in my Sickness* (1720), Swift is explicitly concerned from the start of the poem with generalizing moral definition. He begins with an elegant statement of what he considers to be Stella's major spiritual virtue:

> *PALLAS* observing *Stella*'s Wit
> Was more than for her Sex was fit;
> And that her Beauty, soon or late,
> Might breed Confusion in the State,
> In high Concern for human Kind,
> Fixt *Honour* in her Infant Mind.

And immediately afterwards he sets out to "define" this quality. After raising the rather indefinite idea that honor includes all of the "num'rous Virtues which the Tribe/Of tedious Moralists describe" (ll. 15-16), Swift turns away from purely abstract discussion in order to "Let *Stella*'s fair Example preach/A Lesson she alone can teach" (ll. 33-34). She is thus perceived as a figure who is capable of taking on a didactic function. And in the middle stages of the poem Swift's contemplation of her enables him to base an ethical argument on the example of a real individual, as Stella is seen to demonstrate a sequence of general characteristics such as honesty, "Courage," (l. 66), "Wit" and "Sense" (l. 80). This methodical process of definition is eventually concluded by a summarizing comment:

> Say, *Stella*, was *Prometheus* blind,
> And forming you, mistook your Kind?

No: 'Twas for you alone he stole
The Fire that forms a manly Soul;
Then to compleat it ev'ry way,
He molded it with Female Clay:
To that you owe the nobler Flame,
To this, the Beauty of your Frame.

(ll. 85-92)

The passage is constructed in a very systematic manner; the initial rhetorical question and its answer are followed by two couplets in which Stella's combination of male and female virtues is defined in evenly balanced phrases. Swift's analysis of her character is thus provided with an almost diagrammatic neatness of structure, and the ethical argument appears to have been brought to a conclusion. But at this point Swift turns away from moralistic analysis towards a dramatization of the incident that appears to have prompted the poem:

When on my sickly Couch I lay,
Impatient both of Night and Day,
Lamenting in unmanly Strains,
Call'd ev'ry Pow'r to ease my Pains,
Then *Stella* ran to my Relief
With chearful Face, and inward Grief;
And, though by Heaven's severe Decree
She suffers hourly more than me,
No cruel Master could require
From Slaves employ'd for daily Hire
What *Stella* by her Friendship warm'd,
With Vigour and Delight perform'd.
My sinking Spirits now supplies
With Cordials in her Hands, and Eyes.
Now, with a soft and silent Tread,
Unheard she moves about my Bed.
I see her taste each nauseous Draught,
And so obligingly am caught:
I bless the Hand from whence they came,
Nor dare distort my Face for shame.

(ll. 97-116)

There is a vivid immediacy in this passage which creates the impression that Swift is directly rendering a personal experience. Especially in the last few lines, where he describes Stella tasting the medicine before giving it to him, the circumstantial details do not appear to be included strictly because they further the process of ethical definition. And yet, of course, they do further that process. For as well as being a distinctly individualized human being at this point, Stella is also a supreme example of moral virtue. And the incident that Swift dramatizes, while it is vividly particularized and has the air of being directly rendered, is also structured in a way that enables it to play a significant part in the continuing ethical argument of the poem. Swift describes himself in his sickness as both physically and mentally disturbed, and the "unmanly Strains" to which he gives way are clearly related to the distinction between traditional male and female qualities that he has just enforced. In this state, he finds in Stella a courageous self-control that puts him to "shame." Indeed, the nature of the incident and the thematic structure of the poem are in perfect harmony. Swift recognizes in Stella's personality a kind of stable order that enables him not only to base his idealization of her on the particulars of concrete actuality, but also to make it seem that the structural harmony of the poem in a sense derives from the harmony of her nature.

5

The Design under Stress

IN the poems discussed in the previous chapter, then, Swift approaches his subject matter by means of some noticeably ordered rhetorical forms. In some of these poems, and perhaps most clearly those addressed to Stella, the relationship between the forms and the actualities which they purport to render is both direct and mutually supportive. But in the two Horatian imitations focusing on Swift's friendship with Harley there is a hint of possible irony in the juxtaposition of the rhetorical structure and the defined experience, and such an irony may very well remind us of those poems by Swift in which there is a high degree of tension between orderly designs and other factors which tend to be subversive of them. Now the relationship between form and subject matter that appears in the two Horace imitations is in some ways similar to that which eventually shows itself in *Cadenus and Vanessa* (1713). This poem, of course, may be compared to those addressed to Stella in that it too focuses on an important relationship between Swift and a woman, but the impression that *Cadenus and Vanessa* finally creates is quite different from that of the Stella poems. Here, there is again a noticeable and persistent rhetorical ordering of the experience that is alluded to, but the poem does not suggest that this ordering activity is supported or facilitated by the nature of the experience that it deals with. On the contrary, Swift implies the presence of certain unruly forces that tend to be disruptive of order and that do not appear to be easily contained within the highly structured framework that is imposed on them. Some definitive elements of that framework begin to emerge in the poem's opening lines:

> The *Shepherds* and the *Nymphs* were seen
> Pleading before the *Cyprian* Queen.
> The Council for the Fair began,
> Accusing that false Creature, *Man.*

The initial action of the poem is here located in a pastoral world inhabited by figures of classical myth, and the terms in which that world is evoked are firmly based on a familiar and stylized poetic tradition. Also, the discussion to which Venus is listening takes the form of a lawsuit, and is thus structured according to the terms of a systematic and traditional device of social organization. It soon becomes clear, however, that the subject of the debate is not one to which legal terminology is entirely adequate:

> The Brief with weighty Crimes was charg'd,
> On which the Pleader much enlarg'd;
> That *Cupid* now has lost his Art,
> Or blunts the Point of ev'ry Dart;
> His Altar now no longer smokes,
> His Mother's Aid no Youth invokes:
> This tempts Free-thinkers to refine,
> And bring in doubt their Pow'r divine;
> Now Love is dwindled to Intrigue,
> And Marriage grown a Money-League.
> Which Crimes aforesaid (with her Leave)
> Were (as he humbly did conceive)
> Against our Sov'reign Lady's Peace,
> Against the Statutes in that Case,
> Against her Dignity and Crown:
> Then pray'd an Answer, and sat down.
>   (ll. 5-20)

Even though the pleader approaches the subject of love by means of a strictly traditional set of images, there is a comic contrast in his speech between the emotionally-charged issue at its centre and the formalized phraseology of the lawcourts. This phraseology, as has recently been pointed out, represents an attempt "to reduce the wild question of love to reasonable proportions—to render it orderly, manageable and discussable by circumscribing it with precedents . . . and the rhetoric of logic" (p. 434).[1] So Swift's use of such terms is one of the ways in which, in this opening sequence, he turns towards verbal patterns that systematize and stylize his treatment of the issues. Later in the poem, when the terms of the opening debate are brought to bear upon a difficult and complex experience, the relationship between this process of stylization and the emotions at the center of the narrative comes to involve a considerable degree of irony.

Since the debate over love's decline is cast in the form of a trial, one thing that its participants require is a clear-cut verdict in which blame will be apportioned to one of the two sides. This is what the first pleader has sought to establish, and now the "Defendant's Council" (l. 22) attempts to exonerate the men by blaming the nature of women for the decline of love. His speech contains a rigidly structured argument in which two absolute concepts are juxtaposed so as to lead towards a definitive conclusion. First, he describes the kind of love which was celebrated by the "antient Poets" as "A Fire celestial, chaste, refin'd,/Conceiv'd and kindled in the Mind," an "equal Flame" that effected an ideal spiritual union (ll. 28-34). Then he argues that such love no longer exists because "Women now feel no such Fire,/And only know the gross Desire" (ll. 35-36). Modern love is thus defined as simply a matter of physical lust in which human beings are reduced to the level of animals, and this degeneration has occurred because the emotions of women are now capable of moving only in "lower Spheres" (l. 37). The speaker goes on to insist that modern women can find little time even for this degenerate type of "Love," so engrossed are they by a "thousand Female Toys" (ll. 43-50). Having thus defined woman as a creature of irredeemable baseness and triviality, he next develops a precise illustrative image of a slow-moving stream, and this leads to a confirmatory verdict:

> The Current of a Female Mind
> Stops thus, and turns with ev'ry Wind;
> Thus whirling round, together draws
> Fools, Fops, and Rakes, for Chaff and Straws.
> Hence we conclude, no Women's Hearts
> Are won by Virtue, Wit, and Parts;
> Nor are the Men of Sense to blame
> For Breasts incapable of Flame;
> The Fault must on the *Nymphs* be plac'd,
> Grown so corrupted in their Taste.
>
> (ll. 57-66)

The phrases that the speaker employs suggest that he is engaged in a methodical and logical process of argument; he begins to apply the image with an emphatic "Thus," and his verdict is introduced by "Hence we conclude." As he makes this concluding statement, the structure of his speech becomes even more diagrammatic than before; "Virtue, Wit, and Parts" are opposed to "Fools, Fops, and Rakes," and the blame for love's decline is allocated in a decisive and absolute manner. The speaker's response to the problem under discussion, then, is to construct a highly ordered rhetorical pattern which reduces the issues to a definitive clarity. And when his analysis is concluded, he too invokes the ordering systems of legal procedure by stressing that he has witnesses ready to "attest" (on "Oath") that "ev'ry Article" of his speech is true (ll. 67-74). The speech does not, however, succeed in resolving the issue for Venus, who remains in a state of uncertainty. And indeed, as the poem progresses, it persistently suggests that the type of rationalizing structure upon which the pleader rests his case is inadequate to deal with the problem it is designed to resolve.

Swift now begins to describe Venus's response to the arguments that have been put before her. The debate has left her feeling not only uncertain, but also insecure, because she recognizes that the decline of love constitutes a threat to her reputation and standing among the gods. She therefore seeks a course of action which will both resolve the issues into the form of a decisive verdict and reestablish the authority of her reign:

> The Goddess much perplex'd in Mind,
> To see her Empire thus declin'd,
> When first this grand Debate arose
> Above her Wisdom to compose,
> Conceiv'd a Project in her Head,
> To work her Ends; which if it sped,
> Wou'd shew the Merits of the Cause,
> Far better than consulting Laws.
>
> (ll. 128-35)

It has been pointed out in a recent essay on the poem that Swift's use of the word "Project" in other works invariably carries "pejorative connotations" (520).[2] Also, Venus's plan is later described as an "Experiment" (l. 139), and we know what Swift's attitude to experimental science was. His use of such terms may very well be intended to raise doubts about Venus's plan from the beginning, but it takes some time for its essential inadequacy to emerge. What Venus intends to do is to transform a newly born girl (Vanessa) into a paragon of human excellence, so that the men will no longer be able to complain that womankind is too degenerate a species to provide worthy objects of love:

> Since Men alledge they ne'er can find
> Those Beauties in a Female Mind,
> Which raise a Flame that will endure
> For ever, uncorrupt and pure;
> If 'tis with Reason they complain,
> This Infant shall restore my Reign.

I'll search where ev'ry Virtue dwells,
From Courts inclusive, down to Cells,
What Preachers talk, or Sages write,
These I will gather and unite,
And represent them to Mankind
Collected in that Infant's Mind.

(ll. 142-53)

She is thus seeking to construct an answer to the arguments of
the second pleader in the trial, an answer which will establish
whether or not those arguments were valid. She does not
question the absolutist and categorizing tendencies of his
speech. On the contrary, she too seeks to allocate blame
decisively on one side or another; if Vanessa succeeds in
raising a "Flame that will endure/For ever, uncorrupt and
pure," then it will be proven that the women have been to
blame for the absence of such love prior to Vanessa's appearance, and if she does not succeed, it will be proven that
the men have been at fault. For the purposes of her project,
however, Venus adopts as a premise the notion that the
second pleader's analysis is correct. If it is, then it logically
follows that the creation of Vanessa will be a means of
reestablishing Venus's authority and thus of reviving the old
order in the kingdom of love. This is clearly the major
intention behind her plan, and she sets about implementing
it in a very systematic and thorough fashion. She is going to
probe into every area of human activity so as to "gather" the
virtues that she requires, and then she is going to "unite"
them into the form of a personality that will be both all-
inclusive and harmonious. Venus now proceeds to graft onto
the beauty that Vanessa already possesses such traditional
female qualities as "Sweetness" (l. 161), "Decency of Mind" (l.
164), and a "soft, engaging Air" (l. 178). And she then tricks
Pallas into providing a series of "manly" virtues such as
"Knowledge," "Judgement," "Wit," "Fortitude," and "Honour" (ll. 202-9). Vanessa's personality is thus formed by a
systematic process of selection and organization, and Venus

responds to the initial problem by creating a highly structured artifact that is designed both to resolve her uncertainty
and to render her position secure. Since this fictionalized
creation of Vanessa is intended by Swift as a comment on the
real-life personality of Esther Vanhomrigh, it clearly constitutes an engagement by the author himself in a creative act
which erects a systematized and stylized version of a human
personality. Indeed, the noticeably ordered and idealizing
verbal patterns by which he describes Vanessa at this point
bear a distinct similarity to the patterns by which he
elsewhere describes Stella. However, whereas in the Stella
poems the order embodied by the idealizing definitions is
substantiated and supported by a particularized rendering of
experience, in *Cadenus and Vanessa* the experience that Swift
eventually dramatizes is in radical contrast with that order.
The significance of the contrast is partially defined by
Venus's experience of putting her project into action. She is
confident that the project will lead in an orderly fashion to
certain very decisive consequences:

> She doubted not but such a Dame
> Thro' ev'ry Breast wou'd dart a Flame;
> That ev'ry rich and lordly Swain
> With Pride wou'd drag about her Chain;
> That Scholars wou'd forsake their Books
> To study bright *Vanessa*'s Looks:
> As she advanc'd, that Womankind
> Wou'd by her Model form their Mind,
> And all their Conduct wou'd be try'd
> By her, as an unerring Guide.
>   (ll. 230-39)

She thus attributes to Vanessa not only a power to resolve the
issues of the trial, but also an ability to take on a didactic role
similar to that which we have seen Swift attributing to Stella.
This is what Venus hopes for, but, as Swift warns the reader,
she hopes "in vain" (l. 249).

When Vanessa at last makes her entry into a particularized

world of men and women, the first group of people she confronts is a crowd of "fashionable Fops:"

> They ask'd her, how she lik'd the Play,
> Then told the Tattle of the Day,
> A Duel fought last Night at Two,
> About a Lady — You know who;
> Mention'd a new *Italian*, come
> Either from *Muscovy* or *Rome;*
> Gave Hints of who and who's together;
> Then fell to talking of the Weather:
> Last Night was so extremely fine,
> The Ladies walk'd till after Nine.
>
> (ll. 318-27)

Their talk is an utter chaos of trivial and disconnected items, and it is in sharp contrast with the types of verbal structure that have so far dominated the poem. Vanessa's immediate response to it is "silent Scorn" (l. 334). But she eventually decides to address the fops in a manner that is designed to lead towards an evaluative testing of their intelligence:

> At last she spitefully was bent
> To try their Wisdom's full Extent;
> And said, she valu'd nothing less
> Than Titles, Figure, Shape, and Dress;
> That, Merit should be chiefly plac'd
> In Judgement, Knowledge, Wit, and Taste;
> And these, she offer'd to dispute,
> Alone distinguish'd Man from Brute:
> That, present Times have no Pretence
> To Virtue, in the Noblest Sense,
> By *Greeks* and *Romans* understood,
> To perish for our Country's Good.
>
> (ll. 338-49)

This is only part of Swift's summary of her speech, but it is sufficient to indicate its central characteristics. In some ways, the speech resembles that of the second pleader in the trial at the beginning of the poem. Vanessa insists upon certain clear-cut evaluative distinctions, and she uses carefully balanced rhetorical patterns to enforce them; "Titles, Figure, Shape, and Dress," for instance, are systematically opposed to "Judgement, Knowledge, Wit, and Taste," and the moral character of "present Times" is weighed in the balance with that of the *"Greeks* and *Romans."* What she delivers, in fact, is a formal set piece that resembles a lecture rather than an attempt at conversational interchange. And it appears to emanate from a mind that is confident of its ability to arrange and dispose the materials at its command. But especially when Vanessa goes on to name and describe the "antient Heroes" (l. 350) and to speak of "foreign Customs" (l. 353), it becomes clear that the speech constitutes a withdrawal from the present world she is confronting towards materials that are almost exclusively drawn from her reading. These are the materials that she can arrange into such an orderly pattern. And what Vanessa does is to respond to the chaos that she encounters by constructing a self-contained and highly ordered artifact that separates her from this chaos. Indeed, her behavior at this point in the poem's development is symptomatic of the way she behaves on other occasions during her initial experience of the world. When, a little later, she confronts a crowd of "glitt'ring Dames" (l. 364) whose talk is characterized by a similar disorder and incoherence to that of the fops, she simply stands aloof and withdraws into silence, attempting to maintain some sort of balance and poise in the face of the encroaching chaos. Vanessa's predominant tendency in these early stages is to establish certain areas of order in her experience that separate her from the surrounding confusion. She does not avoid social intercourse altogether, but allows a chosen few into her company:

> Yet some of either Sex, endow'd
> With Gifts superior to the Crowd,
> With Virtue, Knowledge, Taste and Wit,
> She condescended to admit:
> With pleasing Arts she could reduce

Mens Talents to their proper Use;
And with Address each Genius held
To that wherein it most excell'd;
Thus making others Wisdom known,
Cou'd please them, and improve her own.
A modest Youth said something new,
She plac'd it in the strongest View.
All humble Worth she strove to raise;
Would not be prais'd, yet lov'd to praise.

(ll. 444-57)

In her treatment of those with whom she converses, Vanessa resembles an artist who is attempting to create ordered patterns and structures. She is very selective about the materials with which she deals, and she is constantly arranging and disposing those materials in such a way as to arrive at harmonious form. Again, Vanessa appears confident in her ability to order her world, but this world is obviously an exclusive one and its limits are very sharply defined.

It is clear by now that Vanessa's behaviour is not bringing about the kind of consequence that Venus had in mind when she created her; she withdraws from and alienates the majority of the people with whom she comes into contact, and her relationship with the exclusive circle over which she presides is not, it would seem, conducive to the emergence of sexual passion. This developing situation has been closely observed by Venus's son, Cupid, and he now prepares to intervene significantly in the course of the action. He is angered by the apparent defeat of Venus's expectations, and he feels an urgent desire to take "vengeance" on Vanessa for what he conceives to be his mother's "Wrongs" (ll. 466-71). Cupid is thus motivated by an intense emotional response to the course of events, rather than by an objective or rationalistic analysis of it. He is also described as being "full of Mischief" (l. 466), and it is clear that Swift conceives him at this point in his traditional role as an agent of disorder. Cupid, in fact, is bent on destroying the highly ordered experiential world that Vanessa has created for herself. He recognizes that Vanessa's behaviour so far has been directed mainly by the qualities instilled into her by Pallas, and he now plans to bring to fruition those "Seeds" that were sown by Venus and which would naturally be productive of sexual passion (ll. 472-75). For a long time he finds Vanessa "invulnerable" (l. 489), and "hard to be subdu'd" (l. 496). She is characterized by a high degree of ordering self-control, and she is protected by the books which Cadenus, her tutor, constantly places in the way of Cupid's darts. Eventually, in a state of extreme frustration, Cupid attempts to break her resistance by making her fall in love with Cadenus himself, a man who is "Grown old in Politicks and Wit" (l. 509). It is a plan of attack conceived in passion and carried out with the express purpose of destroying Vanessa's poise and making her an object of ridicule.

Swift's rendering of the moment at which Cupid makes his attempt indicates a good deal about his procedure in the rest of the poem:

> *Cadenus* many things had writ;
> *Vanessa* much esteem'd his Wit,
> And call'd for his Poetick Works;
> Mean time the Boy in secret lurks,
> And while the Book was in her Hand,
> The Urchin from his private Stand
> Took Aim, and shot with all his Strength
> A Dart of such prodigious Length,
> It pierc'd the feeble Volume thro',
> And deep transfix'd her Bosom too.
> Some Lines, more moving than the rest,
> Stuck to the Point that pierc'd her Breast;
> And, born directly to the Heart,
> With Pains unknown increas'd her Smart.
> (ll. 510-23)

What Swift describes is the sudden emergence of sexual passion in Vanessa. But the terms of the narrative at this point involve a particularly high degree of formalizing and distancing stylization. First, Swift uses a mythological frame-

work by which Vanessa's emotions are described in the
traditional terms of Cupid shooting his arrows. Then, he tells
us that one of these arrows both penetrated and was made
more effective by a volume of Cadenus's "Poetic Works."
This is an elegant narrative device which provides Swift's
rendering of the moment with a further degree of stylized
patterning. And the fact that no such volume as Swift's
"Poetic Works" existed when he wrote *Cadenus and Vanessa*
only increases our awareness of the distance between actual
experience and the fictionalizing structures that Swift invents. The passage does, however, manage to suggest that
some very strong emotions are at work. When Swift stresses
that Cupid shoots this particular arrow "with all his
Strength," he makes us aware of the accumulated anger and
frustration that are involved in his attitude towards Vanessa.
And when he refers to the "Pains unknown" and the "Smart"
that the piercing of Vanessa's breast creates, he implies that
her experience is one of considerable intensity. Thus, although the passage manifests a tendency towards an elegant
and distancing process of fictionalization, it also makes it
very clear that Vanessa is being affected by powerful emotional forces.

Once these forces take possession of Vanessa, Cadenus
becomes unable to understand her behavior. Up to this point,
it has been possible for him to define his relationship with
her by reference to certain clear-cut categories and structures;
they have been like a "Father" and a "Child," or like a
"Master" and "the finest Boy" (ll. 548-53). But now a "sudden
Change" has come about and she no longer responds to his
"Lessons" in the way that she once did:

> *Cadenus* was amaz'd to find
> Such Marks of a distracted Mind;
> For tho' she seem'd to listen more
> To all he spoke, than e'er before;
> He found her Thoughts would absent range,
> Yet guess'd not whence could spring the Change.
>
> (ll. 562-67)

Vanessa now responds to Cadenus in a much less structured way than she once did; instead of attending to his lessons in order to learn from them, she allows her mind to "range" wildly in a manner that Cadenus can neither predict nor understand. His initial response to the change is to try and define it by means of a traditional category: "And first he modestly conjectures/His Pupil might be tir'd with Lectures" (ll. 568-69). This is an attempt on Cadenus's part to rationalize the disorder he confronts by explaining it in terms of a familiar syndrome. We already know, of course, that it is not an adequate explanation, and the element of comedy in the rhyme appears calculated to make it sound slightly absurd. But this analysis provides Cadenus with an ordering, definitive framework within which to place the new behavior-pattern and thus to render it more manageable than it might otherwise be. He says that he has engaged in an educational "Project" which he now realizes is too "dull" and enclosing for her, and that it has failed because it did not adequately take "Nature" into account (ll. 575-87). The time has therefore come, he argues, for them to part company. Cadenus is thus enabled to reach a conclusion which is not acutely disturbing because it involves reference to certain familiar behavioral landmarks that the teacher has learned to accept. The reader, however, is aware that although his emphasis on "Nature" is indeed relevant to Vanessa's experience, it is relevant in a much more disturbing way than Cadenus understands.

When Vanessa makes it clear that Cadenus's analysis is inaccurate and that she has fallen in love with him, the order of his experiential world immediately collapses:

> *Cadenus* felt within him rise
> Shame, Disappointment, Guilt, Surprize.
> He knew not how to reconcile
> Such Language, with her usual Style:
> And yet her Words were so exprest,
> He cou'd not hope she spoke in Jest.

His Thoughts had wholly been confin'd
To form and cultivate her Mind.
                              (ll. 624-31)

The last couplet in this passage suggests that Cadenus, in his relationship with Vanessa, has been attempting to shape the elements of her mind into an ordered structure somewhat in the way that she herself shaped the materials provided by her social circle. But he now witnesses the disintegration of the order that he thought he had achieved, and the experience causes a radical disturbance of his equanimity. Not only does he become subject to the several emotions referred to in the above passage, but he soon experiences an acute, and very natural, fear of public obloquy and ridicule. And when he eventually tries to construct a response to her declaration, he falters at every word because he is so deeply confused and uncertain (ll. 666-67). At this point Cadenus again tries to rationalize her behaviour by placing it within a manageable category. He suggests that she is engaging in a form of raillery which is called a *"Bite"* and which he does not really approve of because it allows the victim no chance to recognize that a joke is being made (ll. 660-73). But this attempt to take refuge in a defining and categorizing framework is quite transparently a sham, because he is already convinced that she has not spoken in jest (l. 629). Both here and at other points, Swift implies that the descriptive terms on which Cadenus leans are not adequate to cope with his present experience. When he tries to "reconcile/Such Language, with her usual Style," for example, he shows an impulse to consider a declaration of love as if it were a form of rational discourse. His insistent and sometimes desperate response to the confusion induced in him by Vanessa is to erect containing systems of analysis that are inappropriate to the unruly emotions he confronts.

As for Vanessa herself, she too uses some highly structured analytical systems in order to define her emotions. When Cadenus arrives at his initial conclusion that she is simply bored by his teaching, she feels both "Disdain" for his blindness and an impulse towards "Tears" (ll. 594-97). But she has been taught the importance of self-control and "Dignity" (l. 595), and in her declaration of love she attempts to form a rationalistic defence of the passion that Cadenus has aroused. In order to do so, she invokes two "Maxims" that he has taught her; the first is that "Virtue . . . knows nothing which it dare not own," and the second that "common Forms were not design'd/Directors to a noble Mind" (ll. 606-13). She also argues that although Cadenus has warned her about the dangerous "Charms" possessed by "Men of Wit," he has not provided her with the equipment to resist them. And her conclusion is that his "Lessons found the weakest Part,/ Aim'd at the Head, but reach'd the Heart" (ll. 618-23). Vanessa thus employs Cadenus's own teachings so as to build a carefully ordered argument that both defines and justifies an intense emotion. But the fact that she constructs her speech as a deliberate effort to maintain her "Dignity" in the face of disrupting forces suggests that she is aware of a discrepancy between the order embodied by that speech and the experience which it purports to define—if there were not such a discrepancy, she would not have to make such a deliberate effort. Moreover, since her argument refers so consistently to Cadenus's teachings, it creates the impression that she is trying to provide him with the type of analysis which will enable him to accept her love.

Such an impression is even more clearly conveyed at a later stage in the poem, when Vanessa tries to convince Cadenus that her love is based on reason:

> But not to dwell on Things minute,
> *Vanessa* finish'd the Dispute,
> Brought weighty Arguments to prove
> That Reason was her Guide in Love.
> She thought he had himself describ'd,
> His Doctrines when she first imbib'd;
> What he had planted, now was grown;

His Virtues she might call her own;
As he approves, as he dislikes,
Love or Contempt, her Fancy strikes.
Self-Love, in Nature rooted fast,
Attends us first, and leaves us last:
Why she likes him, admire not at her,
She loves herself, and that's the Matter.

(ll. 674-87)

Her first speech was designed to enforce the conclusion that Cadenus's presence aroused an emotional rather than a rational response (his lessons reached her "Heart" rather than her "Head"). But now, after Cadenus's hesitant and embarrassed response, she adopts a different tactic; she argues that since her own virtues have become identifiable with those of her teacher she is acting in accord with the basic human principle of self-love, and that she has been directed into this state by a rational admiration of the virtues Cadenus embodies. The discrepancy between this argument and her earlier one is enough to suggest that Vanessa's speech involves a degree of insincere manipulation on her part and a degree of irony on the part of the author. And the comic rhyme at the end of the passage, combined with the casual glibness of the final line, almost reduces her argument to the level of farce. This is the second occasion on which Swift has introduced a comic rhyme at a point where a speaker is engaged in the rationalistic analysis of passionate behavior, and the effect is again to lightly undercut the speaker's procedure. In this instance the undercutting is a device by which Swift suggests not only that Vanessa's rationalizations are inadequate to define the experience to which they allude, but also that they may not be completely sincere. Vanessa extends the above arguments to considerable length, and in doing so she shows herself very adept at providing Cadenus with the type of rhetorical structure which is most likely to convince him. It seems to me untrue that in this speech she displays the "presumption" of believing that she is "more *animal rationale* than *animal capax rationis*," and that she is "prepared to discount . . . the overpowering role that the passions play in many specifically human actions."[3] On the contrary, there is a good deal of evidence to suggest that she is acutely aware of the role which the passions are now playing in her own experience, but that she is pushed into a process of rationalistic analysis and argument partly by her upbringing and partly by her understanding of Cadenus. It is true that she discusses her love for him as if she were engaged in a formal debate, but the primary impulse towards the structures of such debate appears to come from Cadenus. And there is this crucial difference between them—whereas Cadenus obviously wants to believe that such structures bear a natural and direct correlation with the experience they are both confronting, Vanessa knows from the onset of her emotion that they do not.

Swift, as author, is engaged in a structuring and rationalizing process too, in that he transposes a difficult personal experience into the patterns of orderly debate. And the following analysis of Vanessa's speech indicates a good deal about his procedure:

> Love can with Speech inspire a Mute,
> And taught *Vanessa* to dispute.
> This Topick, never touch'd before,
> Display'd her Eloquence the more:
> Her Knowledge, with such Pains acquir'd,
> By this new Passion grew inspir'd.
> Thro' this she made all Objects pass,
> Which gave a Tincture o'er the Mass:
> As Rivers, tho' they bend and twine,
> Still to the Sea their Course incline;
> Or, as Philosophers, who find
> Some fav'rite System to their Mind,
> In ev'ry Point to make it fit,
> Will force all Nature to submit.
>
> (ll. 712-25)

When Swift describes Vanessa's "Eloquence" in disputing a "Topic" that she and Cadenus have never touched upon before, he uses the debate analogy in such a way as to place their conversation in a familiar conceptual framework that plays down the unsettling aspects of the experience. In this way, he engages in an activity which bears some relationship to that which we have seen Cadenus attempting. But when he goes on to stress the element of "Passion" that inspires Vanessa to eloquence, it becomes clear that the framework provided by the analogy is being introduced ironically, in full recognition of the distance between its comforting intimations of order and the nature of the experience to which it is applied. There is a similar kind of irony in the analogy that Swift uses at the end of the passage. Here, in order to describe the way in which Vanessa brings every item of her "knowledge" to bear upon the expression of her love, he compares her to a philosopher who tries to make everything fit his "System." Swift's use of this analogy has been described as a "charge" against Vanessa that identifies her "with all those projectors who try to make the real world of action conform to an ideal world of abstraction."[4] But the comparison is surely intended to be seen as, in one way at least, comically inappropriate to what is really going on. For Swift again uses terms that are associated with a mode of intellectual argument in order to describe the workings of passion; Vanessa may have been attempting to construct a type of rationalistic "System," but in doing so she has not confronted what she knows to be the central elements of her experience. Despite the element of comic irony, however, the comparison does indirectly define one of the effects that her passion has had on her. For it implies, not that she is characterized by a presumptuous intellectual rigidity, but that she is in the grip of an obsessive emotion that reaches irresistibly into every area of her experience. In the one analogy that does not seem in any way ironic, Swift compares the movement of Vanessa's mind to the movement of a river flowing inexorably to the sea. In doing so, he relates her love for Cadenus to natural forces of great power, and the image represents one of the few occasions on which the central nature of Vanessa's experience is directly confronted, either by the author or by the characters.

After this passage, Swift still maintains the fiction that Cadenus and Vanessa are participants in an intellectual debate; he describes Cadenus as being impressed by her eloquence and by the way in which she so "artfully" applies the "Lessons" in rationalistic analysis that he has taught her (ll. 726-29). But it is soon made clear that these are not really the most appropriate terms by which to describe the effect that she is having on him:

> *Cadenus,* to his Grief and Shame,
> Cou'd scarce oppose *Vanessa's* Flame;
> But tho' her Arguments were strong,
> At least, cou'd hardly wish them wrong.
> Howe'er it came, he cou'd not tell,
> But, sure, she never talk'd so well.
>
> (ll. 744-49)

What Cadenus is trying to "oppose" is not really a debater's argument, but something that is more accurately described by the word "Flame." And even though he still clings to the rationalistic framework by thinking of "Arguments" and of how well Vanessa conducts them, it is clear that the uncertainty to which he is reduced has not been caused by an intellectual appraisal of the points she has made. In these tentative, almost stumbling lines, Swift renders a state of emotional confusion, the causes of which Cadenus cannot adequately "tell" or define. Further evidence of his new state appears when he begins to experience a not particularly admirable but wholly natural sensation of "Pride" at being preferred by Vanessa to a "Crowd of Beaux" (ll. 750-51). Cadenus once more attempts to rationalize Vanessa's behaviour and thus to justify his own sensation:

> So bright a Nymph to come unsought,
> Such Wonder by his Merit wrought;

'Tis Merit must with her prevail,
He never knew her Judgement fail,
She noted all she ever read,
And had a most discerning Head.
                                    (ll. 752-57)

But in the last couplet of this passage, Swift quite openly
ridicules Cadenus's terms of reference, and makes it clear that
the terminology of the classroom is absurdly inappropriate to
the experience it purports to describe. By this point in the
poem it has been established that one of Cadenus's major
characteristics is a compulsive tendency to erect orderly and
reassuring systems of analysis in response to the emotions he
confronts. And this tendency appears to manifest itself once
again when he proposes an alternative to the kind of passion
that Vanessa both feels in herself and wants to arouse in him.
After arguing that his "Dignity" and his "Age" prevent him
from entering into the emotional intensities of *"Love"* (ll.
772-79), he offers a different kind of relationship to Vanessa:

But Friendship in its greatest Height,
A constant, rational Delight,
On Virtue's Basis fix'd to last,
When Love's Allurements long are past;
Which gently warms, but cannot burn;
He gladly offers in return;
His Want of Passion will redeem,
With Gratitude, Respect, Esteem:
With that Devotion we bestow,
When Goddesses appear below.
                                    (ll. 780-89)

This passage is in some ways like certain passages that we
have seen in the Stella poems. It is characterized by a high
degree of logical order, and it achieves great clarity of definition. The relationship it defines is a very stable one, based on
the speaker's admiration for the idealized figure of the
woman, and there is an intrinsic correlation between the
order of the rhetoric and the nature of the speaker's subject. In

the Stella poems, however, such rhetorical structures as this
are brought into harmony with the poet's rendering of emotional experience, indeed, they sometimes give the appearance of deriving from that experience. In this poem,
Cadenus's definition of friendship appears to be another of
those rationalistic verbal systems by which he persistently
seeks to evade Vanessa's passion. It is out of harmony with the
emotional experience at the center of the poem, an experience
which has been made to seem too violent and disruptive to be
reducible to such a framework. Because the terms of Cadenus's definition are irrelevant to the reality of her state,
Vanessa ridicules them as "sublime Conceits . . . Raptures,
Flights, and Fancies" (ll. 793-95). And since she cannot bring
her own desires into any sort of alignment with his proposal,
she can only try and break down his resistance to those
intensities of feeling that have become so central to her own
experience.

Swift does not, of course, provide any resolution to the state
of conflict and tension which has thus been arrived at. By
pointedly refusing to inform the reader whether or not Vanessa's campaign was successful, he deprives the narrative
sequence of a clearly defined ending and places the reader in a
state of uncertainty. At this point, however, he reintroduces
Venus, who has both observed and participated in the action
of the poem, and appears to have reached a decisive conclusion about it. She claims that she is ready to "decide" the
issues of the original debate (l. 837), and she goes on to
pronounce a verdict "against the *Men*" (l. 853) for having
been so undiscriminating as not to fall in love with Vanessa.
Venus has thus, apparently, emerged from the state of uncertainty in which she was left by the speeches of the two
pleaders, and has been enabled to reach the verdict that
initially eluded her. But the speech in which she announces
this verdict is characterized by a strident, frustrated tone,
rather than by the kind of assurance that one ordinarily
associates with reasoned conviction, and it contains much

emotional falsifying of the issues. She complains "grievously" that she has been in some sense "cheated" by the men, that she went to "Lord knows what Expense" to create Vanessa as a "Favour" to them, and that because of their "wretched Taste" they have thrown this favor back in her face (ll. 858-71). What she is reacting to with such bitter emotion, of course, is the failure of her project to achieve its most important aim—to reestablish the authority of her reign. Venus has been forced to recognize that human nature is not amenable to the type of ordering arrangement that she thought she could impose on it. She conceived a project in a methodical, systematic way, and she believed that it would logically make her more certain and more secure. But it has brought about none of the consequences that she predicted. And in the end she simply turns her back on mankind, thus rejecting the materials that she has wanted to bring to a satisfactory and decisive order. She decides to put the "World" into the possession of Cupid, for him to use in whatever way he wants (ll. 880-83). By doing so, she gives it into the possession of arbitrary whim and illogical contingency, which is where it has really been all along. Venus thus acknowledges both her defeat and the reality of the situation, and she finally leaves the "court" in a state of greater confusion than it was at the beginning. In these last stages of the poem Swift completes the elegant framework within which he has set the experience of Cadenus and Vanessa. But at no point does he suggest that the order of this framework, or of the several other frameworks that are erected in the course of the narrative, bears a natural or direct relationship with the emotions at the center of the poem. On the contrary, the prevailing tendency of the poem is to undermine the notion that its many neat structures and systems are adequate means of defining and thus, in a sense, containing the experience to which they allude.

A similar uncertainty about the power of rhetorical systems to contain and subdue the reality that the poet contemplates is also implied by *Verses on the Death of Dr. Swift* (1731). This can best be seen, I think, by considering the particular types of stylistic pattern which dominate the poem's three parts, and which eventually relate to one another in some expressive ways. First, in the opening section, Swift adopts the manner of a rigorously didactic author who subordinates all details to a clearly stated central proposition. He begins by insisting on the truth of La Rochefoucauld's "Maxims," which, he says, are based firmly upon human "Nature" (ll. 1-4), and then he introduces a particularly severe example:

> THIS Maxim more than all the rest
> Is thought too base for human Breast;
> "In all Distresses of our Friends
> "We first consult our private Ends,
> "While Nature kindly bent to ease us,
> "Points out some Circumstance to please us.
>   (ll. 5-10)

The maxim is a brief, epigrammatic verbal configuration which is designed to sum up in a definitive way a large area of human experience. And when Swift proceeds to give a series of examples that demonstrate the accuracy with which it defines human self-interest, his rhetoric continues to manifest the epigrammatic concision of the maxim itself:

> WHAT Poet would not grieve to see
> His Brethren write as well as he?
> But rather than they should excel,
> He'd wish his Rivals all in Hell.
>   (ll. 31-34)

The strictly coordinated sequence of illustrative examples soon leads to some generalized conclusions about the nature of humanity:

> VAIN human Kind! Fantastick Race!
> Thy various Follies, who can trace?

> Self-love, Ambition, Envy, Pride,
> Their Empire in our Hearts divide.
>
> (ll. 39-42)

The first couplet of this may suggest that the "various Follies" of the human race are difficult to define and thus to master, but the systematic phalanx of abstract nouns which follows does not bespeak a lack of confidence or certitude in the author's disposition of his materials. And when Swift turns to the subject of his own experience and his personal attitudes towards his friends, he structures the presentation of that experience in a manner that aligns it very precisely both with the above generalizations and with the initial maxim:

> ARBUTHNOT is no more my Friend,
> Who dares to Irony pretend;
> Which I was born to introduce,
> Refin'd it first, and shew'd its Use.
>
> (ll. 55-58)

Both here and in the accompanying references to Pope and Gay, Swift obviously modifies the actualities of personal experience so as to erect a stylized pattern of confirmatory *exempla*. Indeed, throughout this first section of the poem, his rhetorical procedure is openly formulaic and reductive, and the subordination of detail to the initial emphasis on human self-interest has the appearance of being somewhat rigid. There is, however, an element of irony in the references to his friends, a hint that these formulations do not convey the whole truth about the relationships, which foreshadows the shift in the poem's rhetorical structure that is soon to take place.

After defining the first seventy lines as a "Proem," Swift informs the reader that he is now going to proceed to the "Poem" itself (ll. 71-72), in which he will imagine the occurrence of his own death. In this second part, he moves away from the epigrammatic definition of human behavior towards an extended dramatization of it. The poem now becomes much more expansive, as Swift proceeds to imitate the gossip that he imagines taking place in response to the signs of his approaching death. In some ways, the poem's rhetorical pattern comes to resemble that which appears in *The Journal of a Modern Lady*. For this second section is dominated by the rhythms of naturalistic, disordered speech, rather than by those of didactic exposition. A vivid and typical example occurs when Swift arrives at the point of his death, and dramatizes some of the initial responses to it:

> "O, may we all for Death prepare!
> "What has he left? And who's his Heir?
> "I know no more than what the News is,
> "'Tis all bequeath'd to publick Uses.
> "To publick Use! A perfect Whim!
> "What had the Publick done for him!
> "Meer Envy, Avarice, and Pride!
> "He gave it all:—But first he dy'd.
> "And had the Dean, in all the Nation,
> "No worthy Friend, no poor Relation?
> (ll. 153-62)

Here he allows into the texture of the poem a considerable amount of that disorderly flux which characterizes human talk, and which he purports to be mimicking. The passage is, of course, arranged in such a way as to make it very relevant to the original maxim of La Rochefoucauld, for it clearly exposes the self-absorbed malice with which the main speaker responds to Swift's misfortune. And throughout this section of the poem, Swift never loses contact with the didactic program that he established at the beginning. But a considerable shift in the poem's rhetorical structure has taken place nonetheless. There is now, for instance, a rich abundance of particularized detail; when the queen, upon hearing of Swift's death, expresses her pleasure in having forgotten about some "Medals" that she once promised him, she refers to an actual incident which is obviously introduced for reasons beyond the fact that it can be made to serve the didactic program (ll. 181-88). Also, several passages of protracted mimicry suggest that Swift is now attempting to render the chaos he perceives in a manner that endows it with a fairly high degree of sprawling, autonomous life, rather than to contain it rigorously within a didactic system. One example of this is the celebrated sequence in which he dramatizes the response of his cardplaying "female Friends" (l. 225) to the news of his death. It is typified by the following extracts:

> "The Dean is dead, *(and what is Trumps?)*
> "Then Lord have Mercy on his Soul.
> "(Ladies I'll venture for the *Vole.)*
> "Six Deans they say must bear the Pall.
> "(I wish I knew what *King* to call.)
> "Madam, your Husband will attend
> "The Funeral of so good a Friend.
>
> (ll. 228-34)

However clearly the lines may illustrate the poem's initial "Maxim," there is no doubt that this dramatization of uncoordinated, discontinuous talk, and the extent to which Swift protracts it in the rest of the sequence, exemplify a rhetorical tendency that is quite different from what we confronted in the "Proem." And it is a tendency that manifests an impulse on Swift's part to render the materials he is evaluating with a full sense of their abundant particularity. Perhaps the most dramatic example of this impulse occurs just after the above passage, when Swift dramatizes the response of Lintot, the bookseller, to an inquiry about Swift's works that is made by a "Country Squire" (l. 253) a year after his death. Lintot's speech very clearly illustrates the poem's central theme; after pointing out that he no longer stocks any copies of Swift's works because "His way of Writing now is past" (l. 265), he goes on to recommend a series of more fashionable authors—thus consulting his "private Ends" after a momentary recognition of the transience from which

Swift's reputation has suffered. But although the speech is in this way aligned with the major thematic purpose of the poem, it is protracted to a length of more than forty lines, and in that length there is no significant variation or extension of the thematic relevance which I have described. What soon becomes apparent as the speech develops is that it takes on such dimensions because Swift is interested in the sheer aggregation of certain kinds of detail. When he enumerates the authors whom Lintot recommends as more interesting than himself, he includes a much greater number of particularized references than the satiric and ethical logic of the poem would seem to demand. On the surface, this might appear to demonstrate the energy and zeal with which Lintot pursues his "private Ends." But there is a good deal of evidence to suggest that the primary impulse towards such an accretion of detail comes from Swift rather than from his dramatized speaker. For example, when Lintot recommends "*Wolston*'s Tracts" (l. 281) by emphasizing that they are much in favor with the "Maids of Honour" at the court (l. 287), he follows the reference to the maids of honor with the parenthesis, "(who can read)." Since Lintot is trying to establish the values of the court as positive criteria, this parenthesis is obviously a direct expression of Swift's viewpoint, and it is a typical example of the way in which he so often exploits an inconsistently dramatized speaker for his own moment-to-moment purposes. Also, the primary impulse behind Lintot's protracted recommendation of Woolston is quite clearly a desire on Swift's part to satirize a figure whom he despises, rather than a misguided zeal on the part of the speaker (though, to be sure, such a zeal is one of Lintot's characteristics). This part of Lintot's speech, therefore, like those parts in which he refers to such figures as Walpole and Colley Cibber, is only partially an illustration of how preoccupied he is with "private Ends." Swift's inclusion of so many particularized references suggests that his major interest has shifted beyond the original thematic principle towards some contemporary personalities about whom he feels strongly, and whom he wants to satirize whether or not they are relevant to Rochefoucauld's maxim. And in the speech as a whole, Swift accumulates an abundant multiplicity of detail without rigorously subordinating it to the initially established didactic system.

Immediately after Lintot's speech, the third section of the poem begins. Here, a so-called "indiff'rent" and "impartial" speaker at the Rose Tavern (ll. 299-306) offers a lengthy appraisal of Swift's character and literary career. The analysis begins tentatively, with the speaker confessing himself to be "no Judge" of Swift's literary works and falling back on the fact of their popularity as a means of suggesting their value (ll. 309-12). But in order to establish a more definite initial judgement, he quickly settles upon some formulaic phrases that have traditionally been used to justify the satirist; Swift's works were written with a "moral View," he says, "To cure the Vices of Mankind," and his satire "Expos'd the Fool, and lash'd the Knave" (ll. 313-16). These phrases not only define Swift's work according to certain well-established categories, but they also enforce a vision of him as an ideal satirist. And it soon becomes clear that the speaker's estimate of Swift is dominated by a tendency towards such idealization. His praise of Swift's independent attitude towards influential men rises to an account of him as a figure of absolute integrity, who "never courted men in Station" and who was afraid of "no Man's Greatness" because he "sought for no Man's Aid" (ll. 325-28). And the speaker continues to employ such absolute terms when his praise of Swift's integrity merges into praise of his generosity:

> "Without regarding private Ends,
> "Spent all his Credit for his Friends:
> "And only chose the Wise and Good;
> "No Flatt'rers; no Allies in Blood;
> "But succour'd Virtue in Distress,
> "And seldom fail'd of good Success.
> (ll. 331-36)

It is evident now that the speaker's presentation of Swift's character is being structured according to a somewhat inflexible design. And the type of rhetorical pattern which at this point begins to dominate the poem is thus in radical contrast to that which dominated the second section. In an obtrusively systematic way, the speaker reduces the elements of Swift's personality to a definitive and absolute concept. When he says that Swift consistently "succour'd Virtue in Distress," he furthers the process of idealization by echoing a cliché of heroic romance, and in doing so sets the tone for much of what is to come. The heroic mode soon asserts itself again as the speaker, who has now quite clearly become Swift's eulogist, praises the principles that determined his political action:

> "Fair LIBERTY was all his Cry;
> "For her he stood prepar'd to die;
> "For her he boldly stood alone;
> "For her he oft expos'd his own.
> "Two Kingdoms, just as Faction led,
> "Had set a Price upon his Head;
> "But, not a Traytor cou'd be found,
> "To sell him for Six Hundred Pound.
>
> (ll. 347-54)

In the first four lines of this, Swift's actions in the political arena are defined by an obtrusively stylized, incantatory rhetorical pattern, which again reduces those actions to an inflexible concept. And in the rest of the passage, two different incidents, which were actually separated by an interval of more than ten years,[5] are merged so as to form what sounds like a sequence from a heroic narrative. As the speaker continues to tell the story of Swift's literary-political career, his language is persistently elevated, and at certain points that elevation is pushed to a kind of extreme that makes it very noticeable. After describing the fall of the Tory government, the eulogist comments on the exposed position in which Swift was left:

"WITH Horror, Grief, Despair the Dean
"Beheld the dire destructive Scene:
"His Friends in Exile, or the Tower,
"Himself within the Frown of Power;
"Pursu'd by base envenom'd Pens,
"Far to the Land of Slaves and Fens.

(ll.391-96)

Here the imposing parade of abstract nouns in the first line, the heavy alliteration in the second, and the grandiloquent dramatization of Swift's flight to Ireland, all combine to create a sense that the speaker is bent on creating a narrative of epic scale. Swift is the hero of this narrative, and the general effect of the eulogist's procedure is to transform certain facts of his life into a monolithically structured sequence. We see Swift successively engaged in a noble struggle to avert impending "Ruin" (l. 368), isolated and exposed by a destructive "Tempest" (l. 389), driven into the Irish wasteland, valiantly defending that "helpless" country against English depredation (1.412), and defeating, with the assistance of "Heav'n" (l. 425), a "wicked Monster" which attempted to destroy him (l. 417). It is noticeable that throughout this narrative the speaker does not give the actual names of any of the antagonists with whom the hero does battle. These names, and several specific details about Swift's relationships with the individuals concerned, are consistently relegated to the footnotes, as if the heightened mode of the panegyrist would be disturbed by a descent into such particularity. The rhetoric of the eulogy thus seems deliberately calculated to avoid expressing a sense of that abundantly particularized life which was rendered in the second part of the poem. Also, in constructing such an inflexibly stylized narrative pattern out of the materials of Swift's life, the eulogist engages in a process of schematization that is obviously reductive in its relationship to those materials. His rhetoric shows a further tendency to become reductive in the formulaic phrases that he uses both at the beginning and the end of the eulogy in order to define Swift's quality as a satirist. Towards his conclusion, for instance, he says that "No Individual could resent,/Where Thousands equally were meant" (ll. 461-62), and that "His Satyr points at no Defect,/But what all Mortals may correct" (ll. 462-63), thus once again using some time-honored formulations to provide a definitive image of Swift's work. The rhetoric of the eulogy, therefore, differs from that of the poem's second part, in the further sense that it does not manifest a very distinct apprehension of that disorderly flux which, in the second part, is made so central to the human experience being rendered.

It has often been pointed out that several factors make it extremely difficult to believe that Swift intended us to accept this eulogy of himself at its face value. There are, for instance, some rather dramatic inaccuracies in it; when the speaker says that Swift "To steal a Hint was never known,/But what he writ was all his own" (ll. 317-18), he is allowed by his author to use a literary echo that discredits his own argument, and when he says that Swift "lash'd the Vice but spar'd the Name" (l. 460), he makes an assertion that the preceding parts of this poem demonstrate to be patently untrue.[6] Also, there is the way in which the eulogist's style often comes perilously close to sounding inflated, as it does for example in the incantation about Swift's love of liberty that I quoted earlier. At one point, indeed, Swift provides the speaker with a couplet that has a distinctly comic flavour: when he says that "By Innocence and Resolution,/He bore continual Persecution" (ll. 399-400), he echoes a rhyme from Hudibras that is used to describe the sufferings of the hero's beard, and that in its sound-texture seems appropriate to a comic poem.[7] Perhaps the most powerfully subversive factor is the discrepancy between Swift's initial description of the speaker as "quite indiff'rent in the Cause" (l. 305) and the fact that he turns out to be a partisan of the Opposition politics that Swift espoused and suffered for. This suggests the possibilities, first, that an ironic joke is involved in Swift's initial description of the eulogist, and second, that the eulogy is an essentially self-serving attempt by the speaker to transform Swift into an idealized representative of his own political doctrines. By this analysis, the poem's third part becomes a final demonstration of the truth of La Rochefoucauld's maxim, as the speaker exploits Swift's death in order to serve his own "private Ends."[8]

These factors, as well as others that have been mentioned in the lengthy critical debate that the poem has stimulated, certainly add up to a strong case against an unqualified acceptance of the eulogy. And I think it is central to Swift's intentions in the poem that we should be made to question the validity of what the speaker says. Yet there are still several problems lying in the way of an interpretation which would argue that the burden of the panegyric is completely negated by these qualifying factors. For one thing, if the major purpose of the sequence is to demonstrate a further example of self-interest, this time on the part of the eulogist, it is difficult to understand why Swift should protract it to a length that almost equals the whole of the poem's middle section; the sheer extent of the eulogy, and the standing which it is implicitly given, suggest that Swift's interests go beyond such an enforcement of a satiric point that has already been rather fully made. Moreover, although the panegyrist is a distinctly dramatized and individuated figure, Swift's characterisation of him is not entirely consistent, and there are moments in his speech at which a considerable degree of "primary self-assertion"[9] on the part of the author appears to be taking place. When the speaker describes Swift's exile in Ireland, for instance, and stresses the fact that he would not tolerate the company of "Rural Squires" (l. 443), he suddenly launches into a passage of extended satire on the profiteering techniques of the Irish upper classes and on the political system that they exploit (ll. 443-54); the passage involves a fairly high degree of localized topical commentary that does

not significantly further the process of the hero's eulogiza-
tion, and it is clear that Swift is taking the opportunity to
make some attacks that are not really subordinated to the
characterization of his fictional speaker. A little further on,
after the eulogist has defended Swift's satire by means of some
formulaic phrases that appear both secondhand and inaccurate, his analysis suddenly begins to take on a new precision;
when we hear him arguing that Swift "spar'd a Hump or
crooked Nose,/Whose Owners set not up for Beaux" (ll.
467-68) and that "True genuine Dulness mov'd his Pity,/
Unless it offer'd to be witty" (ll. 469-70), it sounds rather as if
the author of the poem is, after all, making a serious attempt
to defend his satiric procedures. Finally, it has quite correctly
been pointed out that the eulogist praises many achievements
of which Swift was "genuinely proud," and which he is
obviously not "repudiating" through his ironic manipulation of the speaker (219-20).[10] In the panegyric, several very
great human values are praised and given dramatic substance
by the speaker's narrative of Swift's career. And because of
this, one cannot disconnect the sequence entirely from the
great tradition of the satirist's *apologia*. After all, this tradition has never required that the *apologia* should be true to the
actualities of the satirist's personal life; as Maynard Mack has
emphasized, the "contours of a formal verse satire . . . are part
of a fiction" (p. 85), and the *apologia* is one element in that
fiction. For the satirist, "the establishment of an authoritative *ethos* is imperative" (p. 86), [11] and the panegyric which
appears at the end of the *Verses* certainly establishes an image
of the moral attributes that would characterize an ideal
satirist. If the sequence is in some sense a genuine *apologia*,
then it is very strategically placed in the developing pattern of
the poem. For Swift has taken on the task of demonstrating
the truth of a maxim which enforces a very severe judgment of
mankind, and it would be logical for him to conclude the
demonstration with a sequence which established both the
positive values in which he believes and his own ethical

credentials. Moreover, the panegyric does not really conflict with Swift's earlier statement that he is subject to envious feelings towards his friends; such a statement only makes it plain that the generous *actions* described in the panegyric emerge from a struggle with the unavoidable realities of human nature.

But in this poem the qualifying factors are too numerous and too subversive for the *apologia* to emerge unscathed. Such discrepancies as that between praise of Swift for sparing the name and the actuality of the poem itself cannot be explained away by reference to the fictions of satire. And the relationship between the rhetoric of the eulogy and that of the poem's middle section implies that the type of reductive framework employed by the eulogist involves an avoidance of contact with the particularized texture of reality. The *apologia* is thus neither completely genuine nor completely negated by irony.[12] But once one has said this, one is left with the question of whether there is any meaningful relationship between the main burden of the *apologia* and the qualifying factors. And in order to approach this question, I think it is useful to return to the fact that the primary function of the satirist's *apologia* is that it establishes an ethical standpoint from which his attacks are launched. Traditionally, the attribution of an ideal *persona* to the satirist provides a moral basis that justifies his aggressive engagement with a corrupt world and establishes his own spiritual strength. It thus creates an area of firm ground amidst the chaos that he confronts. In Pope's poetry it does this, and one is impressed by the certainty and the sense of authority which the creation of an ideal *persona* brings to his work. But in Swift's poem, although a similar *persona* is attributed to the satirist, various elements work to subvert the qualities of firmness and certainty which the construction of such a *persona* traditionally provides. Swift erects the image of the satirist as an ideal hero and good man, only to make the reader insecure about how he is to view this image. And the sequence thus becomes an example of what C.J. Rawson is referring to when he says that Swift's style tends to "undermine certainties, including the certainties it consciously proclaims."[13] In the poem as a whole, Swift has sought to demonstrate the truth of a rigorous maxim, and has concluded with a sequence that ostensibly provides a solid basis for this demonstration. Such a manifestly ordered framework would in itself appear to express a secure authorial confidence in the disposition of his materials. But in the middle section of the poem, instead of rigorously subordinating those materials to the satiric argument that is being conducted, Swift renders them with a full sense of their abundant and unruly particularity. And in the concluding section, he makes it impossible for the reader to feel that he has arrived at the certainty of stance which the satirist's *apologia* traditionally assumes. Thus, although Swift constructs a very coherent overall design, which is useful for the purposes of satiric argument and which celebrates some great human values, he carefully avoids the appearance of being certain that the reality he perceives can be fully reduced to or contained by the kind of order which the design embodies.

In both of the above poems, then, some stringent rhetorical systems coexist in a state of uneasiness with other factors that disturb or undermine the authority of those systems. And a similar state of uneasy tension tends particularly to arise in poems that focus on what Swift perceives as unruly elements in human experience, such as the sometimes radically disturbing forces of human sexuality. One confrontation with these forces occurs in *Phillis, or, the Progress of Love* (1719), where Swift constructs a systematically arranged and to some extent formulaic narrative in order to render the disturbing effects of sexual passion on an individual personality. The opening lines of the poem define its heroine, Phillis, as being endowed with "ev'ry Talent of a Prude," and thus suggest that she is an adept in the controlled practice of certain techniques. But Swift also implies that she is subject to some very powerful forces of which those techniques are a ritualized expression:

> In Church you heard her thrô the Crowd
> Repeat the Absolution loud;
> In Church, secure behind her Fan
> She durst behold that Monster, Man:
> There practic'd how to place her Head,
> And bit her Lips to make them red:
> Or on the Matt devoutly kneeling
> Would lift her Eyes up to the Ceeling,
> And heave her Bosom unaware
> For neighb'ring Beaux to see it bare.
>
> (ll. 9-18)

This is the first of several occasions in the poem on which some form of order is implicitly contrasted with the reality of Phillis's nature and experience. Here, the order of the church ceremony provides an environment within which she feels that she can safely give covert expression to desires that obviously disturb and frighten her. It may appear that in a certain sense there is an element of ordered ritual in her behavior just as there is in the church service. But Swift makes it vividly apparent that the impulses which give rise to this behavior derive from a powerful repressed sexuality, and it is with the increasingly disruptive effects of this sexuality that the poem's narrative is concerned. At first, Phillis prepares to enter into a sexual relationship in a manner that is sanctioned by both social and religious tradition:

> At length a lucky Lover came,
> And found Admittance from the Dame.
> Suppose all Partyes now agreed,
> The Writings drawn, the Lawyer fee'd,
> The Vicar and the Ring bespoke:
> Guess how could such a Match be broke.
>
> (ll. 19-24)

Her behavior at this point remains firmly within the context of orderly public arrangements and ceremonies. But the last line of the passage invites us to consider the possibility that the order embodied by these arrangements may be more fragile than those who are involved in them suspect. And, indeed, it is soon discovered that Phillis has run away with John the butler. Her family is thus forced to witness the collapse of the ordered pattern that they had felt was so secure. And after several moments of farcical chaos, they find a letter from Phillis addressed to her "much honor'd Father" (l. 46):

> ('Tis always done, Romances tell us,
> When Daughters run away with Fellows)
> Fill'd with the choicest common-places,
> By others us'd in the like Cases.
> That, long ago a Fortune-teller
> Exactly said what now befell her,
> And in a Glass had made her see
> A serving-Man of low Degree:
> It was her Fate; must be forgiven;
> For Marriages are made in Heaven.
>   (ll. 47-56)

It is now clear that the details of Swift's narrative are being largely determined by an antiromantic program. However, he does not simply satirize romantic fiction in this passage, but also defines a special kind of inadequacy in Phillis's response to her experience. For she attempts to place that experience within a conceptual framework that brings to it a considerable degree of reassuring order; not only can she use the romantic stereotype to claim that her action was directed by "Heaven" and "Fate," but she can also define her relationship with John by the traditionally structured image of the rich man's daughter falling in love with the "serving-Man of low Degree." Swift means the reader to understand that the intimations of order to which she clings in her letter are false to the reality of her action, because that action was caused by a giving way to irrational instinct that can only be productive of chaos. In the succeeding narrative, it becomes clear that the relationship between Phillis and John, based as it is exclusively on sexual passion, cannot survive the physical difficulties and discomfort that they immediately encounter:

> The loving Couple well bemir'd,
> The Horse and both the Riders tir'd:
> Their Vittells bad, their Lodging worse,
> Phil cry'd, and John began to curse;
> Phil wish't, that she had strained a Limb
> When first she ventur'd out with him.
> John wish't, that he had broke a Leg
> When first for her he quitted Peg.
> (ll. 77-84)

In this passage, the selection and arrangement of detail are so rigorously directed by Swift's antiromantic purpose that the poem's development takes on the structure of a diagram. Moreover, as he charts the inexorable process of deterioration, his rhetoric becomes marked by an obtrusively systematic balancing of related phrases. What is being defined in such an orderly manner is the physical and emotional chaos which, in Swift's view, follows logically upon Phillis's unthinking submission to sexual impulse. And in the last stages of the poem, her situation becomes ugly and humiliating in the extreme:

> But what Adventures more befell 'um
> The Muse has now not time to tell 'um.
> How Johnny wheadled, threatned, fawnd,
> Till Phillis all her Trinkets pawn'd:
> How oft she broke her marriage Vows
> In kindness to maintain her Spouse;
> Till Swains unwholsome spoyld the Trade,
> For now the Surgeon must be paid;
> To whom those Perquisites are gone
> In Christian Justice due to John.
> (ll. 85-94)

This passage describes a further stage in Phillis's admonitory "progress," and it thus plays an important part in the poem's ethical argument. But although Swift is once more engaged in a process of formulaic arrangement, he also endows his materials with a degree of complex life and a continuing power to disturb. For one thing, Phillis is now rather clearly presented as a victim, not only of sexual impulse but also of John's callous manipulation, and the moralistic evaluation of her becomes complicated by an element of pity. Also, the savage irony that Swift directs at John in the last line of the passage suggests a considerable intensity of animus in the author's response to his materials. For reasons such as this, the poem finally creates the impression that its rigorously structured design is a response on Swift's part to elements in human experience that he recognizes to be acutely disturbing and not easily reducible to rationalizing systems.

In *The Progress of Marriage* (1722) Swift again constructs a systematic narrative that focuses on the effects of sexual impulse, but in this case the order of the narrative design is not so consistently sustained as in the above poem. The story is about a marriage between a "rich Divine," who is fifty-two years old, and a "handsome young imperious *Girl*" (ll. 2-3). Swift conceives the marriage as a ludicrous mistake, and at the beginning of the poem he defines its inadequacy by a list of mythological figures who are imagined as being invited to the wedding:

> They first invite the Cyprian Queen,
> 'Twas answered, she would not be seen.
> The Graces next, and all the Muses
> Were bid in form, but sent Excuses:
> Juno attended at the Porch
> With farthing Candle for a Torch,
> While Mistress Iris held her Train,
> The faded Bow distilling Rain,
> Then Hebe came and took her Place
> But showed no more than half her Face.
> (ll. 7-16)

This is a very systematic, step-by-step way of drawing attention to what is either missing from or only partially present

in the relationship, and the passage suggests that Swift's
major concern at this point is with precise thematic definition. His procedure also has the effect of stylizing and distancing the fictional materials, as the nature of the marriage
is described by means of an elegant pattern of traditional
references. Soon after this, however, when Swift suddenly
takes us into the bedroom of the married couple, his presentation of their experience becomes more direct:

> The Bridegroom dresst, to make a Figure,
> Assumes an artificiall Vigor;
> A flourisht Night-cap on, to grace
> His ruddy, wrinckled, smirking Face,
> Like the faint red upon a Pippin
> Half wither'd by a Winters keeping . . .
>   (ll. 21-26)

Here, the minutely observed physical details suggest an interest on Swift's part in the particularized rendering of experience, as well as in its thematic definition, and indeed, the
passage involves an acute and almost embarrassing immediacy. At the same time, however, it does play an important
part in the poem's thematic development, because it defines
both the self-delusion which has prevented the dean from
recognizing the absurdity of his action and the actuality upon
which the marriage is going to founder. After this passage,
Swift begins to chart the inexorable progress of the marriage's disintegration, and in doing so, he immediately establishes a very stringent pattern of analysis:

> Both from the Goal together start;
> Scarce run a step before they part;
> No common Ligament that binds
> The various Textures of their Minds,
> Their Thoughts, and Actions, Hopes, and Fears,
> Less corresponding than their Years.
> Her Spouse desires his Coffee soon,
> She rises to her Tea at noon.

> While He goes out to cheapen Books,
> She at the Glass consults her Looks.
>
> (ll. 31-40)

The initial generalizing statement of an absolute division
between the two characters leads to some specific examples of
it, and those examples are arranged in a regularly alternating
sequence. After this, Swift juxtaposes a summary of the wife's
pattern of behavior with a summary of the husband's; she is
self-confidently absorbed in expensive trivia, and he anx-
iously contemplates a life-style that he can neither participate
in nor understand. In this manner, the contrast between them
is defined with great clarity, and it leads to an admonitory
comment on the part of the author:

> Canst thou imagine, dull Divine,
> 'Twill gain her Love to make her fine?
> Hath she no other wants beside?
> You raise Desire as well as Pride,
> Enticing Coxcombs to adore,
> And teach her to despise thee more.
>
> (ll. 71-76)

Swift sounds as if he is lecturing the husband in a scornfully
aloof manner at this point, delivering a psychological lesson
to a man he regards as too "dull" to recognize the error of
what he is doing. The impression is created, therefore, that
Swift is disposing the materials of his narrative in an authoritatively didactic way, and that these materials are being
reduced to the form of certain admonitory propositions. But
as the narrative progresses, Swift's rendering of the characters' experience does not contain it quite so completely
within a rationalizing framework as these terms imply:

> If in her Coach she'll condescend
> To place him at the hinder End
> Her Hoop is hoist above his Nose,
> His odious Goun would soil her Cloaths,

And drops him at the Church, to pray
While she drives on to see the Play.
He like an orderly Divine
Comes home a quarter after nine,
And meets her hasting to the Ball,
Her Chairmen push him from the Wall:
He enters in, and walks up Stairs,
And calls the Family to Prayrs,
Then goes alone to take his Rest
In bed, where he can spare her best.

(ll. 77-90)

Now it is clear that the details of this passage have been arranged so as to stress certain definitive thematic contrasts; there is, for example, the juxtaposition of "Church" and "Play," and the distinction between the "orderly" pattern of the husband's life and the implied chaos of the wife's. These contrasts enforce a moral-satiric evaluation of the kind of life-style that the wife's behavior represents, and they also bring a high degree of emblematic structuring to Swift's narration of the characters' experience. But one impression that the passage rather strongly creates is that the author's reprimanding attitude towards the husband is becoming complicated by an element of pity. As the picture of his humiliation is intensified, especially by the images of his being pushed aside by the chairmen and of his exhausted withdrawal "alone" to bed, he becomes an acutely pathetic figure and Swift's rendering of his experience takes on tragic overtones. What the discrepancy between the order of the dean's life-style and the disorder of his wife's now most strongly enforces is a sense of the suffering which it brings to the dean. And a tone of bitterly sardonic hostility now enters into the author's presentation of the wife's behavior.

From this point on, the rigorously diagrammatic structures which Swift has been using in order to define the characters' experience give way to rather different types of configuration. When the wife's failure to become pregnant after a year of marriage is attributed to the fact that the dean is "past his Prime" (l. 104), it is decided that she must be submitted to the waters at Bath:

> For Venus rising from the Ocean
> Infus'd a strong prolifick Potion,
> That mixt with Achelous Spring,
> The *horned* Floud, as Poets sing:
> Who with an English Beauty smitten
> Ran under Ground from Greece to Brittain,
> The genial Virtue with him brought,
> And gave the Nymph a plenteous Draught:
> Then fled, and left his Horn behind
> For Husbands past their Youth to find;
> The Nymph who still with Passion burn'd,
> Was to a boiling Fountain turn'd,
> Where Childless wives crowd ev'ry morn
> To drink in Achilous' Horn.
> And here the Father often gains
> That Title by anothers Pains.
>
> (ll. 107-22)

Here, Swift engages in the elaborately extended development of an image which suggests that certain very powerful forces are now determining the course of the poem's action. The waters in which the dean's wife is about to be immersed are described as having been infused by a "strong prolifick Potion," originating with Venus and brought into England by the sexually aroused river-god, and they are thus provided with a mythological background that associates them with an abundant and powerful sexuality. The last couplet of the above passage suggests the manner in which, in practice, the waters have developed their potent reputation, as also does a cancelled couplet in which Swift refers to the Cross Bath as a place where "fruitfull Matter chiefly Swims."[14] And it is not surprising that the dean attempts to resist the notion of his wife's visit. But he is easily manipulated into agreement, and he is soon watching from a distance as his wife bathes in the Cross Bath with the "Belles and Beaux" (l. 144). The author comments:

So have I seen within a Pen
Young Ducklings, fostered by a Hen;
But when let out, they run and muddle
As Instinct leads them, in a Puddle;
The sober Hen not born to swim
With mournful Note clocks round the Brim.
(ll. 145-50)

This is an image of a further kind of chaos in which his wife
enthusiastically participates and with which the dean cannot
cope. What he confronts now are the workings of "Instinct,"
and his wife's behavior again reduces him to a state of
pathetic isolation and helplessness. Although the analogy by
which Swift describes their experience has a certain distancing effect, in that it places the experience within a neat
emblematic framework, the sensation of disgust that is communicated by the word "Puddle" suggests a considerable
intensity of engagement on the part of the author. And when
Swift turns to a more direct rendering of the characters'
behavior, his response to the fictional materials rises to a
violent crescendo. First, he briefly describes the death of the
old dean, who exhausts himself upon his wife's body and
thus becomes a "Victim" of sexual forces that make too great
a demand on his "declining" strength (ll. 151-56). Then he
concludes the poem by uttering an angry curse upon the wife:

The Widow goes through all her Forms;
New Lovers now will come in Swarms.
Oh, may I see her soon dispensing
Her Favours to some broken Ensign
Him let her Marry for his Face,
And only Coat of tarnish't Lace;
To turn her Naked out of Doors,
And spend her Joynture on his Whores:
But for a parting Present leave her
A rooted Pox to last for ever.
(ll. 157-66)

This is not the kind of conclusion that the ordering analytical
structures of the poem's early stages would appear to predict,

and it suggests that the author has not found those structures adequate to a full expression of his response to what he narrates. Herbert Davis finds evidence in this conclusion of Swift's inability to keep up the "good behaviour" that he maintains for much of the poem: "He is not content to let the story of this foolish marriage between a rich old Dean and an extravagant young beauty carry its own obvious moral. The telling of it stirs his anger and fury; and as he leaves the rich young widow surrounded with swarms of lovers, he pours out the filthiest curses upon her. . . ."[15] This comment very accurately describes the intensity of Swift's response to the materials of his narrative. But I would suggest that the concluding curse, rather than representing an unfortunate loss of control on Swift's part, involves a deliberate attempt to dramatize the disturbing nature of the experience he confronts. Swift's contemplation of that experience initially leads him to establish stringent systems of analysis that both define and contain it, but he eventually departs from such systems in order to suggest the radical unruliness of the forces that determine the action of the poem.

The Progress of Beauty (1719) also begins in a manner which suggests that Swift is going to render the central experience by means of a rigorously structured system. In the first three stanzas he establishes the terms of the analogical argument which will constitute that system:

> When first Diana leaves her Bed
> Vapors and Steams her Looks disgrace,
> A frouzy dirty colour'd red
> Sits on her cloudy wrinckled Face.

> But by degrees when mounted high
> Her artificiall Face appears
> Down from her Window in the Sky,
> Her Spots are gone, her Visage clears.

> 'Twixt earthly Femals and the Moon
> All Parallells exactly run;
> If Celia should appear too soon
> Alas, the Nymph would be undone.

The poem is apparently going to have a very definite antiromantic program; it will involve a comparison between the moon and a woman, but it will overturn the traditional manner of developing such a comparison. One can feel in these opening stanzas a careful and precise selection of details which will serve such a program; Diana's face is "frouzy" and "wrinckled" when it is seen close up at the time of her first emergence, but once she has withdrawn to a greater distance it "clears" and takes on an "artificiall" beauty. When Swift asserts that " 'Twixt earthly Femals and the Moon/All Parallells exactly run," he implies that the analogical argument is going to be worked out with great precision. And in the following stanza he begins to describe more precisely the aspects of the woman's early-morning appearance which make her comparable to the moon:

> To see her from her Pillow rise
> All reeking in a cloudy Steam,
> Crackt Lips, foul Teeth, and gummy Eyes,
> Poor Strephon, how would he blaspheme!

What at once becomes apparent is that Swift's description of the woman involves a much greater violence of phrasing than does his description of the moon. Words such as "reeking," "foul," and "gummy" arouse acute sensations of physical disgust that make the initial account of the moon's ugliness seem comparatively mild. No doubt this is caused by the fact that a greater physical immediacy is possible in a description of a woman's face than in a description of the moon. But the stanza nevertheless provides some indication of an imbalance in the poem's analogical structure that is soon going to become extreme. Indeed, from this point until more than halfway through the poem, Swift becomes involved in an account of the nocturnal disintegration of Celia's face and of her attempts to repair it that is not parallelled by details relating to the moon. John M. Aden has suggested that the poem involves an "appropriately alternating . . . formula of attrition: now the myth, now the mortal. . . ." (p. 16).[16] But for a very considerable part of the poem there is no such alternating pattern. The structure of this poem is therefore rather different from that of *The Progress of Poetry,* in which, as we saw in the previous chapter, Swift also works out an extended analogy, but through an almost symmetrical arrangement of parallel details. Here, Swift suggests that he is going to proceed with a high degree of structural rigor and exactitude of parallellism, but it soon becomes apparent that the details of the poem are not being completely subordinated to the initially established analogical system. Swift's account of how Celia's facial makeup disintegrates during the night is logically related to the initial comparison, of course, in that it defines the process by which her face takes on the ugliness that has already been compared to the moon's. But since no parallel is drawn between this process and any process by which the moon arrives at her initially "frouzy" appearance, Swift's account of it involves a departure from strictly balanced analogical patterning. Moreover, the description is so protracted and so richly detailed that it takes on a vigorous life of its own and makes the initial comparison recede into apparent irrelevance. The sequence begins in the following manner:

> The Soot or Powder which was wont
> To make her Hair look black as Jet,
> Falls from her Tresses on her Front
> A mingled Mass of Dirt and Sweat.
>
> Three Colours, Black, and Red, and White,
> So gracefull in their proper Place,
> Remove them to a diff'rent Light
> They form a frightful hideous Face,
>
> For instance; when the Lilly slipps
> Into the Precincts of the Rose,
> And takes Possession of the Lips,
> Leaving the Purple to the Nose.

The details of this passage are largely determined by the fact that Swift is engaged in a process of parody; the blackness of "Jet," the whiteness of the "Lilly," and the redness of the "Rose" are poetic commonplaces that are brought into the service of his antiromantic program. But such an explanation does not fully account for the extent to which Swift protracts a sequence which is already, as we have seen, somewhat out of harmony with the initially established analogical design. Indeed, as he continues to particularize the several shifts of color that disfigure Celia's face, it becomes difficult to escape the impression that he is dwelling on the subject, in an insistent and somewhat repetitive manner that does not make the now unfashionable notion of Swift's obsessiveness seem entirely inappropriate:

> So Celia went entire to bed,
> All her Complexions safe and sound,
> But when she rose, the black and red
> Though still in Sight, had chang'd their Ground.
>
> The Black, which would not be confin'd
> A more inferior Station seeks
> Leaving the fiery red behind,
> And mingles in her muddy Cheeks.

It has been clear from the beginning of the sequence that, however drily analytic the author's language at several points may be, the process that he is describing arouses in him an acutely emotional response—such a response is articulated, for example, by his description of the "mingled Mass of Dirt and Sweat" forming on Celia's breast. And now the sequence reaches a climactic intensity of phrasing:

> The Paint by Perspiration cracks,
> And falls in Rivulets of Sweat,
> On either Side you see the Tracks,
> While at her Chin the Conflu'ents met.
>
> A Skillful Houswife thus her Thumb

> With Spittle while she spins, anoints,
> And thus the brown Meanders come
> In trickling Streams betwixt her Joynts.

In the second of these stanzas, Swift's major concern appears to be with arousing in the reader the kind of discomfort which leads to feelings of disgust or distaste for the ugliness of Celia's ruined face, and the sequence thus involves an element of fairly conventional satire on the offensive falsity of cosmetics. But it also goes beyond this kind of satiric attack to suggest that Celia is engaged in a struggle against over-whelming disruptive forces. What Swift describes is a process by which the order that she has momentarily achieved col-lapses into chaos. And although that order is quite clearly spurious, the major emphasis of the passage is not on its falsity, but on the inexorable process of its disintegration. It is the contemplation of this process that provokes in Swift the kind of verbal response that I have described, a response that is not strictly aligned with an initial system of parallellism, that is insistently and even obsessively protracted, and that involves a high degree of emotional intensity. Such a re-sponse attributes to the process being described a considera-ble power to disturb. And although Swift goes on to describe the techniques by which Celia can "with ease" (l. 44) re-create the order that has collapsed during the night, the force of the above passage is not really counteracted. What is made viv-idly apparent is that the order she achieves is both fragile and limited; her repaired face is as brittle as "China ware" (l. 64), and Celia is advised not to allow it to be observed too closely (ll. 65-68). When Swift compares her cosmetic artistry to that of "Other Painters" (l. 51), he widens the context in which we contemplate her nocturnal defeat so as to suggest that there is something archetypal about her experience. And this adds a further degree of significance to the fact that the poem's initially established design becomes disturbed as Swift con-fronts that experience.

It is after stressing that Celia's newly restored "beauty" will not survive very close examination that Swift finally returns to the analogical system with which the poem began. He suggests that Celia should follow the moon's example by allowing herself to be seen only "from far" and mainly "by Night" (ll. 71-72). And from this point until the end of the poem the analogy is consistently sustained. Along with this return to structural rigor there comes a further development in the poem's meaning, for Swift now argues that although Celia's "Art" can for a while offer some degree of resistance to the ravages of the night, there will come a time when it will be permanently defeated by certain more fundamental disruptions:

> But, Art no longer can prevayl
> When the Materialls all are gone,
> The best Mechanick Hand must fayl
> Where Nothing's left to work upon.
>
> Matter, as wise Logicians say,
> Cannot without a Form subsist,
> And Form, say I, as well as They,
> Must fayl if Matter brings no Grist.
> (ll. 77-84)

The processes of decay that are confronted here would seem to be more radically disturbing than those described earlier in the poem. But the manner in which Swift approaches them makes it seem that he is entering rather jauntily into an intellectual debate; he adopts the terminology of the "Logicians," and he asserts that he has as much right as they have to put forward his own propositions. Moreover, when he goes on to apply these propositions to the poem's original analogy, he ostentatiously parades his astrological references:

> And this is fair Diana's Case
> For, all Astrologers maintain
> Each Night a Bit drops off her Face
> When Mortals say she's in her Wain.

> While Partridge wisely shews the Cause
> Efficient of the Moon's Decay,
> That Cancer with his pois'nous Claws
> Attacks her in the milky Way:
>
> But Gadbury in Art profound
> From her pale Cheeks pretends to show
> That Swain Endymion is not sound,
> Or else, that Mercury's her Foe.
>
> (ll. 85-96)

One purpose of this passage, of course, is to ridicule the astrologers to whom Swift ironically refers as if they were legitimate authorities. But what is also evident is that he is now developing the analogy between moon and woman with the kind of precision and exactitude of parallellism that he claimed he would achieve at the beginning of the poem. Around this point, therefore, Swift both adopts the rhetoric of intellectual debate and becomes very rigorous in his adherence to the poem's stated analogical system. At the same time, he focuses on some particularly harsh realities of human experience, exemplified in the above passage by the references to cancer and venereal disease. The poem thus takes on some of the characteristics of those poems I discussed in the second chapter, in which there is a contrast between an obtrusively systematized structure and a violent central image. In this instance, however, the contrast between structure and theme is disturbing in a way that those other poems are not, because the processes that are being referred to are so central to human experience. What is happening at this point is very different from what happened in the earlier part of the poem, in that Swift now brings his account of the disruptive forces to which humanity is subject into strict and systematic alignment with an ordering framework. But there is enough irony in his treatment of the comparison to suggest that the materials with which he is dealing are not very comfortably contained within such a framework. Indeed, throughout the poem there is some tension between Swift's perception of Celia's experience and the high degree of order that is implied or actually achieved by the analogical system. This order is not confidently established as the embodiment of a positive value by which Celia's moral degeneration is judged. Instead, it is placed under a considerable degree of stress by Swift's contemplation of the forces to which she is subject.

In *The Lady's Dressing Room* (1730) Swift constructs a brief narrative which, in its basic outline, has the thematic discipline of a moral tract. It focuses on the experience of Strephon, who at first regards the "Lady," Celia, as a "Goddess"; he has only seen her when she has been arrayed in "Lace, Brocades and Tissues" (ll. 3-4), and he is prone to romantic idealization. When he enters her dressing room, however, and makes a "strict Survey" (l. 7) of her dirty underwear and cosmetic apparatus, the falsity of his initial vision is brutally exposed. Towards the end of his survey, Strephon discovers what appears to be a highly decorated "Cabinet" (l. 78), and he opens it with feelings of *"Hope"* (l. 88). But when the cabinet turns out to be Celia's lavatory, Strephon's idealization of her suffers a conclusive setback:

> The Vapours flew from out the Vent,
> But *Strephon* cautious never meant
> The Bottom of the Pan to grope,
> And fowl his Hands in Search of *Hope*.
> (ll. 91-94)

There is an elegantly didactic symbolism in this incident, especially in the image of the decorated commode, by which Swift enforces the poem's central contrast between artificial surfaces and the realities that lie beneath them. And Strephon's experience of this contrast forces him to a terribly clear recognition:

> Thus finishing his grand Survey,
> Disgusted *Strephon* stole away,

Repeating in his amorous Fits,
Oh! *Celia, Celia, Celia* shits!

(ll. 115-18)

He cannot cope rationally with what has been revealed to him, and from this point on his tendency towards romantic idealization is replaced by a bitter disgust for all women. His experience in Celia's dressing room has thus led him from one unbalanced extreme to another. And Swift concludes the poem's ethical argument by recommending a compromise that he has himself adopted, and that he proposes as a solution to the difficulties created by Strephon's experience; he urges Strephon to take pleasure in the fact that so much "Order" as that which is embodied by Celia's public appearance can emerge from so much "Confusion" as that which is to be found in her dressing room (ll. 141-44). In this manner, a systematically structured narrative is concluded by the author's prescription for a balanced acceptance of what that narrative has revealed.[17]

But although Swift's narrative does possess this rather obtrusive rhetorical and thematic design, there are also several elements in the poem which are not completely subordinated to that design. To begin with, the description of the "Litter" (l. 8) in Celia's dressing room is protracted far beyond the point that is necessary for enforcing the argument against irrational idealization. *The Lady's Dressing-Room* is a poem, of course, and should not be subjected to the kind of analysis that would be appropriate to more strictly rationalistic forms of discourse. But my point is simply that the impulse to demonstrate the truth of a didactic proposition does not appear to be the only impulse directing the aggregation of detail in this sequence. It might be said in response to this that such a prolonged exposure to the kind of reality contained in Celia's bedchamber is what is necessary for Strephon to be shaken out of an attitude that is rather firmly fixed in his mind. Also, since the poem appears to be very much concerned with an evaluation of the irrational response that Strephon eventually makes, it would seem logical to subject him to an experience of fairly considerable proportions—otherwise, we might find it impossible to believe in that response when it occurs. Such arguments as these provide a degree of logical and thematic justification for the sequence by focusing on Strephon's role as protagonist in a morally illustrative drama. And further rationalization of this kind has been provided by the argument that Strephon sees such an enormous amount of filth only because he is determined to do so; the description of Celia's dressing room is "largely evoked from and aimed at Strephon, who is hoist on the petard of his own voyeurism."[18] Strephon is indeed a compulsive voyeur, and Swift frequently suggests both that he is our guide to the dressing room and that he is obsessively bent on showing us everything; he describes Strephon as a "Rogue" (l. 13) whose eye "No Object" escapes (l. 47), who is "Resolv'd to go thro' thick and thin" (l. 80), and at one point Swift asks "Why *Strephon* will you tell the rest?" (l. 69). It is thus implied that the aggregation of repulsive details is so obsessively prolonged because Strephon cannot hold himself in check, and the sequence thus becomes a further instance of his paranoia. But at several points the role of guide shifts from Strephon to the author himself:

> No Object *Strephon*'s Eye escapes,
> Here Pettycoats in frowzy Heaps;
> Nor be the Handkerchiefs forgot
> All varnish'd o'er with Snuff and Snot.
> The Stockings, why shou'd I expose,
> Stain'd with the Marks of stinking Toes;
> Or greasy Coifs and Pinners reeking,
> Which *Celia* slept at least a Week in?
> (ll. 47-54)

In the first couplet of this passage, Swift insists that it is Strephon who is forcing the reader to see so much. But in the second, the responsibility for mentioning the handkerchiefs appears to be moving to the author. And in the third, it is very clearly Swift himself who cannot refrain from exposing the ugly marks on the stockings; at this point he dramatizes himself, rather than Strephon, as the compulsive observer. A degree of collusion between author and protagonist now appears to be developing, and a little later Swift comes to an item which, he says, "we" must include:

> The Virtues we must not let pass,
> Of *Celia*'s magnifying Glass.
> When frighted *Strephon* cast his Eye on't
> It shew'd the Visage of a Gyant.
> A Glass that can to Sight disclose,
> The smallest Worm in *Celia*'s Nose,
> And faithfully direct her Nail
> To squeeze it out from Head to Tail;
> For catch it nicely by the Head,
> It must come out alive or dead.
>
> (ll. 59-68)

In this passage, Swift drops the fiction that he is recording what Strephon saw, to describe in lingering detail the uses to which he visualizes Celia putting her magnifying glass. He makes it quite clear that he is now dramatizing an act of imagination on the part of the author rather than of compulsive observation on the part of the protagonist, and it is thus Swift himself who at this point appears to be thorough and inclusive in his aggregation of details. Therefore, the massive and protracted accumulation of repulsive items is not presented as simply the product of Strephon's neurotic voyeurism. And it also follows that the intense revulsion with which those items are presented is an element in the author's, as well as the protagonist's, perception of the dressing room. It is not only for Strephon, evidently, that the experience of visualizing the contents of that room is a powerfully disturbing one. After describing his protagonist's exploration of Celia's commode, Swift comments, "O may she better learn to keep/ 'Those Secrets of the hoary deep!'" (ll. 97-98). The reference is to Milton's account of Chaos, and the most logical interpretation is no doubt to regard the lines as being conventionally mock-heroic, intended to "put excretion in proper perspective" by contrasting it with the genuinely massive;[19] but it is a truism that the mock-heroic style sometimes has a rather different effect from this on the way we perceive the subject's dimensions, and when one considers this particular allusion in the light of what has gone before, it is not difficult to sense its potentiality for suggesting that what has been confronted in the dressing room is a disorder of staggering proportions. Swift has made the recognition of this disorder such a disturbing experience that one can hardly be surprised when Strephon finds it difficult to cope with. Moreover, the poem has not really established a sufficient distance between author and protagonist for it to be clear that when Strephon comes to feel such an overwhelming disgust for womankind he is simply being defined as a misguided neurotic. His situation is rather like that which Gulliver is finally left in; his "Imagination" has become "foul" (l. 121) because he has confronted some genuinely disturbing realities, and the manner in which Swift has rendered his experience has suggested that the retention of mental balance after it would be a difficult matter. It is not surprising, therefore, that the poem's final passage does not really offer such a clear-cut resolution of Strephon's dilemma as my initial account of it suggested:

> I pity wretched *Strephon* blind
> To all the Charms of Female Kind;
> Should I the Queen of Love refuse,
> Because she rose from stinking Ooze?
> To him that looks behind the Scene,
> *Satira*'s but some pocky Quean.
> When *Celia* in her Glory shows,
> If *Strephon* would but stop his Nose;
> (Who now so impiously blasphemes
> Her Ointments, Daubs, and Paints and Creams,
> Her Washes, Slops, and every Clout,
> With which he makes so foul a Rout;)
> He soon would learn to think like me,

And bless his ravisht Sight to see
Such Order from Confusion sprung,
Such gaudy Tulips rais'd from Dung.

(ll. 129-44)

The prescription itself is clear enough, but it is hedged about with so many ironies and ambiguities that it is impossible to take it at its face value. For instance, when Swift suggests that Strephon "impiously blasphemes" in cursing Celia's cosmetic apparatus, he ironically adopts an attitude very similar to that of Pope's Belinda; certainly Strephon's behavior is an offense against the "Sacred Rites" of the dressing table, but for Swift to emphasize this constitutes an implicit endorsement of his attitude rather than a rejection of it—the author himself is clearly a heretic with regard to this particular religion too. Also, to advise Strephon to "stop his Nose" is to recommend a nonrecognition that his experience has obviously made impossible, and which, as a way out of his dilemma, is a desperate form of evasion. The compromise that is finally offered does, however, involve a clear recognition of the "Confusion" that the poem has made so vividly evident. But the "Order" which Swift professes to admire is a manifestly spurious one, and while its achievement is no doubt a source of "wonder," that achievement is more or less on the level of an impressive conjuring trick.[20] The passage as a whole expresses an underlying sympathy with Strephon's attitude, and a bitter sense of the shifts and evasions that must be resorted to if one is to maintain a balanced response to the experience in which the author and his protagonist have participated. The poem's conclusion does not, therefore, suggest that a really adequate solution to Strephon's dilemma has been reached.

In the poem as a whole, then, Swift on the one hand establishes a morally evaluative framework that often seems capable of bringing its subject matter to a kind of order by placing it firmly within a coherent ethical structure. But he also at several points in the poem renders that subject matter in such a way as to suggest that it is not being entirely subdued by the rationalizing framework, and that it is in the end too radically disturbing and unruly to be subject to that kind of ordering containment. What we confront here is not the usual discrepancy between the coherence of the satirist's style and the disorder of the subject he is defining, but a contrast between two different modes of rendering that subject. In spite of the revisions that have been made to some old assumptions about eighteenth-century literature, I think it is still true that the highly ordered narrative and ethical framework of *The Lady's Dressing Room* represents one major tendency in the poetry of Swift's time. In this case, Swift makes the framework a particularly obtrusive one, as if to establish an extreme model of a kind of order to which both he and his contemporaries frequently aspired. And the poem as a whole expresses both an impulse towards this order and a considerable degree of uncertainty about its power to subdue experience.

A somewhat related effect to that which I have described above is also given by *Strephon and Chloe* (1731). An extremely visible aspect of this poem is the coherence of its narrative and ethical structure, which appears to be built according to a rigorously formulated plan. The poem is intended to demonstrate the dangers to which the romantic idealization of woman can lead, and the story which it tells is systematically directed towards this end. First, the reputation of Chloe is established:

> Of *Chloe* all the Town has rung;
> By ev'ry size of Poets sung:
> So beautiful a Nymph appears
> But once in Twenty Thousand Years.
> (ll. 1-4)

She is regarded as an absolute ideal of female beauty, and the flawlessness of that ideal is the subject of much poetic hyperbole. Not surprisingly, she is adored and pursued by multitudes of men, exalted to such a degree that she has become, Swift mockingly suggests, a rival to Venus herself. Strephon soon becomes a victim of the universal romantic prostration, and after much "loud and strong" sighing (l. 39), his suit is rewarded. The marriage is attended by a lengthy parade of mythological deities, as in the best epithalamic tradition. And the two figures are finally brought together in the bedroom. Swift has set the situation up very carefully, stressing at every point the atmosphere of romantic idealization in which the union is established. And now Strephon faces a difficult problem:

> BUT, still the hardest Part remains.
> *Strephon* had long perplex'd his Brains,
> How with so high a Nymph he might
> Demean himself the Wedding-Night:
> For, as he view'd his Person round,
> Meer mortal Flesh was all he found.
> (ll. 71-76)

Having worshipped a woman as if she were a goddess, he is baffled by the problem of how to make physical contact with her, and is thus caught in the trap of his own romantic idealism. Turning to classical precedent in order to explain his dilemma to himself, Strephon derives some hope from the example of Thetis and Peleus. But this is immediately counteracted by his remembrance of Semele's death in Jove's embrace, and he experiences a fear that Swift defines with great clarity: "But, what if he should lose his Life/By vent'ring on his heav'nly Wife?" (ll. 103-4). Strephon's insecurity very soon appears to be justified, when Chloe rejects his initial advances. However, in what turns out to be a dramatic turning point in the progression of his experience, Strephon is forced to recognize that Chloe's behaviour is not caused by the semidivine chastity of her nature, but by the fact that she needs to urinate. His cry of protest is both as anguished and as thematically illustrative as that uttered by the other Strephon in *The Lady's Dressing Room*:

> *STREPHON* who heard the fuming Rill
> As from a mossy Cliff distill;
> Cry'd out, ye Gods, what Sound is this?
> Can *Chloe*, heav'nly *Chloe* —?
>
> (ll. 175-78)

The goddess turns out to be a woman after all, and for a few moments Strephon cannot cope with the overthrow of his idealizing vision. But he does recover, and is faced with the fact that to perceive Chloe's physical reality necessarily involves a total readjustment of his attitude to her and to women in general:

> ADIEU to ravishing Delights,
> High Raptures, and romantick Flights;
> To Goddesses so heav'nly sweet,
> Expiring Shepherds at their Feet;
> To silver Meads, and shady Bow'rs,
> Drest up with *Amaranthine* Flow'rs.
>
> (ll. 197-202)

Now the loss of such attitudes is clearly a good thing and should be capable of leading him towards a more rational and balanced viewpoint than he has so far demonstrated. But what happens instead is that Strephon and Chloe now go to another extreme, an extreme of vulgarity and obscenity in which they leave "all Constraint" (l. 205) behind them. Swift's implication is that the destruction of one kind of imbalance has led to the establishment of another, and that Strephon has failed to cope rationally with his experience. He then asserts that the behavior of Strephon and Chloe illustrates the vital importance of "Decency" in human relationships (l. 219). As he stresses this, Swift introduces a series of carefully balanced aphorisms such as "If Decency brings no Supplies,/Opinion falls, and Beauty dies" (ll. 225-26), which are intended to sum up the ethical significance of the preceding narrative. And this sententious manner reappears in the poem's concluding passage, which is typified by the following lines:

> Rash Mortals, e'er you take a Wife,
> Contrive your Pile to last for Life;
> Since Beauty scarce endures a Day,
> And Youth so swiftly glides away;
> Why will you make yourself a Bubble
> To build on Sand with Hay and Stubble?
>
> (ll. 301-6)

The rhetorical structure of the passage is obtrusively ordered, making the points in a neat and solidly consecutive fashion, and it appears that Swift is rounding off the poem with a high degree of authoritative finality. Moreover, these conclusions are derived in a logical way from the preceding narrative, which has possessed something like the illustrative clarity of a diagram. One very strong impression that the poem gives, therefore, is that it has been systematically structured so as to demonstrate the truth of certain ethical propositions.

But even though the didactic framework is so rigorously structured, there are again several elements in the poem which are not so authoritatively contained by that framework as Swift's concluding lines appear to suggest. The poem constantly creates the impression that the material with which it deals is not easily subject to the kind of didactic resolution which appears in the concluding lines and in so many aspects of the poem's structure. In particular, what the poem deals with and eventually rationalizes about is the inescapable physicality of human beings. And often Swift's confrontation with this physicality leads him beyond what would seem to be the logical necessities of the satiric or didactic argument. At the beginning of the poem, for instance, after stressing that Chloe's perfection ("faultless to a single Hair") makes her seem to be "of no mortal Race," Swift goes on to define that perfection in very precise physical terms:

> And then, so nice, and so genteel;
> Such Cleanliness, from Head to Heel:
> No Humours gross, or frowzy Steams,

No noisom Whiffs, or sweaty Streams,
Before, behind, above, below,
Could from her taintless Body flow.

(ll. 9-14)

Since the object of Swift's satire in this poem is the failure of idealizing romantics to confront a very physical reality, the high degree of specificity about the human body ("Before, behind, above, below") which appears in these lines is very relevant to the didactic theme. And there is, of course, a substantial literary tradition behind what Swift is doing here.[21] But he does not stop at this point, even though this stage of the satiric argument seems to have been more than adequately developed. He continues for several more lines to dwell on the same theme:

Would so discreetly Things dispose,
None ever saw her pluck a Rose.
Her dearest Comrades never caught her
Squat on her Hams, to make Maid's Water.
You'd swear, that so divine a Creature
Felt no Necessities of Nature.
In Summer had she walkt the Town,
Her Arm-pits would not stain her Gown:
At Country Dances, not a Nose
Could in the Dog-Days smell her Toes.

(ll. 15-24)

Much of the detail here seems gratuitous, as if Swift is pushing his emphasis a great deal further than is either necessary or logical.[22] The immediate impression that the passage is likely to create is that the poem is becoming structurally unbalanced at an early stage of its development, and a natural reflex action in the reader is to start thinking about Swift's "obsessions." But the very obsessiveness of the passage's development, which almost disrupts the logical frame of the didactic argument at an early stage, is one of a complex of forces which eventually gives the poem greater richness than that frame could of itself provide. For Swift does not at this point register Chloe's personality in the manner of a serenely balanced didactic author, confidently expressing his ability to rationalize the material he confronts. He registers it in a lingering and unsettling protracted way. And in doing so, he expresses an acute and uncomfortable sense of the unruliness of the poem's material, a sense that it may not be easily reducible to the order of didactic formulation. Swift's contemplation of it leads him into what C. J. Rawson has called a kind of "overplus,"[23] here an overplus of specific detail, which tends to create unease rather than the security which the later aphorisms seem designed to induce.

As we have seen, Strephon faces a baffling dilemma when he finds himself in bed with Chloe, and that dilemma is defined with a great deal of thematic clarity. But while his experience is made to fit neatly into the progressive didactic argument of the poem, it is not always rendered in such a way as to make it seem easily manageable by the greater rationality of the author and the reader:

> His Hand, his Neck, his Mouth, and Feet
> Were duly washt to keep 'em sweet;
> (With other Parts that shall be nameless,
> The Ladies else might think me shameless.)
> The Weather and his Love were hot;
> And should he struggle; I know what—
> Why let it go, if I must tell it—
> He'll sweat, and then the Nymph may smell it.
> (ll. 77-84)

In the last few lines of this passage, Swift is seeking to dramatize a degree of struggle and difficulty not only in the experience of the protagonist, but also in that of the author. Granted, the rhetorical maneuver is here a little contrived and not entirely convincing. But a certain sense is nevertheless given that Strephon's physicality is something which is difficult to confront and to cope with, and not only because of the tendency towards romantic idealization which separates Strephon from the author.

A little later, just before Chloe feels the urge to urinate,
Swift utters an ominous warning:

> NOW, *Ponder well ye Parents dear;*
> Forbid your Daughters guzzling Beer;
> And make them ev'ry Afternoon
> Forbear their Tea, or drink it soon;
> That, e'er to Bed they venture up,
> They may discharge it ev'ry Sup;
> If not; they must in evil Plight
> Be often forc'd to rise at Night.
>
> (ll. 115-22)

He stresses again the facts that the human body is subject to
certain "Necessities of Nature" and that those who ignore
this do so at their peril. The comments are thus closely related
to a central theme of the poem's didactic argument. But
although in this passage Swift does adopt the stance of an
authoritative didactic guide, his intention seems to be to
parody it; the opening line transforms that stance into an
attidude of absurd pomposity, and the tone of the advice
which follows is calculated to increase the comic effect.[24] In
the next few lines Swift again seems to parody the manner of
the didactic author:

> Keep them to wholsome Food confin'd,
> Nor let them taste what causes Wind;
> ('Tis this the Sage of *Samos* means,
> Forbidding his Disciples Beans)
>
> (ll. 123-26)

A footnote to the couplet in parenthesis states that this is "A
well known precept of Pythagoras, not to eat Beans." Thus,
the tendency of didactic moralists to invoke the authority of
classical precedent is mimicked in such a way as to make it
sound absurd. And the tone around this point has a pecu-
liarly subverting relationship to the later statement that,
"AUTHORITIES both old and recent,/Direct that Women

must be decent" (251-52). Why Swift should want to parody
the manner of didacticism at this point in the poem when at
others he seems to adopt it quite seriously is not immediately
clear. But to examine the way in which the passage continues
is, I think, capable of providing an explanation:

> O, think what Evils must ensue;
> Miss *Moll* the Jade will burn it blue:
> And when she once has got the Art,
> She cannot help it for her Heart;
> But, out it flies, even when she meets
> Her Bridegroom in the Wedding-Sheets.
> *Carminative* and *Diuretick*,
> Will damp all Passion Sympathetick;
> And, Love such Nicety requires,
> One *Blast* will put out all his Fires.
>
> (ll. 127-36)

In the first line of this Swift continues the mock-solemnity
that we have just seen. And what we encounter in the following lines is a further example of the kind of "overplus" that
occurred at the beginning of the poem. Swift elaborates on
the problem raised by the "Sage of Samos" to an extent which
goes far beyond the necessities of logical satiric discourse. It is
possible, I suppose, to argue that what the passage shows is
an obsessive fascination with the bodily functions. But one
would not have to discount this psychological interpretation
in order to suggest that the passage also communicates a
sense that the physicality of human beings is a disturbing
fact. Swift's emphasis on this physicality has been so insistent
and repetitive in this sequence, and has been carried so far
beyond the expected limits, that the "Love" which is mentioned at the end is made to seem hopelessly fragile. I would
suggest that this aspect of the passage is closely related to the
comic parody of didacticism which also keeps on appearing
in it. For in the face of what we are made to confront here, the
authoritative rationalizations of the didactic author seem like
futile gestures. As we read this passage we are plunged into an

absurd chaos of disruptive physical forces, and the experience
it creates is such that when we come to the neat didactic
formulations of the later stages we may very well feel that they
are inadequate to define or contain what Swift has dramatized.

After Strephon's idealizing vision has finally been shattered, the author comments on his experience and on what he
suggests is his own greater rationality:

> O *Strephon*, e'er that fatal Day
> When *Chloe* stole your Heart away,
> Had you but through a Cranny spy'd
> On House of Ease your future Bride,
> In all the Postures of her Face,
> Which Nature gives in such a Case;
> Distortions, Groanings, Strainings, Heavings;
> 'Twere better you had lickt her Leavings,
> Than from Experience find too late
> Your Goddess grown a filthy Mate.
> Your Fancy then had always dwelt
> On what you saw, and what you smelt;
> Would still the same Ideas give ye,
> As when you spy'd her on the Privy.
> And, spight of *Chloe*'s Charms divine,
> Your Heart had been as whole as mine.
>
> (ll. 235-50)

In the last couplet Swift claims to possess a wisdom which is
unavailable to Strephon. When he says that his heart is
"whole" in a way that Strephon's is not, he obviously means
that it is invulnerable to female beauty. But this invul-
nerability is also being offered as a testament to the author's
rationality in the face of what has led Strephon into an
unbalanced state. It seems, therefore, that the author is being
firmly separated from his protagonist, and that he is judging
that protagonist from the standpoint of his own balanced
wisdom. And yet such a claim is made at the end of a passage
in which the author himself has appeared to be intensely
disturbed by those physical facts with which Strephon has

been unable to cope. The description of Chloe on the lavatory, full of violently repulsive images, seems to come from a man who is himself tormented by the physicality of human beings. And Swift implies that his heart is "whole" only because he is made invulnerable by disgust. The human body thus becomes an overpowering presence once again, and the way in which Swift establishes that presence has the effect of undermining the pose of secure authorial distance which is adopted in the last couplet of the passage.

Denis Donoghue has described "the executive nature of Swift's mind, its expression in lucid arrangements," and the way in which his rhetoric appears to "subdue experience by imposing administrative pressure upon it." He argues that Swift's mind was acutely aware of "occasions of violence for which the official terms were inadequate," but that his response to such occasions is to protect himself against them "by constructing a working model of life which enables him to hold the essential forts. . . . The best model is not the most capacious or the most liberal; it takes possession of a certain area of experience and fends off rival forces. . . . The ideal analogue is the self-enclosed diagram in geometry, the triangle, or the square, anything that exhibits a blocked-off unity of apprehension, no loose edges."[25] These comments are extremely pertinent not only to *Strephon and Chloe* but also to the other poems I have discussed in this chapter, for the highly ordered structures which Swift builds in them are examples of the kind of "model" that Donoghue describes. But whereas he argues that these structures are techniques by which Swift keeps unruly, disruptive elements "at a safe distance" (p. 28), I would suggest that, in the above poems at least, such elements are very strongly present. It has been said that one of Swift's predominant stylistic tendencies is "to suggest forces which cannot be contained."[26] And he often renders such forces in poems that have particularly obtrusive rhetorical or didactic systems. A major consequence of this is that Swift seems on the one hand to be setting up extreme

models (in the case of *Strephon and Chloe* almost a caricature) of a kind of order to which he undoubtedly aspired, and
on the other to be subjecting those models to stresses that are
intended to create some degree of doubt about their ultimate
authority over the materials with which they deal.

Conclusion

It may very well seem that there is a fundamental duality in the above study from which it is difficult to draw any very clear conclusions. For I have argued on the one hand that Swift sometimes creates verbal patterns which violate certain orthodox "Augustan" principles of organization and on the other that he sometimes creates verbal patterns that are closely aligned with such principles. And indeed, there is a considerable variety in Swift's poetic output that should make us cautious about definitive generalizations, especially when we are focusing upon the matters with which this study is concerned. However, although in several poems, some of which I have discussed in chapter four, Swift does erect noticeably orthodox thematic or didactic patterns without in any way subverting their authority from within, I believe that there is a good deal of evidence to suggest that such poems are not the ones which are most typical of him. Certainly, in the poems addressed to Stella there is an impressive and often moving harmony between ordered rhetorical patterns and the experience which those patterns define. But in some other poems that I have also discussed in the fourth chapter there are hints that the relationship between a systematic structure and the defined subject involves a degree of conscious irony. And in chapter five I have argued that certain poems which are obviously central to Swift's work, such as *Cadenus and Vanessa, Verses on the Death of Dr. Swift,* and *Strephon and Chloe,* need to be considered in terms of this irony.

The irony that I am referring to is not the same as that which has been recognized as a typical characteristic of Augustan literature. In Dryden and Pope there is often an ironic contrast between rhetorical systems and the disorderly subject matter which those systems define, but this contrast tends to diminish the subject matter by making it seem to fall woefully short of the authoritative order embodied by the rhetoric; the adequacy of the rhetorical structure as a means of defining or subduing the material to which it alludes is not usually subjected to challenges from within the poem. Similarly, while it has been suggested that there is an "irony of form" in Fielding's *Tom Jones,* and that there is a fundamental contrast in that work between its "neat structure" and the "perceived life it contains," this contrast does not lead to doubts about the adequacy of the structure so much as to an admiration of the author's "esthetic skill" and his ability to create a sense of "order behind scattered incidents."[1] The kind of irony that I have attempted to describe in Swift involves, on the contrary, an apparent questioning of the structure itself.

It is not, however, an utterly negating kind of irony, or one that is intended to demolish the status of the forms towards which it expresses an attitude. I do not wish to suggest that such overtly structured sequences as Cadenus's speech on the value of friendship, the "indiff'rent" speaker's eulogy of Swift, or the author's didactic commentary on the experience of Strephon are simply being made to look ridiculous. There is clearly in Swift an impulse to believe in the validity of such forms as means of rendering experience, and the irony with which he approaches them is more complex than one that would seek simply to destroy the reader's perception of their authority. But these ordered and ordering forms are placed in contexts that are capable of generating doubts about their efficacy as responses to the materials with which Swift is dealing, and the irony with which he approaches them is a conscious expression of uncertainty.

The effect of the poems in which this occurs is different from the effect of those that I discussed in the second chapter, where Swift caricatures the procedures of a systematic logician and makes radical and seriously damaging fun of them. In the poems discussed in chapter five we do not confront absurd parodies of the ways in which a formal, academic logician might structure an argument, but imitations of tendencies that were much more central to the literature of his time, in fact of some characteristically "Augustan" means of bringing aesthetic order to the artist's experience; some examples are the elegantly stylized comic narrative in *Cadenus and Vanessa,* the satirist's *apologia* in *Verses on the Death of Dr. Swift,* the didactic structuring of the narrative in *Strephon and Chloe,* and the development of an illustrative analogy in *The Progress of Beauty.* Swift's approach to these modes of literary organization does in one way resemble his approach to the procedures of the academic logician, however, in that he carries them to extremes that occasionally verge on caricature; the comic stylization of experience is obtrusively elegant, the satirist's *apologia* is a narrative of consistent heroism, didactic organization is diagrammatic in its clarity, and the development of analogy is (for part of the time, at least) rigidly systematic. In fact, when Swift does seek to introduce orthodox types of formal organization into his poems, the structures that result tend to be very obtrusive, much more obtrusive than they are, for example, in the poetry of Pope. And that is why critics such as Ong and Donoghue have commented so emphatically on the closed systems that they perceive in Swift's work.[2] The extreme rigor that characterizes so many of these systems may be the consequence of an attempt on Swift's part to set up rather clear-cut contrasts between ordering designs and other elements which challenge or subvert those designs. And it may also suggest the intensity of his impulse towards the severe forms of organization that the systems often represent; certainly, Donoghue's comments about Swift's need for "military" gestures as means of "keeping the world in its place" would seem to support such a notion.[3] But however strong such an impulse may have been, it is persistently accompanied by intimations of uncertainty about how powerful such forms are as expressions of authorial dominance of the materials they dispose, and by a sense of the essential unruliness of those materials. This means that there is rather frequently in Swift's poetry a degree of tension between rigidity and flux, between "ordering designs" and elements within the poetry which challenge or subvert the authority of those designs.

This uncertainty about and questioning of certain orthodox modes of formal organization seems closely connected with Swift's interest in those contrasting types of verbal pattern that I described in the first three chapters of this study. What I have attempted to demonstrate in those chapters are certain interests that may very well seem surprising in a writer who sometimes appears to subscribe quite straightforwardly to certain "Augustan" literary values. It has been recognized, of course, that Swift often violates orthodox modes of literary organization in his work, but it is usually suggested that he does this in order to express his essential belief in the validity of these modes; Martin C. Battestin, for example, has said of *A Tale of a Tub* that "the formal principles of Augustan aesthetics are self-consciously violated . . . to affirm the ideals of rationality and regularity by ironically enacting their contraries."[4] But, as I have already pointed out, there is some evidence to suggest that Swift may have found the style of the *Tale* expressive in a way that such a comment does not really countenance. Certainly there are in Swift's poems several violations of "rationality and regularity" that are not adequately described as parodies intended to affirm the value of opposite forms of organization. In many widely differing poems such as *On Poetry; A*

Rapsody, The Bubble, and *The Legion Club,* the disruptions of formal order are felt to have their own value as expressive forms rather than as ironic affirmations of contrasting structures.

In his seminal work, *The Providence of Wit,* Battestin has argued that the Augustan poet's pursuit of harmony and proportion in literature was an effort to imitate "the fiat of Genesis, by which the idea of Order in the mind of God was bodied forth in Nature, . . . anarchy was dispelled, the jarring elements harmonized, due bounds prescribed, and all things given form" (pp. 79-80). We have seen that in several of Swift's poems images accumulate in anarchic superabundance, unrelated elements are juxtaposed without being coordinated into thematic harmonies, and details insist on their recalcitrance to literary structures that would seek to enclose and subdue them. Often these poems seem to have been designed so as to suggest that it is very difficult for a human artist to achieve the ideal of order that Battestin describes. But this does not mean that in them Swift is dramatizing failures to arrive at an order to which he aspires but which he finds difficult to attain. On the contrary, his perceptions in these poems lead towards alternative forms of literary organization which become for him intensely expressive. And if the degree of value these alternative forms have for him often depends upon the extent to which they depart from principles to which his major contemporaries rather steadily adhered, this should not seem surprising when one considers the uncertainty and ambivalence that are so often present in his approach to those principles.

Notes

Introduction

1. Denis Donoghue, *Jonathan Swift: A Critical Introduction* (Cambridge: at the University Press, 1969), pp. 198-203.

2. John M. Aden, "Those Gaudy Tulips: Swift's 'Unprintables,'" in *Quick Springs of Sense: Studies in the Eighteenth Century*, ed. Larry S. Champion (Athens, Ga.: University of Georgia Press, 1974), pp. 15-32.

3. Donald Greene, "'Logical structure' in Eighteenth-Century Poetry," *Philological Quarterly* 31 (1952):315-36.

4. Peter Thorpe, "The Nonstructure of Augustan Verse," *Papers on Language and Literature* 5 (1969):235-51.

5. David M. Vieth, "Toward an Anti-Aristotelian Poetic: Rochester's *Satyr Against Mankind* and *Artemisia to Chloe*, with notes on Swift's *Tale of a Tub* and *Gulliver's Travels*," *Language and Style* 5 (1972):123-45.

6. Martin C. Battestin, *The Providence of Wit: Aspects of Form in Augustan Literature and the Arts* (Oxford: Clarendon Press, 1974), p. vii.

Chapter 1: "Wild Excursions"

1. Geoffrey Walton, *Metaphysical to Augustan: Studies in Tone and Sensibility in the Seventeenth Century* (London: Bowes & Bowes, 1955), p. 83.

2. Walter J. Ong, S.J., "Swift on the Mind: The Myth of Asepsis," *Modern Language Quarterly* 15 (1954): 208-21.

3. *The Correspondence of Jonathan Swift*, ed. Harold Williams, 5 vols. (Oxford: Clarendon Press, 1963), 1:9.

4. See, for example, George N. Shuster, *The English Ode from Milton to Keats* (New York: Columbia University Press, 1940), p. 114, and Robert Shafer, *The English Ode to 1660* (Princeton, N.J.: Princeton University Press, 1918), p. 156.

5. *The Works of Mr. Abraham Cowley*, 4th ed. (London: Printed by John Murray for Henry Herringman, 1674), from "The Preface of the Author" (no page numbers).

6. Ibid., "Pindarique Odes," p. 19.

7. *The Praise of Pindar*, lines 12-15, in ibid., p. 18.

8. From the Preface to *Ovid's Epistles*, in *The Works of John Dryden*, ed. Edward Niles Hooker and H. T. Swedenberg, Jr. (Berkeley and Los Angeles, Calif.: University of California Press, 1956), 1:117.

9. Quotations are from *The Poems of Jonathan Swift*, ed. Harold Williams, 2d ed., 3 vols. (Oxford: Clarendon Press, 1958).

10. Robert W. Uphaus, "From Panegyric to Satire: Swift's Early Odes and *A Tale of a Tub*," *Texas Studies in Language and Literature* 13 (1971-72):55-70.

11. Martin Price, *Swift's Rhetorical Art: A Study in Structure and Meaning* (New Haven, Conn.: Yale University Press, 1953), p. 44.

12. In "'Occasions So Few': Satire as a Strategy of Praise in Swift's Early Odes," *Modern Language Quarterly* 31 (1970): 22-37, Kathryn Montgomery Harris makes a point that is very similar to this. She also recognizes that Swift's technique involves a radical "departure from . . . traditional modes of praise" (p. 31).

13. Jonathan Swift, *"Tale of a Tub." To Which Is added "The Battle of the Books" and "The Mechanical Operation of the Spirit,"* ed. A.C. Guthkelch and D. Nichol Smith, 2d ed. (Oxford: Clarendon Press, 1958), p. 209.

14. "To my Honored Friend, Sr. Robert Howard, On his Excellent Poems," line 34. *The Poems of John Dryden*, ed. James Kinsley, 4 vols. (Oxford: Clarendon Press, 1958), 1:14. Kathleen Williams makes the same comparison in *Jonathan Swift and the Age of Compromise* (Lawrence, Kans.: University of Kansas Press, 1958), p. 25.

15. Eugene F. Timpe has referred to the sequence as a "clumsy" attempt at "raillery." "Swift as Railleur," *Journal of English and Germanic Philology* 69 (1970):41-49.

16. Swift, *A Tale of a Tub*, ed. Guthkelch and Smith, p. 59.

17. The full title was *The Athenian Gazette: or Casuistical Mercury, Resolving all the most Nice and Curious Questions Proposed by the Ingenious.*

18. Swift, *Correspondence*, 1:8. Also, in *The Life and Errors of John Dunton* (London: Printed for S. Malthus, 1705), p. 261, Dunton informs us that Temple submitted several queries to the *Gazette*.

19. See Swift, *Poems*, ed. Harold Williams, 1:33-34.

20. Swift, *Correspondence*, 1:13-14.

21. Swift, *Poems*, 1:49.

22. Since these characteristics of the *Tale* have been often and amply described, it does not seem to me necessary to provide particular illustrations of them.

23. Uphaus, "From Panegyric to Satire," pp. 55-70.

24. C. J. Rawson, *Gulliver and the Gentle Reader: Studies in Swift and our Time* (London and Boston: Routledge & Kegan Paul, 1973), p. 2.

25. John Traugott, *"A Tale of A Tub,"* in *Focus: Swift*, ed. C.J. Rawson (London: Sphere Books, 1971), pp. 76-120.

26. Samuel Johnson, *A Dictionary of the English Language*, 2 vols. (1755; reprint ed., New York: AMS Press, 1967).

27. *The First Epistle of the Second Book of Horace*, lines 340-41. *The Poems of Alexander Pope*, Twickenham ed., *Imitations of Horace with An Epistle to Dr. Arbuthnot and The Epilogue to the Satires*, ed. John Butt (London and New Haven: Yale University Press, 1939), 4:225. Robert W. Uphaus has also noted this parallel; see "Swift's Poetry: The Making of Meaning," *Eighteenth-Century Studies* 5 (1971-72):569-86.

28. David Ward has referred to this as parody of "the late Metaphysical habit of the decorative conceit." But he also recognizes that Swift gives us "some of the delight we feel in the deliberately outrageous metaphor" *(Jonathan Swift: An Introductory Essay* [London: Methuen, 1973], p. 200). In other words, Swift engages in this wild proliferation of images for its own sake as well as for its parodic function.

29. James L. Tyne, S.J., discusses these parodies in detail in "Swift's Mock Panegyrics in 'On Poetry: A Rapsody,'" *Papers on Language and Literature* 10 (1974):279-86.

30. In the three blank spaces marked by dashes or asterisks the reader is meant to supply "George," "Monarch," and "Jove" (this last, of course, being an implicit reference to the Christian God). See Swift, *Poems*, 2:657.

31. C.J. Rawson describes a quality of "open-endedness" that he sees in the poem's conclusion. *Gulliver and the Gentle Reader*, p. 72.

Chapter 2: The Subversive Image

1. See Irvin Ehrenpreis, *Swift: The Man, His Works, and the Age* (Cambridge Mass.: Harvard University Press, 1962-), 1:200, and John M. Bullitt, *Jonathan Swift and the Anatomy of Satire* (Cambridge, Mass.: Harvard University Press, 1953), pp. 116-22.

2. My argument around this point has been considerably influenced by Martin Price's comments on *The Fable of Midas* in *Swift's Rhetorical Art* (New Haven, Conn.: Yale University Press, 1953), pp. 48-49.

3. See *The Poems of Jonathan Swift*, ed. Harold Williams, 2d ed. (Oxford: Clarendon Press, 1958), 1:89-90. Williams includes both the 1703 manuscript version and the revision published by Swift in the *Miscellanies* of 1711.

4. Martin C. Battestin, *The Providence of Wit* (Oxford: Clarendon Press, 1974) p. 219.

5. *The Self Observed: Swift, Johnson, Wordsworth* (Baltimore, Md.: Johns Hopkins University Press, 1972), p. 64.

Chapter 3: Enumerations, Miscellanies, and the Irreducible Particular

1. See *The Poems of Jonathan Swift*, ed. Harold Williams, 2d ed. (Oxford: Clarendon Press, 1958), 1:88-95 and 110-17. Williams includes the early manuscript version and the revision published in the *Miscellanies* of 1711.

2. Eric Rothstein, "Jonathan Swift as Jupiter: 'Baucis and Philemon,'" in *The Augustan Milieu: Essays Presented to Louis A. Landa*, ed. Henry Knight Miller, Eric Rothstein, and G.S. Rousseau (Oxford: Clarendon Press, 1970), pp. 205-24.

3. Irvin Ehrenpreis, *Swift: The Man, His Works, and the Age* (Cambridge, Mass.: Harvard University Press, 1962-), 2 (1967):245-46.

4. "Swift and the Poetry of Allusion: 'The Journal,'" in *Literary Theory and Structure: Essays in Honor of William K. Wimsatt*, ed. Frank Brady, John Palmer, and Martin Price (New Haven, Conn.: Yale University Press, 1973), pp. 227-43.

5. Roger Savage, "Swift's Fallen City: A Description of the Morning," in *The World of Jonathan Swift: Essays for the Tercentenary*, ed. Brian Vickers (Oxford: Basil Blackwell, 1968), pp. 171-94.

6. *The Tatler*, No. 9, in *The Lucubrations of Isaac Bickerstaff, Esq.*, 4 vols. (London: Charles Lillie and John Morphew, 1710-11), pp. 68-69.

7. David M. Vieth, *"Fiat Lux:* Logos versus Chaos in Swift's 'A Description of the Morning,'" *Papers on Language and Literature* 8 (1972):302-7.

8. Rachel Trickett, *The Honest Muse: A Study in Augustan Verse* (Oxford: Clarendon Press, 1967), p. 121.

9. Kathleen Williams, *Jonathan Swift and the Age of Compromise* (Lawrence, Kans.: University of Kansas Press, 1958), p. 19.

10. *The Poems of John Dryden*, ed. James Kinsley, 4 vols. (Oxford: Clarendon Press, 1958), 2:931-32.

11. Brendan O Hehir, "Meaning of Swift's 'Description of a City Shower,'" *ELH* 27 (1960):194-207.

12. Joseph Addison, "An Essay on Virgil's *Georgics*" (1697), in *Eighteenth-Century Critical Essays*, ed. Scott Elledge, 2 vols. (Ithaca, N.Y.: Cornell University Press, 1961), 1:1-8.

13. O Hehir points out that sempstresses and templars were often equated with prostitutes and their clients. But what is important is the manner in which these figures are presented in the poem.

14. Dryden's translation, bk. 1, lines 444 and 451-52, in *Poems*, ed. James Kinsley, 2:930.

15. In "Apparent Contraries: A Reading of Swift's 'A Description of a City Shower,'" *Tennessee Studies in Literature* 19 (1974):21-34, John I. Fischer develops an argument which is in certain ways similar to my own.

16. I realize that Horace's structures are by no means always particularly rigorous (see, for example, Donald Greene's comments in "'Logical Structure' in Eighteenth-Century Poetry," p. 333, and Peter Thorpe's in "The Nonstructure of Augustan Verse," p. 249). However, in this instance Horace's ode is a model of coherent organization in comparison to Swift's satire.

17. See Swift, *Poems*, 3:828.

18. "Virgil and the Dean: Christian and Classical Allusion in *The Legion Club*," *Studies in Philology* 70 (1973):427-38.

19. Robert C. Elliott, *The Power of Satire: Magic, Ritual, Art* (Princeton, N.J.: Princeton University Press, 1960).

20. Bronislaw Malinowski, *Argonauts of the Western Pacific* (London: Routledge and Kegan Paul, 1932), p. 432.

21. Denis Donoghue, *Jonathan Swift: A Critical Introduction* (Cambridge: at the University Press, 1969), p. 215.

22. Quotations are from Jonathan Swift, *Journal to Stella*, ed. Harold Williams, 2 vols. (Oxford: Clarendon Press, 1948).

23. Donoghue, *Jonathan Swift: A Critical Introduction*, p. 196.

Chapter 4: The Ordering Design

1. In this respect, one might usefully compare the passage with Pope's description of Belinda's awakening at the start of *The Rape of the Lock*.

2. This is included by the editor in *The Poems of Jonathan Swift*, ed. Harold Williams, 2d ed., 3 vols. (Oxford: Clarendon Press, 1958), 2:471-74.

3. See ibid., 2:481-82.

4. Irvin Ehrenpreis, *Swift: The Man, His Works, and the Age,* 2:743-44.

Chapter 5: The Design under Stress

1. Gareth Jones, *"Swift's Cadenus and Vanessa:* A Question of 'Positives,' " *Essays in Criticism,* 20 (1970):424-40.

2. James L. Tyne, S.J., "Vanessa and the Houyhnhnms: A Reading of 'Cadenus and Vanessa,'" *Studies in English Literature* 11 (1971):517-34.

3. Ibid., p. 529.

4. Ibid., p. 530.

5. *The Poems of Jonathan Swift,* ed. Harold Williams, 2d ed., 3 vols. (Oxford: Clarendon Press, 1958), 2:566-67.

6. These points are made by Barry Slepian in "The Ironic Intention of Swift's Verses on His Own Death," *Review of English Studies* 14 (1963):249-56. Slepian acknowledges that he is not the first to have recognized these inaccuracies, or to have found them a problem. They are also discussed by the many subsequent contributors to the debate that Slepian's article stimulated.

7. " 'Twas bound to suffer Persecution/And Martyrdome with resolution" (part 1, canto 1, lines 259-60). Samuel Butler, *Hudibras,* ed. John Wilders (Oxford: Clarendon Press, 1967), p. 9.

8. Peter J. Schakel analyses the eulogy in this way in "The Politics of Opposition in 'Verses on the Death of Dr. Swift,' " *Modern Language Quarterly* 35 (1974): 246-56.

9. C.J. Rawson, *Gulliver and the Gentle Reader* (London and Boston: Routledge & Kegan Paul, 1973), p. 2.

10. Arthur H. Scouten and Robert D. Hume, "Pope and Swift: Text and Interpretation of Swift's Verses on His Death," *Philogical Quarterly* 52 (1973):205-31.

11. Maynard Mack, "The Muse of Satire," *Yale Review* 41 (1951-2):80-92.

12. Scouten and Hume, in the above-mentioned article, arrive at a similar conclusion. But when they go on to ask why Swift should have adopted such a procedure, they argue that he "burlesques his praise just enough that the reader should be too delighted by the multiple ironies to resist the apologia" (231). This reduces Swift's irony to an entertaining device by which he "insinuates a half-genuine apologia" into the reader's consciousness. And I think that something more significant than that is going on.

13. Rawson, *Gulliver and the Gentle Reader,* p. 40.

14. Swift, *Poems,* 1:293.

15. Herbert Davis, "A Modest Defence of 'The Lady's Dressing Room,' " in *Restoration and Eighteenth-Century Literature: Essays in Honor of Alan Dugald McKillop* (Chicago: University of Chicago Press, 1963), pp. 39-48.

16. John M. Aden, "Those Gaudy Tulips: Swift's 'Unprintables,'" in *Quick Springs of Sense: Studies in the Eighteenth Century,* ed. Larry S. Champion (Athens, Ga.: University of Georgia Press, 1974), pp. 15-32.

17. The above account of the poem is similar to the one given by Donald Greene in "On Swift's Scatological Poems," *Sewanee Review* 75 (1967): 672-89.

18. Aden, "Those Gaudy Tulips: Swift's 'Unprintables,'" p. 22.

19. Peter J. Schakel, "Swift's Remedy for Love: The 'Scatological' Poems" (Paper delivered at the annual meeting of the Modern Language Association, New York, December, 1976), p. 2.

20. Christine Rees has defined the spurious nature of this "Order" with great clarity in "Gay, Swift, and the Nymphs of Drury Lane," *Essays in Criticism*, 23 (1973):15-16. I am also referring here to a comment by John M. Aden, "Those Gaudy Tulips," p. 21.

21. Robert W. Uphaus, among others, has made this point in "Swift's Poetry: The Making of Meaning," *Eighteenth-Century Studies* 5 (1971-72):569-86.

22. John M. Aden suggests that the paragraph contains "more than one puzzling if not pointless repetition" and that it creates an "impression of redundancy." His view is that the poetry is "flawed" because of this, and that *Strephon and Chloe* is an "overladen" poem which "fails of poetical economy." ("Those Gaudy Tulips," pp. 23-24).

23. Rawson, *Gulliver and the Gentle Reader*, p. 36.

24. Thomas B. Gilmore, Jr., has commented rather differently on this passage in "The Comedy of Swift's Scatological Poems," *PMLA* 91 (1976):33-43. The comic intentions of the opening line seem to be reinforced by the fact that the italicized words are a song title the air of which was included in *The Beggar's Opera* (Air 12). John Gay, *The Beggar's Opera*, ed. Peter Elfed Lewis (Edinburgh: Oliver & Boyd, 1973), p. 64.

25. Denis Donoghue, *Jonathan Swift: A Critical Introduction* (Cambridge: at the University Press, 1969), pp. 28, 30, and 36.

26. Rawson, *Gulliver and the Gentle Reader*, p. 55.

Conclusion

1. Sheridan Baker, "Fielding and the Irony of Form," *Eighteenth-Century Studies* 2 (1968-69):138-54.

2. See above, chaps. 1, 5.

3. Denis Donoghue, *Jonathan Swift: A Critical Introduction* (Cambridge: at the University Press, 1969), p. 28.

4. Martin C. Battestin, *The Providence of Wit* (Oxford: Clarendon Press, 1974), p. ix.

Bibliography

Addison, Joseph. "An Essay on Virgil's *Georgics*" (1697). In *Eighteenth-Century Essays,* edited by Scott Elledge. 2 vols. Ithaca, N.Y.: Cornell University Press, 1961, 1: 1-8.

Aden, John M. "Corinna and the Sterner Muse of Swift." *English Language Notes* 4 (1966): 23-31.

————. "Those Gaudy Tulips: Swift's 'Unprintables.'" In *Quick Springs of Sense: Studies in the Eighteenth Century,* edited by Larry S. Champion, pp. 15-32. Athens, Ga.: University of Georgia Press, 1974.

Athenian Gazette, The, or Casuistical Mercury, Resolving all the most Nice and Curious Questions proposed by the Ingenious. 2 vols. London: Printed for John Dunton, at the Raven in the Poultry, 1691.

Baker, Sheridan. "Fielding and the Irony of Form." *Eighteenth-Century Studies* 2 (1968-69): 138-54.

Ball, F. Elrington. *Swift's Verse: An Essay.* London: John Murray, 1929.

Bateson, F. N. W. *English Poetry: A Critical Introduction.* London and New York: Longmans, Green, 1950.

Battestin, Martin C. *The Providence of Wit: Aspects of Form in Augustan Literature and the Arts.* Oxford: Clarendon Press, 1974.

Bullitt, John M. *Jonathan Swift and the Anatomy of Satire.* Cambridge, Mass.: Harvard University Press, 1953.

Butler, Samuel. *Hudibras.* Edited by John Wilders. Oxford: Clarendon Press, 1967.

Cowley, Abraham. *The Works of Mr. Abraham Cowley.* 4th ed. London: Printed by John Murray for Henry Herringman, 1674.

Davis, Herbert. *Jonathan Swift: Essays on his Satire and Other Studies*. New York: Oxford University Press, 1964.

———. "A Modest Defence of 'The Lady's Dressing Room.'" In *Restoration and Eighteenth-Century Literature: Essays in Honor of Alan Dugald McKillop*. Chicago: University of Chicago Press, 1963, pp. 39-48.

Donoghue, Denis. *Jonathan Swift: A Critical Introduction*. Cambridge: At the University Press, 1969.

Dryden, John. *The Poems of John Dryden*. Edited by James Kinsley. 4 vols. Oxford: Clarendon Press, 1958.

———. *The Works of John Dryden*. Edited by Edward Niles Hooker and H.T. Swedenberg, Jr. vol 1. Berkeley and Los Angeles, Calif.: University of California Press, 1956.

Dunton, John. *The Life and Errors of John Dunton*. London: Printed for S. Malthus, 1705.

Ehrenpreis, Irvin. *Swift: The Man, His Works, and the Age*. Cambridge, Mass.: Harvard University Press, 1962-.

Elliott, Robert C. *The Power of Satire: Magic, Ritual, Art*. Princeton, N.J.: Princeton University Press, 1960.

Fischer, John Irwin. "Apparent Contraries: A Reading of Swift's 'A Description of a City Shower.'" *Tennessee Studies in Literature* 19 (1974):21-34.

———. "How to Die: *Verses on the Death of Dr. Swift*." *Review of English Studies*, new series 21 (1970):422-41.

———. "The Uses of Virtue: Swift's Last Poem to Stella." In *Essays in Honor of Esmond Linworth Marilla*, edited by Thomas Austin Kirby and William John Olive, pp. 201-9. Baton Rouge, La.: University of Louisiana Press, 1970.

Fisher, Alan S. "Swift's Verse Portraits: A Study of his Originality as an Augustan Satirist." *Studies in English Literature* 14 (1974):357-71.

Gay, John. *The Beggar's Opera*. Edited by Peter Elfed Lewis. Edinburgh: Oliver & Boyd, 1973.

Gilmore, Thomas B., Jr. "The Comedy of Swift's Scatological Poems." *PMLA* 91 (1976):33-43.

Golden, Morris. *The Self Observed: Swift, Johnson, Wordsworth*. Baltimore, Md.: Johns Hopkins University Press, 1972.

Greene, Donald. "'Logical Structure' in Eighteenth-Century Poetry." *Philological Quarterly* 31 (1952):315-36.

———. "On Swift's Scatological Poems." *Sewanee Review* 75 (1967):672-89.

Griffin, Dustin H. *Satires Against Man: The Poems of Rochester.* Berkeley and Los Angeles, Calif.: University of California Press, 1973.

Harris, Kathryn Montgomery. "'Occasions So Few': Satire as a Strategy of Praise in Swift's Early Odes." *Modern Language Quarterly* 31 (1970):22-37.

Hill, Geoffrey. "Jonathan Swift: The Poetry of Reaction." In *The World of Jonathan Swift: Essays for the Tercentenary,* edited by Brian Vickers, pp. 195-211. Oxford: Basil Blackwell, 1968.

Jarrell, Mackie L. "'Ode to the King': Some Contests, Dissensions, and Exchanges among Jonathan Swift, John Dunton, and Henry Jones." *Texas Studies in Language and Literature* 7 (1965-66):145-59.

Jefferson, D.W. "The Poetry of Age." In *Focus: Swift,* edited by C.J. Rawson, pp. 121-37. London: Sphere Books, 1971.

Johnson, Maurice. *The Sin of Wit: Jonathan Swift as a Poet.* Syracuse, N.Y.: Syracuse University Press, 1950.

———. "Swift's Poetry Reconsidered." In *English Writers of the Eighteenth Century,* edited by John H. Middendorf, pp. 233-48. New York: Columbia University Press, 1971.

Johnson, Samuel. *A Dictionary of the English Language.* 2 vols London, 1755. Reprint. New York: AMS Press, 1967.

Johnston, Oswald. "Swift and the Common Reader." In *In Defense of Reading,* edited by Reuben A. Brower and Richard Poirier, pp. 174-190. New York: E.P. Dutton and Co., 1962.

Jones, Gareth. "Swift's *Cadenus and Vanessa:* A Question of 'Positives.'" *Essays in Criticism* 20 (1970):424-40.

Mack, Maynard. "The Muse of Satire." *Yale Review* 41 (1951-2):80-92.

Mayhew, George P. "'Rage or Raillery': Swift's *Epistle to a Lady* and *On Poetry: A Rapsody.*" *Huntington Library Quarterly* 23 (1960):159-80.

Mell, Donald C. "Elegiac Design and Satiric Intention in *Verses on the Death of Dr. Swift.*" *Concerning Poetry* 6 (1973):15-24.

O Hehir, Brendan. "Meaning of Swift's 'Description of a City Shower.'" *ELH,* 27 (1960):194-207.

Ohlin, Peter. "'Cadenus and Vanessa': Reason and Passion." *Studies in English Literature* 4 (1964):485-96.

Ong, Walter J., S.J. "Swift on the Mind: The Myth of Asepsis." *Modern Language Quarterly* 15 (1954):208-21.

Parkin, Rebecca P. "Swift's *Baucis and Philemon:* A Sermon in the Burlesque Mode." *Satire Newsletter* 7 (1970):109-14.

Paulson, Ronald. "Swift, Stella, and Permanence." *ELH* 27 (1960):298-314.

Pope, Alexander. *The Poems of Alexander Pope.* Twickenham edition, edited by John Butt and others. 11 volumes. London and New Haven: Yale University Press, 1939-69. Vol. 4, *Imitations of Horace with An Epistle to Dr. Arbuthnot and The Epilogue to the Satires.* Edited by John Butt.

Price, Martin. *Swift's Rhetorical Art: A Study in Structure and Meaning.* New Haven, Conn.: Yale University Press, 1953.

Rawson, C. J. *Gulliver and the Gentle Reader: Studies in Swift and Our Time.* London and Boston: Routledge & Kegan Paul, 1973.

Rees, Christine. "Gay, Swift, and the Nymphs of Drury Lane." *Essays in Criticism* 23 (1973):15-16.

Rogers, Katharine M. "'My Female Friends': The Misogyny of Jonathan Swift." *Texas Studies in Language and Literature* 1 (1959):366-79.

Rogers, Pat. *The Augustan Vision.* London: Weidenfeld and Nicolson, 1974.

Rothstein, Eric. "Jonathan Swift as Jupiter: 'Baucis and Philemon.'" In *The Augustan Milieu: Essays Presented to Louis A. Landa,* edited by Henry Knight Miller, Eric Rothstein, and G.S. Rousseau, pp. 205-24. Oxford: Clarendon Press, 1970.

Said, Edward W. "Swift's Tory Anarchy." *Eighteenth-Century Studies* 3 (1969): 48-66.

Sams, Henry W. "Swift's Satire of the Second Person." *ELH* 26 (1959):36-44.

San Juan, E., Jr. "The Anti-Poetry of Jonathan Swift." *Philological Quarterly* 44 (1965):387-96.

Savage, Roger. "Swift's Fallen City: A Description of the Morning." In *The World of Jonathan Swift: Essays for the Tercentenary,* edited by Brian Vickers, pp. 171-94. Oxford: Basil Blackwell, 1968.

Schakel, Peter J. "The Politics of Opposition in 'Verses on the Death of Dr. Swift.'" *Modern Language Quarterly* 35 (1974):246-56.

―――― "Swift's 'dapper Clerk' and the Matrix of Allusions in 'Cadenus and Vanessa.'" *Criticism* 17 (1975):246-61.

―――― "Swift's Remedy for Love: The 'Scatological' Poems." Paper delivered at the annual meeting of the Modern Language Association, New York, December 1976.

―――― "Virgil and the Dean: Christian and Classical Allusion in *The Legion Club.*" *Studies in Philology* 70 (1974):427-38.

Scouten, Arthur H. and Robert D. Hume. "Pope and Swift: Text and Interpretation of Swift's Verses on His Death." *Philological Quarterly* 52 (1973):205-31.

Scruggs, Charles. "Swift's Views on Language: The Basis of his Attack on Poetic Diction." *Texas Studies in Language and Literature* 13 (1972):581-92.

Shafer, Robert. *The English Ode to 1660.* Princeton, N.J.: Princeton University Press, 1918.

Shuster, George N. *The English Ode from Milton to Keats.* New York: Columbia University Press, 1940.

Slepian, Barry. "The Ironic Intention of Swift's Verses on His Own Death." *Review of English Studies* 14 (1963):249-56.

Smith, Frederik N. "Swift's Correspondence: The 'Dramatic' Style and the Assumption of Roles." *Studies in English Literature* 14 (1974): 357-71.

Swift, Jonathan. *The Correspondence of Jonathan Swift.* Edited by Harold Williams. 5 vols. Oxford: Clarendon Press, 1963-65.

——. *Journal to Stella.* Edited by Harold Williams, 2 vols. Oxford: Clarendon Press, 1948.

——. *The Poems of Jonathan Swift.* Edited by Harold Williams. 2 ed. 3 vols. Oxford: Clarendon Press, 1958.

——. *The Prose Works of Jonathan Swift.* Edited by Herbert Davis. 14 vols. Basil Blackwell, Oxford: 1939-68.

——. *A Tale of a Tub: To Which Is added The Battle of the Books and the Mechanical Operation of the Spirit.* Edited by A.C. Guthkelch and David Nichol Smith. 2d ed. Oxford: Clarendon Press, 1958.

Thorpe, Peter. "The Nonstructure of Augustan Verse." *Papers on Language and Literature* 5 (1969): 235-51.

Timpe, Eugene F. "Swift as Railleur." *Journal of English and Germanic Philology* 69 (1970): 41-49.

Traugott, John. "*A Tale of a Tub.*" In *Focus: Swift,* edited by C.J. Rawson, pp. 76-120. London: Sphere Books, 1971.

Trickett, Rachel. *The Honest Muse: A Study in Augustan Verse.* Oxford: Clarendon Press, 1967.

Tyne, James L., S.J. "Swift's Mock Panegyrics in 'On Poetry: A Rapsody.'" *Papers on Language and Literature* 10 (1974):279-86.

——. "Vanessa and the Houyhnhnms: A Reading of 'Cadenus and Vanessa.'" *Studies in English Literature* 11 (1971):517-34.

Uphaus, Robert W. "From Panegyric to Satire: Swift's Early Odes and *A Tale of a Tub.*" *Texas Studies in Language and Literature* 13 (1971-72):55-70.

_____ "Swift's Poetry: The Making of Meaning." *Eighteenth-Century Studies* 5 (1971-72):569-86.

_____ "Swift's Stella Poems and Fidelity to Experience." *Éire-Ireland* 5 (1970):40-52.

_____ "Swift's 'Whole Character': The Delany Poems and 'Verses on the Death of Dr. Swift.'" *Modern Language Quarterly* 34 (1973):406-16.

Vieth, David M. *"Fiat Lux:* Logos versus Chaos in Swift's 'A Description of the Morning.'" *Papers on Language and Literature* 8 (1972):302-7.

_____ "Toward an Anti-Aristotelian Poetic: Rochester's *Satyr Against Mankind* and *Artemisia to Chloe,* with notes on Swift's *Tale of a Tub* and *Gulliver's Travels." Language and Style* 5 (1972):123-45.

Waingrow, Marshall. "'Verses on the Death of Dr. Swift.'" *Studies in English Literature* 5 (1965):513-18.

Walton, Geoffrey. *Metaphysical to Augustan: Studies in Tone and Sensibility in the Seventeenth Century.* London: Bowes & Bowes, 1953.

Ward, David. *Jonathan Swift: An Introductory Essay.* London: Methuen, 1973.

Williams, Aubrey. "Swift and the Poetry of Allusion: 'The Journal.'" In *Literary Theory and Structure: Essays in Honor of William K. Wimsatt,* edited by Frank Brady, John Palmer, and Martin Price, pp. 227-43. New Haven, Conn.: Yale University Press, 1973.

Williams, Kathleen. *Jonathan Swift and the Age of Compromise.* Lawrence, Kans.: University of Kansas Press, 1958.

Index

239